Four Crises of American Democracy

Also by Alasdair Roberts

Blacked Out: Government Secrecy in the Information Age
The Collapse of Fortress Bush: The Crisis of Authority in American Government
The Logic of Discipline: Global Capitalism and the Architecture of Government
America's First Great Depression: Economic Crisis and Political Disorder after the Panic of 1837
The End of Protest: How Free-Market Capitalism Learned to Control Dissent

Four Crises of American Democracy

Representation, Mastery, Discipline, Anticipation

ALASDAIR ROBERTS

Oxford University Press is a department of the University of Oxford. It furthers
the University's objective of excellence in research, scholarship, and education
by publishing worldwide. Oxford is a registered trade mark of Oxford University
Press in the UK and certain other countries.

Published in the United States of America by Oxford University Press
198 Madison Avenue, New York, NY 10016, United States of America.

Library of Congress Cataloging-in-Publication Data
Names: Roberts, Alasdair (Alasdair Scott), author.
Title: Four crises of American democracy : representation, mastery, discipline,
anticipation / Alasdair Roberts.
Description: New York, NY : Oxford University Press, [2017] | Includes bibliographical
references.
Identifiers: LCCN 2016016716 (print) | LCCN 2016031202 (ebook) | ISBN 9780190459895
(hardcover : alk. paper) | ISBN 9780190459901 (E-book) | ISBN 9780190459918 (E-book)
Subjects: LCSH: Democracy—United States. | United States—Politics and government.
Classification: LCC JK1726 .R67 2017 (print) | LCC JK1726 (ebook) | DDC 320.973—dc23
LC record available at https://lccn.loc.gov/2016016716
ISBN 978–0–19–045989–5

9 8 7 6 5 4 3 2 1

Printed by Sheridan Books, Inc., United States of America

CONTENTS

ACKNOWLEDGMENTS

This short book is based on the S. T. Lee Lecture in Political Science and Government that I delivered at All Souls College, University of Oxford, in February 2015. I am grateful to Professor Sir John Vickers, Warden of All Souls College, and Professor Christopher Hood, for the invitation to deliver the Lee Lecture, and their hospitality during my visit to the College.

Four Crises of American Democracy

The Return of Democratic Malaise

The West is suddenly suffused with self-doubt.... The rise of authoritarian capitalism has been a blow to assumptions, made popular by Francis Fukuyama, that liberal democracy has proved to be the most reliable and lasting political system.

—Steven Erlanger, *New York Times*, September 13, 2015

[It is] increasingly difficult to portray the capitalist societies that emerged from the ruins of the Communist system, or those that renewed themselves in the post-Communist era, as exemplars of economic stability, full employment, continuous growth, social equality, or individual freedom in any meaningful sense of the word. Having defeated its old enemy ideologically and economically, the triumphant West is now living through the twilight of democracy.

—Tariq Ali, *The Extreme Centre*, 2015

The crisis of governance in Western democracies has undermined blind faith in electoral democracy and opened the normative space for political alternatives.... Actually existing democracy in the Western world no longer sets a clear-cut positive model for other countries.

—DANIEL BELL, *The China Model,* 2015

Democracy is a system of government in which people have the right to select, judge, and replace their rulers. Sometimes people who live in the wealthy and stable countries of the Western world take it for granted. We should not. For ordinary people— those of us who are not rich, well-connected, famous, or otherwise powerful—democracy is a crucially important thing. As the philosopher Karl Popper once said, it might be the only device by which we can protect ourselves against the abuse of political power. "Any government that can be thrown out," Popper observed, "has a strong incentive to act in a way that makes people content with it."[1]

Democracy might be desirable, but is it a viable system of government? For a long time—from the collapse of the ancient Greek states until the middle of the eighteenth century—the conventional wisdom was that democracy could not work on a large scale or for a long period of time. It was said that ordinary people were too stupid, fickle, and selfish to be trusted with real power. If democratic states could be established at all, it was expected that they would quickly fall into anarchy. And if a democratic state did not collapse by itself, it would soon be conquered by a less democratic and more disciplined rival.[2]

At first glance, modern history might seem to prove that fears about the viability of democratic governance were unjustified. If you do not scrutinize the record too closely, the democratic ideal appears to have made steady progress since the eighteenth century. By 1900, there were almost a dozen nations, including the United States, the United Kingdom, and France, that described themselves as democracies. These were stable and prosperous societies. A century later, it was estimated that 60 percent of the world's population lived under democratically elected leadership, and sixty countries could be counted as stable democracies.[3] In 1995 an international blue-ribbon commission reported "a consensus that democracy . . . is a global entitlement, a right that should be available and protected for all."[4] The scholarly *Journal of Democracy* boasted in 1996 that democracy "has gained enormous ground . . . Attacks on it still emanate from the few remaining Marxist regimes, from Islamic fundamentalists, and from some Asian authoritarians, but today democracy reigns supreme in the ideological sphere."[5]

On a closer examination, however, democracy's progress has never been straightforward. Throughout the modern era, there have been moments when there were real doubts about whether democratic institutions could be established at all, whether those institutions were capable of managing public affairs competently, and whether democracies could defend themselves from internal and external threats. Sometimes it was not just elite opinion that turned against democracy. Ordinary citizens—the people for whom democratic institutions were the only real guarantee of political influence—also began to criticize the performance of those institutions. These were moments of democratic malaise. At these times, the mood in leading democracies was sour: people were preoccupied with failure, and pessimistic about the future. These were also moments of risk for democracy. When faith in democracy was shaken, powerful interests and demagogues recognized an opportunity to take power out of the hands of ordinary people.

We are suffering from a bout of democratic malaise right now. It has been building up for several years, especially since the global financial crisis of 2007–2008. It is manifested by a softening in public support for democratic institutions, a rising chorus of complaints from intellectuals and activists about the performance of democratic systems, skepticism about the capacity of leading democracies to fix their problems, and apprehensions about the rise of non-democratic states such as China.

The worldwide decline of public confidence in democracy has been widely noted.[6] In the United States, for example, only 15 percent of respondents told the Gallup Poll in 2014 that they had a great deal of trust in the judgment of the American people about issues facing the country. The proportion expressing reservations about the judgment of the American people was the highest since the Gallup Poll started asking the question in 1974. Half of respondents to that poll said they had little or no trust in the men and women who hold public office, and 60 percent said that they had little or no confidence in the capacity of the US federal government to deal with domestic problems.[7] This decline in faith is not unique to the United States; researchers in Europe have observed a similar trend. Moreover, it has been suggested that the collapse in confidence is causing a decline in voting and other forms of participation in the democratic process.[8]

The complaints that are made against democracy, as it is currently practiced around the world, can be organized into four categories. There are complaints about the lack of real public control over government, which I will call complaints about *representation*. There are complaints about the inability of government to deal competently with problems identified by the public, which I will call complaints about *mastery*. There are complaints about the excessive or unreasonable demands that people impose on their governments, which I will call complaints about *discipline*. And finally there are complaints about the failure of democracies to address long-term problems, which I will call complaints about *anticipation*. Critics of democracy usually focus on one of these categories and ignore the other three. Indeed, they may not even recognize that there are several other ways of describing democratic failure. (Or they may not see how these four complaints may be inconsistent with one another. For example, complaints about representation usually address a perceived shortfall in public influence over government, while complaints about discipline address an excess of public influence.) So we are improving the conversation about democratic failure just by recognizing these distinct categories. Let us examine each category in a little more detail.

Representation. The Universal Declaration of Human Rights, adopted by the United Nations in 1948, says that the "will of the people shall be the basis of the authority of government."[9] This is also known as the principle of popular representation. Complaints about representation arise when ordinary people feel that they no longer exercise real control over their government— or to put it another way, when government appears to be serving some group or special interest other than the general public. We might say that government institutions that are supposed to serve the public have been captured by such interests.[10]

This is especially galling when a regime continues to insist on its respect for democratic principles. For example, the Treaty of European Union, which sets the terms for cooperation among twenty-eight European countries, says that its aim is to "develop and consolidate democracy." But skeptics say that the process of economic integration has produced a "facade of democracy" that disguises the reality of rule by bureaucrats in powerful EU institutions.[11] A more extreme case is Russia, described by President Vladimir Putin as a "modern and open" democracy, which critics say has actually degenerated into rule by a "close-knit cabal" of officials and businessmen who enrich themselves while using democracy "for decoration rather than direction."[12] Similarly, Prime Minister Prayut Chan-o-cha insisted in May 2015 that Thailand was a "free, democratic country" despite a military takeover in 2014.[13] (In his role as army chief, Prayut himself led the takeover.) And some parts of the Mexican government are said to have been "captured" by drug cartels, producing a system of narco-rule rather than the democracy promised by the Mexican constitution.[14]

There are also complaints about "state capture" in the United States. In 2009 the economist Simon Johnson argued that the financial crisis was the direct result of policies that had been pressed upon the US federal government by powerful business interests. The United States, Johnson argued, had become the world's "most advanced oligarchy."[15] Two years later, the Occupy Movement restated the case: economic inequality has produced political inequality as well, as the rich buy control of the political process. The Nobel-winning economist Joseph Stiglitz warned in

2012 that economic inequality was causing "the evisceration of our democracy."[16] Fellow economist (and *New York Times* columnist) Paul Krugman agreed: the concentration of income and wealth, he said, threatened to make the United States "a democracy in name only."[17]

Mastery. Assume for the moment that a country does take democracy seriously: everyone has the right to vote, elections are well organized, and elected officials really do hold the reins of power. That is not the end of the story. There has to be some capacity for formulating and executing policies that respond to problems that have been identified by voters and politicians—some capacity for establishing social and economic order and producing public services. In long-established democracies like the United States, this capacity tends to be taken for granted. The idea that a government would be completely incapable of exercising influence over the world around it—by repelling military threats, controlling borders, stopping riots and crime, collecting taxes, issuing pension checks, running schools, inspecting factories, and so on—is largely unfamiliar to those living in well-established democracies. But there are still many countries whose governments lack this capacity. Even if they are democratically established, they are incapable of exercising adequate control—or mastery, to use the term suggested by the American writer Walter Lippmann—over their environment.[18] And they may fail as democracies for that reason. For example, a recent study of Latin American voters found that their support for democracy arose "not just as a result of belief in its intrinsic legitimacy … but mainly because of [its perceived] ability to deliver expected results."[19] In other words, well-run elections are not enough: the machinery of government has to be adept at solving problems too.

Complaints about mastery arise when democratically elected governments are incapable of controlling their environments in ways that satisfy the expectations of voters. For the political scientist Joshua Kurlantzick, this is the main reason for democratic malaise around the world: governments have not met the middle class's demands for steady growth, social order, and key services such as education and healthcare. The result, he argues, is a "wave of antidemocratization" that might be more serious than the setbacks of the 1930s.[20] Other researchers have also attributed democratic reversals in developing nations to shortfalls in administrative capacity that make it hard to deliver core public services.[21] But the problem may not be limited to poor countries. *Financial Times* columnist Gideon Rachman worried in 2015 about the "loss of faith in the ability of established democracies to deliver competent government."[22] For example, the political scientists Anthony King and Ivor Crewe have written a sharp critique of "operational disconnects" within the British government: politicians make promises that bureaucrats cannot fulfill.[23]

Concern about the broken-down machinery of government can be heard in the United States as well. "There is a growing sense," political scientist Larry Diamond said in 2015, "that democracy in the United States has not been functioning effectively enough to address the major challenges of government."[24] In the same vein, Thomas Friedman and Michael Mandelbaum have worried about the loss of the nation's "capacity for collective action," while Thomas Mann and Norman Ornstein have lamented a declining "capacity to govern."[25] Legislative gridlock is not the only sign of breakdown within the governmental machine. A respected observer of the federal bureaucracy, Donald Kettl, has recently said that it is "struggling, with greater frequency and ever greater failure" to cope with major social and economic problems.[26] In a comprehensive 2014 book, *Why Government Fails So Often*, law professor Peter Schuck described a pattern of "endemic failure" within programs administered by federal agencies.[27] In his own bestselling 2014 book, Francis Fukuyama suggested that part of the problem might be the public's unwillingness to eliminate the red tape that makes it difficult for federal bureaucrats to manage programs efficiently. American democracy, Fukuyama said, was in a state of "political decay," marked in part by its neglect of the "state capacity" that was needed to address major problems.[28]

Discipline. There is a third category of complaints against democracy, the substance of which is concerned less with the machinery of government and more with the demands that are placed upon it. The worry here is that people expect too much of their governments, or alternately that democratic institutions make it too easy for people to pressure government to satisfy those expectations. In other words, it is a worry about an excess rather than a deficiency of democracy—a fear that "voters demand too much" of their governments.[29] The political scientist Matthew Flinders has recently argued that a combination of factors—including a decline in deference to authority, better education, and improved communications technologies—are causing an increase in demands for services and benefits to a level that exceeds what can realistically be delivered by politicians and bureaucrats. The result is an "expectations gap" that has fed public disillusionment with government. The rescue of democracy, Flinders says, depends on reducing the public's "insatiable" demands.[30]

Two symptoms of excessive democracy are said to be "non-stop government growth" and unprecedented levels of peacetime indebtedness.[31] In their popular 2014 book *The Fourth Revolution*, two writers from *The Economist* magazine—John Micklethwait and Adrian Wooldridge—argued that "democracy has become too sloppy and self-indulgent over the recent decades of prosperity." The result is that Western governments have become "bloated and overwhelmed ... supersized by ambition and pulled hither and thither by conflicting aims." Voters "overloaded the state with their demands," Micklethwait and Wooldridge concluded, then became "furious that it works so badly."[32] In his 2012 book *The Great Degeneration*, the historian Niall Ferguson agreed that "something is amiss" with Western democracy. He says there is "an institutional malaise" that threatens to undo "the achievements of half a millennium of Western institutional evolution." The clearest symptom of this malaise, according to Ferguson, is the "feckless" attitude of Western democracies toward spending and indebtedness: "We bay for tougher regulation, though not of ourselves." The result, Ferguson has warned, could be a "fiscal death spiral" that plunges Western democracies into default, hyperinflation, or economic stagnation.[33]

Anticipation. The final category of complaints against democracy has to do with its perceived inability to anticipate and manage long-term problems. Critics have always complained about the shortsightedness of democracies, which is said to be caused by the self-absorption of ordinary people, compounded by the fixation of politicians on winning the next election. But now the problem of shortsightedness seems to be more complicated, in two ways. First, the horizon is more distant: we are now dealing with next-generation problems, rather than next-year problems. This raises questions about our willingness and capacity to look very far into the future, and also about our duties toward people who may not yet be born. And second, the costs of shortsightedness appear to be much larger, and perhaps even cataclysmic.

In the United States and other advanced democracies, four critical long-term problems are usually identified. One is the failure to make adequate investments in the infrastructure that is essential for economic growth, such as roads, high-speed rail, ports, airports and air traffic control, and electric and water utilities.[34] Another is inattention to the effects of an aging population on the cost of pension and healthcare programs for the elderly—a fiscal challenge so large that one American expert has argued it could "threaten democracy itself."[35] And a third is the rise of China, a non-democratic state that will soon become the world's largest economy, and perhaps a threat to the United States' status as global superpower. This is a development that has been described as "the most serious challenge that liberal democracy has faced since fascism in the 1930s."[36]

The fourth and most compelling example of a neglected long-term problem is global warming. Experts warn that the world might experience cataclysmic climate change if severe restrictions on the emission of greenhouse gases are not imposed immediately. But politicians and voters in many of the wealthy democracies have been reluctant to accept such restrictions. "We are criminally failing our children and future generations," one environmentalist has said, because elected officials are "obsessed with opinion polls and maintaining constant popularity."[37] The political scientist John Dunn, a respected commentator on democracy, says that the failure to anticipate this "biological disaster" is evidence of a "dismaying collective fecklessness."[38] The Australian scholars David Shearman and Joseph Wayne Smith have gone further. They argued in 2007 that democracy had failed humanity, and that an authoritarian form of government is necessary instead.[39]

We can see, then, that existing democracy appears to have many serious problems. We might not worry about this if we thought that democratic systems were good at recognizing and fixing such problems. But today's fears about democratic failure are heightened because of a widely held belief that democracies cannot heal themselves, or that they will be outpaced by non-democratic rivals.

The belief that democracies cannot heal themselves is predicated on two assumptions. The first is the notion that democracies are not very creative when it comes to repairing weaknesses in existing institutions. This was the view taken by the distinguished political scientist Samuel Huntington, at least in the American case. Huntington argued in 1968 that Americans had an obsession with reforms that limited and divided power and were "peculiarly blind to the problems of creating effective authority" in government.[40] Francis Fukuyama has recently echoed Huntington's position. "The traditional American solution to perceived governmental dysfunction," Fukuyama said in 2014, "has been to try to expand democratic participation and transparency.... No-one dares suggest that what the country needs is a bit less participation and transparency."[41] If you believe that the declining performance of American government is caused by an excessive number of democratic controls on the bureaucracy, as Fukuyama does, this is a serious problem: the only medicine that Americans are willing to take actually makes the illness worse.

Fukuyama is not alone in his belief in the ineptitude of American democracy in crafting responses to institutional failures. The conservative commentator David Frum also says that the United States is caught in a vicious cycle of dysfunctionality:

> When government seems to fail, Americans habitually resort to the same solutions: more process, more transparency, more appeals to courts. Each dose of this medicine leaves government more sluggish. To counter the ensuing disappointment, reformers urge another dose.... For fifty years, Americans have reformed their government to allow for ever more participation, ever more transparency, ever more reforms and appeals, and ever fewer actual results.[42]

And the legal scholar Richard H. Pildes has made the same argument:

> The central impulse behind many of our democratic reform efforts is not to criticize or challenge the individualist conception of democracy, but to insist on yet more "participation" and other ways of "empowering" individual citizens as the solution to our democratic disaffections.... Our culture seems to reel from one democratic dysfunction, to which the solution is more citizen empowerment, to another, in which we must face up to the perverse consequences of this prior solution, only to try yet another way to ensure more transparency and citizen control.[43]

The second assumption that encourages skepticism about the self-healing capacities of democracies has to do with the perceived inflexibility of existing institutions. After all, creativity in devising solutions for dysfunctionality does little good if it proves impossible to implement those solutions by changing existing institutions. But it is now widely accepted among researchers that governmental institutions cannot be adjusted easily. "Institutions," one academic has recently observed, "are like dried cement."[44]

This is an observation about institutions in any form of government, but some people go further and argue that democratic institutions are particularly hard to change, precisely because it is so easy to mobilize opposition to any possible reform. Modern democracies, the respected political scientists James March and Johan Olsen have argued, "seem to have limited capacity for institutional design and reform."[45] Indeed, Tariq Ali has recently claimed that "the political structure of the United States has barely changed for a hundred and fifty years"—that is, since the end of the Civil War.[46] "State-building in the United States," affirms another scholar, "has been a slow and convoluted process."[47] Authoritarian regimes, by contrast, seem to adapt with an enviable rapidity. The Chinese state, for example, has recently been praised as "a highly dynamic institution . . . Based on experimentation and trial and error, it has been continuously restructured, with institutions regularly re-purposed and incentivized."[48]

As this praise suggests, democratic malaise has been aggravated by the perception that other nations are doing much better even though their commitment to democracy is weak or nonexistent. Even before the rise of China seized the attention of the West, there were the four "Little Dragons"—South Korea, Taiwan,

Hong Kong, and Singapore: nations that achieved remarkable improvements in living standards even though they were under military, colonial, or one-party rule. All four nations have moved toward Western-style democracy in the last two decades, but critics of the Western approach observe that rapid development came before democratization—and furthermore, that democratization may have slowed the pace of development while increasing internal disorder and corruption.[49]

Even in 2013, the pro-democracy group Freedom House said flatly that Singapore was still "not an electoral democracy. Elections are free from irregularities and vote rigging, but the ruling [party] dominates the political process."[50] And yet for many people, Singapore remains a model of rapid growth, social order, and efficient administration. Westerners, the Singaporean writer Kishore Mahbubani said in 2013, cannot see that democracy "is neither a necessary nor a sufficient condition for good governance."[51] When Singapore's long-serving prime minister, Lee Kuan Yew, died in 2015, a former dean of Harvard University's Kennedy School of Government seemed to agree:

It is hard to deny that the nation Lee built has for five decades produced more wealth per capita, more health, and more security for ordinary citizens than any of his competitors. Thus Lee Kuan Yew leaves students and practitioners of government with a challenge. If Churchill was right in his judgment that democracy is the worst form of government except for all the others, what about Singapore?[52]

"To whom will monuments be built a century from now?" added the philosopher Slavoj Žižek. "Among them, perhaps, will be Lee

Kuan Yew . . . the creator of authoritarian capitalism, an ideology set to shape the next century as much as democracy shaped the last."[53]

Of course, China seems to be an even more powerful example of a nation that is thriving despite its hostility toward Western-style democracy. Forty years ago, the American economy was twenty times bigger than the Chinese economy, but soon the Chinese economy will be the larger of the two.[54] Economic reforms have lifted hundreds of millions of Chinese out of poverty. In just thirty years, the population of Chinese cities has grown by more than half a billion people, and in some places the quality of Chinese urban infrastructure exceeds that of major Western cities.[55] Supporters of the "China model of development" argue that it is based on many of the principles that were once thought to be the exclusive advantages of democracy: pragmatism, decentralized experimentation, rapid adoption of innovations, and close attention to the "hearts and minds of the people."[56] In fact, the Gallup World Poll has reported that public confidence in the national government is higher in China than in most of the advanced democracies.[57] But China itself is not a democracy, of course. Its leaders are not elected. Nor is there perceived to be any immediate need to follow the West in this practice. Western democracy is "in crisis," according to Weiwei Zhang, a bestselling Chinese political scientist. The democratic political model, he says, has "deep-seated problems," including simple-minded populism, complacency, short-sightedness, and political rigidity.[58]

Now we know the case against democracy. It seems to suffer from multiple defects, is not very good at repairing itself, and is being outmaneuvered by non-democratic rivals. This is a grim diagnosis. But we should acknowledge that it is not universally shared. There are some people who argue that democracy is not really in crisis at all.

Some defenders of democracy remind us to look at the big picture. For example, even if some newly established democracies have encountered trouble over the last fifteen years, it remains the case that the democratic model is much better established than it was one or two generations ago. Freedom House calculated that there were 69 electoral democracies in 1989, covering 40 percent of the world's population; by 2014, there were 125, covering 63 percent of the world's population. Granted, there has been no significant expansion of democracy since 2000—but taking the long view, this seems more like stalemate than "democracy in retreat."[59] And while the mood in established democracies might be gloomy, it is probably too much to say that these countries are in crisis—if by this we mean a moment in which the collapse of the political system is a real possibility. No one is predicting a junta in Washington or a dictator in Downing Street.

Others point out that the criticism of democracy is too broad and indiscriminate, ignoring those countries where it still works well. Advocates of the "Asian model" have sometimes been criticized for attacking "Western democracy" without recognizing that the structure of politics varies widely from one advanced democracy to the next.[60] The criticism has merit, but advocates of the Asian model are hardly alone in making the mistake. As we can see from the preceding discussion, Western authors routinely fall into the same trap, loosely passing judgment on "Western democracy," the "advanced" or "established" democracies, or simply democracy *tout court*—and sometimes interchanging all of these concepts thoughtlessly. We forget that the world's first and third most populous democracies—India and Indonesia—are not usually counted as part of the Western world. Moreover, several advanced democracies are clearly not in crisis, as some writers concede. Thus, we find Adrian Wooldridge and John Micklethwait of *The Economist* claiming that "democracy is becoming increasingly dysfunctional," while also acknowledging that democracies such as Australia, Canada, and New Zealand are "among the world's best governments."[61]

There is another reason why we might be inclined to ignore today's warnings about the impending collapse of democracy: we have been here before. Since 1900, there have been three other periods in which all of the elements of today's democratic malaise—a shaky economy, a collapse in public confidence, handwringing by intellectuals, and competition from a non-democratic rival—have been combined. And every time, intimations of doom have proved to be unjustified.

For example, the advanced democracies suffered a severe bout of malaise in the mid-1970s. After decades of rapid growth, the industrialized economies stagnated in the 1970s. Many nations suffered from political turbulence—protest, domestic disorder, and the rapid turnover of governments. And at this time, the non-democratic Soviet Union still seemed like a powerful threat to the democratic West. In 1975, an influential study from the Trilateral Commission, a private group of businessmen and intellectuals, fretted about the "bleak future for democratic government" in major Western countries.[62] The following year, the political scientist Richard Simeon described "a political malaise which is in some respects more severe than that of the Great Depression, and which may constitute a threat to the continued existence of representative government itself."[63] "The sickness of democracy," *New York Times* columnist James Reston confirmed, "is no longer a subject for theoretical debate."[64] And yet the sickness appeared to pass: by 1990, the number of democratic states had doubled, and academics were celebrating a global "wave" of democratization.[65]

As Simeon suggested, the established democracies had also suffered from malaise forty years earlier, in the 1930s. Economic conditions at that time were undeniably bleak: the world economy had sunk into a deep depression. The leading democracies—the United States, Britain, and France—were seized with domestic unrest, and many people believed that the democratic system was unequal to the task of recovery. The political scientist Harold Laski lamented the "malaise in representative democracy" and observed that in the United States there was "a wider disillusionment with democracy, a greater skepticism about its institutions, than at any period in its history."[66] The fascist regimes of Italy and Germany appeared to be more effective in reviving their economies and asserting national power. The newly elected American President, Franklin Roosevelt, conceded that he was "deeply impressed" by the accomplishments of Benito Mussolini, Italy's dictator.[67] Again, though, the malaise passed: by the late 1940s, the fascist regimes had collapsed, and democracy had regained the high ground.

And it had been a similar story a few decades earlier. The years preceding World War I were also marked by economic turbulence, although not so severe as the Great Depression. In the United States, the financial crisis of 1907 triggered a 30 percent decline in business activity, and a wave of industrial unrest that persisted for several years.[68] "We are in a period of clamor, of bewilderment, of an almost tremulous unrest," an editor of *The New Republic* wrote in early 1914. "The thought arises: 'Is democracy after all a failure?'"[69] At the same time, H. G. Wells warned of a "growing discord between governments and governed in the world . . . [I]t is an almost worldwide movement . . . an almost universal disappointment with so-called popular government."[70] British and French writers lamented the incompetence of their governments and looked enviously at the "Prussian efficiency" of Kaiser Wilhelm's Germany. Woodrow Wilson was also an admirer of some German methods, and one of his advisors dreamed of replacing the clumsy American democracy with a benevolent dictatorship.[71] But again the malaise passed: the German regime collapsed, and the Allied powers celebrated the "triumph of democracy over autocracy."[72]

So we can put today's "democratic crisis" in context: it is the fourth serious bout of malaise that democratic states have suffered since 1900. In every previous instance, warnings of impending disaster have proved to be wrong. Perhaps the real trouble with democracies is that they suffer from a sort of systemic hypochondria. The political scientist David Runciman has recently argued democracies are "hypersensitive . . . to the impending sense of catastrophe" and therefore live in "a semipermanent state of crisis." American democracy in particular is said to be marked by "its endless questioning of its own survival prospects."[73] We can see why democracies might have this tendency. In the scramble for public attention, everyone has an incentive to exaggerate the risks associated with neglect of their cause. The lesson, it might seem, is that we should not always take the rhetoric of crisis at face value. From this perspective, malaise is a recurrent and transient phenomenon: democracies always claim to be fatally ill, but they always recover.

So what is the truth, after all—is democracy really in trouble today, or are we simply exaggerating minor ailments? In this book, I will propose a way of thinking about democratic crises that will help us to make sense of our experiences over the last century, and also our current malaise. I intend to tread a path between dismissal and despair. On one hand, we must take declarations of malaise seriously. It is not just hypochondria. When democracies declare themselves to be in a deep funk, there usually is something seriously wrong with the polity. We will not deny that the democratic world confronted grave problems in 1910, 1933, and 1974, and that it confronts grave problems again today. However, we must do some investigation to find out exactly what is wrong at any particular moment in history. Not all bouts of malaise have the same features and causes.

On the other hand, we will take warnings of impending catastrophe with a grain of salt. Conditions are not always so bad as critics of democracy may think at the darkest moments. In fact, many democracies have a well-honed capacity to reinvent themselves in response to new challenges. The architecture of government is overhauled, so that the practical meaning of democracy—that is, what it actually involves as a matter of everyday government—is changed substantially. When we recognize this capacity for reinvention, our view of malaise is likely to change. Rather than being a portent of imminent collapse, malaise may be a sign that a process of democratic reconstruction is under way.

I propose to illustrate this argument by looking at the four "crises of democracy" that have afflicted national politics in the United States since 1900. In doing this, I am trying to avoid an all-encompassing argument about the virtues or weaknesses of established democracies, or Western democracies, or democracy as an ideal. That approach is too broad to be useful. It makes sense to focus on the United States because, in the global contest of ideas, the experience of the democratic superpower is given great weight. In fact, it often becomes clear on close reading that many books and articles criticizing democracy in general are really motivated by the perceived failures of American democracy at the national level. Frustrating though it may be for the citizens of other nations, the United States is viewed as the model of democratic practice. I suspect that some of the claims I make about the character of democratic crises in the United States could be applied to other countries. But this book will be concerned mainly with the American experience.

I will begin by arguing that not all bouts of malaise are alike. Earlier, I noted the common features of democratic crises, such as a sour public mood, a declining economy, and a perceived threat from a non-democratic rival. But if we look at the American experience since 1900, there are deeper differences between the four moments of crisis. In each case, American democracy was wrestling with a fundamentally different problem of governance. The problem was not entirely new, but presented itself with unprecedented intensity, and it was this fact that created the sense of crisis. At each of the four moments, the American polity found itself on an unfamiliar frontier.

The first crisis that I will examine (in chapter 2) roughly spans the years from 1890 to 1920. I will argue that in this period, national politics in the United States was preoccupied with a *crisis of representation*. Such a crisis arises when large parts of a governed population protest against their inability to influence the exercise of power. The central question that is asked by these excluded people is whether their system of government can properly be characterized as a democracy at all, given the fact of their exclusion from that system. In the years before World War I, half the adult American population was disenfranchised because of their sex, and another 5 percent was disenfranchised because of race, while a substantial proportion of the remaining population believed that the institutions of government had been captured by moneyed interests. For this large and restless majority, American democracy was a fraud. The dominant question in this era was how to restructure national government so that its legitimacy would be restored.

The second period that I will examine (in chapter 3) roughly spans the years from 1917 to 1948, and includes the moment of deep malaise of the mid-1930s. I will argue that in these years, national politics was seized with a *crisis of mastery*. In the vocabulary of the time, the United States was being acted upon by powerful social and economic forces, which the national government—with its rudimentary bureaucracy and armed services—appeared to be incapable of controlling. Democracy seemed to be a hollow accomplishment because it lacked the administrative capacity that was necessary to allow the exercise of power. Elected officials were like workmen without tools. Many people wondered whether democracies like the United States had the capacity to overcome their aversion to strong government, so that they could build the bureaucratic and military institutions that were necessary to address grave threats.

The third period that I will examine spans the years between 1970 and 2007, and includes the moment of deep malaise of the mid-1970s (chapter 4). By this time, the United States had broadened voting rights and substantially expanded the capabilities of national government. It was much easier for citizens to make demands on government, and easier for politicians to respond to those demands. But the question arose as to whether it might be possible for citizens to demand too much, and politicians to respond too quickly. Many people argued that the circuitry of government had been overloaded, and that steps were necessary to reduce public expectations about the provision of public services and benefits. I will argue that in this period, national politics in the United States was seized by a *crisis of discipline*.

The fourth period that I wish to examine is one that began with the financial crisis of 2007–2008 and continues today. As I suggested earlier, we are still sorting out precisely what kind of malaise we are suffering from today. There are people who think that our main problem is the capture of democratic institutions by moneyed interests, which suggests that this might be another crisis of representation. There are people who dwell on our deficient "capacity for collective action"—which sounds much like a crisis of mastery. And there are people who suggest that the core problem is the insatiability of public expectations, which suggests that this is merely a continuation of the crisis of discipline. In other words, all of these people tend to see the current malaise as a reprise of an earlier episode in American history.

It is conceivable, though, that the current crisis is something different. In chapter 5, I will argue that it might be construed as a *crisis of anticipation*—that is, the sort of crisis that arises because of doubts about the capacity of a democracy to deal with problems that have long-delayed but very serious consequences. For Americans, this includes climate change, the rise of China as a competing power, decaying infrastructure, and fiscal pressures associated with an aging population. I do not mean to suggest that this is necessarily the right interpretation of the current crisis: this is a matter to be debated. Still, it makes sense to give serious attention to the possibility that we might be dealing with a crisis of anticipation. We do not want to fall into the habit of assuming that the future is just a replay of the past. And as we shall see, the management of these long-term problems could require innovations that fundamentally reshape our understanding of what a viable democracy looks like. I will focus on climate change, which is arguably the most serious of the long-run threats facing the United States today.

It is useful at this point to address three possible objections to the argument that I intend to make. The first is that the periods of crisis that I have described cover most of the last century of American history: the implication might seem to be that I believe that American democracy is always in crisis. Here I admit to some looseness in the use of language. Each of the past three periods spans two or three decades. Within each of these periods, there was a shorter moment in which there was indeed a widely shared sense of crisis. However, there were many other years within each period in which there was no such anxiety, but in which national politics was still dominated by the task of renovating institutions to deal with the conditions that triggered anxiety. For convenience, I will refer to whole periods as crises; in fact, each period usually consists of a moment of deeply felt crisis, and a phase of less anxious institutional adjustment. (An implication is that we are still in the early phases of a fourth period of adjustment, which may last for another ten or twenty years.[74])

A second objection has to do with the demarcation of these four periods. Any attempt to define distinctive phases of history is liable to criticism.[75] For example, am I really going to argue that all problems of enfranchisement were dealt with by 1920, the end of my "crisis of representation"? After all, Congress did not seriously address the problem of African American exclusion until it passed the Voting Rights Act in 1965. Similarly, am I really saying that problems of building administrative capacity never arose before the "crisis of mastery" began in 1917? This seems to be contradicted by the immense build-up of military capabilities that was necessary to fight the Civil War. And am I really saying that the only thing that preoccupied Americans after 1974—the starting point for my "crisis of discipline"—was limiting public expectations about what government would do? After 2001, for example, the federal government rushed to satisfy new demands for improved homeland security and built substantial new capacity to satisfy these demands.

Here, again, I must ask readers to tolerate a little looseness. The four periods that I describe are not watertight compartments. In any period, government deals to some extent with problems of representation, mastery, discipline, and anticipation. Indeed, we could think of these as the four fundamental problems of democratic governance. Still, not all tasks present themselves with equal urgency at all times; and it can be shown that in each of these periods the dominating theme had to do with one of these tasks rather than the other three. I also recognize that every crisis leaves unfinished business for the next generation. For example, I concede that the problem of African American voting rights was not seriously addressed until the 1960s, and arguably not adequately addressed even then. But this does not detract from the point that the politics of 1890–1920 was dominated by controversies over disenfranchisement.

A third objection might be that I am oversimplifying the character of national politics in each of these periods. It might seem very neat: a problem is recognized, and then the problem is fixed. I do not want to convey this impression at all. Problems are never self-evident: evidence about democratic failure may only emerge in pieces, and be liable to multiple interpretations. Only time and public debate result in the coalescence of a dominant interpretation of events.[76] Similarly, solutions are never obvious. New institutional arrangements have to be invented, and sometimes these new inventions challenge traditional understandings about the role of government, or appear to threaten widely held values. Often, new institutions have to be modified to accommodate political opposition, or deal with unanticipated problems that arise after their establishment. The process of inventing, implementing, and adapting institutions can also be contentious—and indeed, is never really finished.

But a critical point is that the institutions of American democracy do change—and have changed radically in response to repeated bouts of malaise. Granted, the pace of reform never satisfies the impatient reformer, for whom the deficiencies of the status quo are obvious and ought to be fixed immediately. But it is not clear why this should be our standard for judging the rate of adaptation within a large democracy like the United States. We ought to take a longer view. Tariq Ali is flat-out wrong when he says that "the political structure of the United States has barely changed for a hundred and fifty years."[77] Any writer of 1865 would be stunned to see the governmental apparatus of 2015. The meaning of American democracy, as it is expressed through its institutions, has been transformed in that time.

Moreover, there has been more creativity in the renovation of American government than is generally recognized. Certainly, there have been instances in which the response to perceived failures has been the imposition of "more democracy"—or, as David Frum has put it, "more process, more transparency, more appeals to courts."[78] But this has hardly been the typical or habitual response to crises. The crisis of mastery produced an expansive federal bureaucracy, a more powerful presidency, and the foundations of the national security state. The crisis of discipline also reinforced the presidency, bolstered the power and autonomy of the Federal Reserve, and led us into an age of spending controls, international trade agreements, and deregulation. All of this was authorized by democratically elected officials—that is, by the people's representatives. Even so, all of these reforms actually complicated the task of exercising democratic control over government. Indeed, one of the distinctive features of the last century has been the extent to which elected officials have been prepared to experiment with reforms that are anti-democratic in spirit but suited to the needs of the moment. I will discuss this practice of playing with anti-democratic reforms more fully in chapter 6.

What gives American democracy the capacity to adapt, and is there anything about the American system that might make it better at adaptation than non-democratic states? I will also examine these questions in chapter 6. Some considerations come quickly to mind—such as ideological pragmatism, a decentralized structure that encourages experimentation, and close attention to the public mood. As I noted earlier, it has been argued that non-democratic states like China also possess these three virtues, but we should be skeptical about that claim. And the democratic approach has other advantages as well: notably, the capacity to foster intense debate about problems and solutions, and to allow for the swift replacement of rulers. Certainly, democracy may be prone to malaise, like all systems of government—but a well-functioning democracy also provides the cure.

"SIXTY-ONE AND NINETEEN-NINE.——WHO WILL MARCH TO SET US FREE?"

Fig. 2.1 "Sixty-one and nineteen-nine—who will march to set us free?" Print by Keppler & Schwarzmann, New York, 1909. A gloved hand labeled "Plutocracy" with a design showing the US Capitol crushes a group of citizens with its thumb; while on the left, in the clouds of the past, a Union army marches into battle as Abraham Lincoln frees the slaves. (Library of Congress)

Representation

We have not a democracy today. We have a monarch, and his name is J. P. Morgan.

> —Gertrude Atherton, *San Diego (CA) Union*,
> October 4, 1912

Democracy means rule of the people. But the people of the United States do not rule: only men rule.

> —Alice Davis, *Atlanta (GA) Jeffersonian*, November 4, 1909

This Negro will not be satisfied until he gets a fair chance to vote. And until that chance is given, "Our Democracy" is merely a sham and a farce.

> —R. R. Wright Jr., "What Does the Negro Want in
> Our Democracy?" *Proceedings of the National Conference
> of Social Work*, 1910

We are not dealing with immigration in any ordinary sense of the word, but with an inundation and a conquest. We have put our American institutions into imminent peril.

> —John H. Denison, Testimony to Dillingham Commission
> on Immigration, 1910

Whose country is it? Whose government?
—*ROCKFORD (IL) MORNING STAR*, August 30, 1912

At the end of the nineteenth century, the intellectual elites of the United States and the United Kingdom were tightly connected, and within that community, James Bryce was "almost a legendary figure."[1] At the age of 26, he published an acclaimed study of the Holy Roman Empire; at 32, he became a professor at the University of Oxford; at 42, he was elected as a member of the British House of Commons; at 54, he joined the cabinet of Prime Minister William Gladstone. And he traveled constantly across the United States. He met an aging Longfellow and a young Theodore Roosevelt, watched Boss Tweed orchestrate a Democratic Party convention, and saw the driving of the last spike on the Northern Pacific's transcontinental railroad. American audiences were captivated by his erudition and "brilliant gray eyes."[2] In 1915, after Bryce served as Britain's ambassador to Washington, Woodrow Wilson called him the greatest living Englishman.[3]

The thing that cemented Bryce's fame in the United States was his three-volume book, *The American Commonwealth*. First published in 1888, it was hailed by Theodore Roosevelt as a match for Tocqueville's *Democracy in America*.[4] Woodrow Wilson himself called it a "great work."[5] It was still a textbook in American schools when Bryce died in 1922 and acclaimed as "the best discussion of American institutions and public life ever written by anybody."[6] What particularly impressed Americans was Bryce's sympathy toward the country's experiment with democracy. In no other country, Bryce said, did the "opinion of the whole nation" have such power over the nation's leaders. In the United States, "every man knows that he is himself a part of the government . . . [and] that the government is his own."[7]

Still, the system that Bryce called a democracy was imperfect. Bryce conceded that Congress was dominated by "railroad men, land speculators, and manufacturers"—but the federal government played such a small role in everyday life that this did not seem to be a major difficulty. Bryce also recognized that women could not vote, but dismissed this as a "minor question." Nor was Bryce troubled that southern elections were manipulated to exclude African American males because they were "as unfit for political rights as any population could be." Similarly, Bryce felt the delay in providing statehood to Arizona and New Mexico was justified because the Southwest was "populated by Indo-Spanish Mexicans . . . obviously ill fitted for self-government." Bryce thought that American cities showed the dangers of extending voting rights too quickly. These cities were corrupt and ill-managed, Bryce said, because they had "a vast population of ignorant immigrants . . . not fit for the suffrage."[8]

If statements like these were made today, we would consider them inflammatory. Bryce and his American friends did not give them a second thought. But this complacency evaporated over the next three decades. The question of whether the United States could be described accurately as a democracy—in Bryce's own words, a form of government in which power was vested "in members of the community as a whole"[9]—seized American politics (fig. 2.1). Many people who already had the right to vote believed that their actual influence over government was slipping away, either because politicians had been captured by "moneyed interests" or because immigration was "diluting the body politic."

And at the same time there were louder protests by millions of disenfranchised women and African Americans. The dire condition
of American politics was illustrated by the presidential election of
1912. Bryce, serving as Britain's ambassador in Washington, con-
gratulated Woodrow Wilson for an impressive victory.[10] It was
not: Wilson became president of the "leading democracy of the
world" with the votes of only one-tenth of the adult population.[11]

Between 1890 and 1920 the United States suffered a crisis of
representation, provoked by widespread doubts about whether
American government could accurately be described as a system of rule by the people. In one respect, this was simply a question of whether votes mattered: that is, whether the decisions of
politicians were actually guided by preferences expressed in the
voting booth. (It is not an accident that this era saw the advent
of the voting machine, described in a 1907 patent application as
a "simple yet highly efficient" device for recording voter choices
that would thwart efforts by "unprincipled politicians to stuff the
ballot."[12]) But the more difficult question was who ought to be
counted among "the people," and therefore entitled to vote. This
was not a purely philosophical matter. The existing electorate—
that is, the population of adult white male citizens—was being
asked to surrender some share of its political power. The mystery
was why they would do this voluntarily.[13]

In chapter 1, we noted a common complaint about the
American response to crises of governance: that it habitually
consists of demands for more democracy, more participation,
and more transparency. As we shall see in following chapters,
this is clearly not true of the crises of the 1930s and the 1970s.
A stronger case can be made for the years 1890–1920. Many
of the reforms adopted in this period really were about "more

democracy": more people were allowed to vote, they were given more to vote for, and steps were taken to make elections fairer and more open. But even in this period, the response to crisis also took other forms, aimed at constraining rather than expanding self-rule. The system was still demonstrating its ability to adapt to new challenges, but in an unhealthy way: it revealed a pathological inventiveness as it restricted the political rights of African Americans, immigrants, and radicals. Fortunately, the system retained enough openness that some of the wrongs committed in this era could be corrected decades later.

The years between 1890 and 1920 were dominated by the fear that the United States had ceased to be a democracy and was instead a plutocracy, a system of "government by the rich for the rich."[14] The burst of industrialization after the Civil War produced a new class of powerful corporations and a new aristocracy of wealthy entrepreneurs, who seemed able to flout the law, or make their own law by buying the service of voters and politicians. The main impulse of politics in this period was to reform institutions so that the "power of centralized and predatory wealth" was checked, and sovereignty restored to the people.[15]

This was an era of extraordinary changes in the structure of the American economy. Two aspects of this transformation were especially troubling. The first was the emergence of vast and powerful industrial enterprises. By 1888 the Pennsylvania Railroad alone had 100,000 employees, almost as many as the whole federal government.[16] Railroads often enjoyed regional monopolies and dictated the price at which farmers, manufacturers, and traders shipped their goods. Regulation was weak—at the federal level, almost nonexistent—and abuses of monopoly

power were frequent. In 1901 the journalist Frank Norris condemned California's Central Pacific Railway as "an excrescence,
a gigantic parasite fattening upon the lifeblood of an entire commonwealth."[17] Rage against the industry mounted as railroads
combined to form super-systems in the 1890s. By 1906, according to the historian Alfred Chandler Jr., consolidation had "prac-
tically eliminated" competition between major railroads.[18]

The phenomenon of corporate growth and consolidation was
not limited to the railroads. Every part of the commercial world
was touched by the effort to control production and fix prices.[19]
The US Steel Corporation, formed in 1901, controlled over
250 mining and manufacturing companies and accounted for
60 percent of all iron and steel production in the United States.[20]
At the same time, John D. Rockefeller's Standard Oil combination controlled most of the nation's oil pipelines and refiner-
ies, and in some parts of the country it was the only available
purchaser of crude oil.[21] In an exposé for *McClure's* magazine,
the journalist Ida May Tarbell said that Rockefeller wielded
"autocratic powers in commerce": Standard Oil's practices were
ruthless and sometimes corrupt.[22] A congressional inquiry led
by Louisiana Representative Arsène Pujo found that there was
a "money trust" too—a combination to control money and
credit led by the financier J. P. Morgan.[23] Boston lawyer Louis
Brandeis—soon to be appointed to the Supreme Court—said
that bankers had established a "financial oligarchy."[24] It was
even alleged that the money trust had engineered the financial
crisis of 1907 to "break down" the reform-minded president,
Theodore Roosevelt.[25]

Fears about corporate power were combined with alarm about
the unprecedented concentration of wealth in the hands of a few

Americans. There had always been a division of rich and poor people in the United States, but the separation had never been so stark as it was at the advent of the twentieth century. In 1893 the statistician George Holmes reported that 9 percent of American families owned 70 percent of the nation's wealth, and that there was even further concentration of wealth within that small group. Holmes calculated that the richest four thousand households in the United States owned more than poorest eleven million. "The results seem almost incredible," Holmes conceded.[26] But his findings were bolstered by another study three years later. Ten percent of American families, Charles Spahr found, earned the same income as the remaining 90 percent, and the top 1 percent earned the same total income as the bottom 50 percent.[27] A decade later, another writer said the situation had become even worse. One percent of the population, Henry Lauren Call concluded, owned at least 90 percent of the total wealth of the country.[28] Call was denounced as a socialist, but this image of the spoiled 1 percent—the "luxury class"—became lodged in popular consciousness.

The image was reinforced by stories of extraordinary wealth and spectacular consumption. In 1909 John D. Rockefeller was on track to become the first billionaire in history: with an estimated worth of seven hundred million dollars, he alone could have financed the entire expenditure of the federal government in that year.[29] Newspapers speculated that the Astors—"the synonym of unspeakable wealth"—were almost that rich as well.[30] Andrew Carnegie was said to have more wealth than "all the greatest names in history" combined.[31] The new Vanderbilt summer home in Newport, Rhode Island, was hailed as a "veritable palace," grander than any castle in Europe.[32] When a Vanderbilt scion was married there in 1903, one newspaper described the wedding as "an orgy of vulgarity . . . a struggle to spend as much as much money as possible."[33]

Such gross economic inequality was offensive in its own right. Added to this was the fear that the rich were using their money to acquire special privileges in politics as well. "We cannot join economic inequality and political equality," the theologian Walter Rauschenbusch wrote in 1907. "If we have a class which owns a large part of the national wealth . . . it is idle to suppose that this class will not see to it that the vast power exerted by the machinery of government serves its interests."[34]

Economic inequality was transformed into political inequality through the corruption of democratic institutions. On election day, voters were presented with a list of candidates chosen by party bosses who were paid off by special interests. And elections themselves were often rigged: parties invented clever ways of stuffing ballot boxes, paid for the loyalty of election officials, or simply bought the voters themselves.[35] This was made easier when voting was done with colored ballots that were provided by the parties and cast into a glass ballot box that was open to public inspection. The loyalty of politicians could also be acquired after their election. City councilors took bribes for making appointments to the municipal payroll and dispensing streetcar and utility franchises on favorable terms. "General corruption," the journalist Lincoln Steffens said in 1906, was "the shame of the cities."[36] State legislatures were scarcely better. Illinois governor Edward Dunne argued that the legislative power of states was actually shared by "a third house, not recognized by the laws or constitution."[37] This was the corporate lobby, consisting largely of railroad lawyers, "continually on guard in the legislative halls."[38]

Corruption within state legislatures was especially problematic because those bodies were charged with the responsibility of electing the members of the US Senate. One expert observed in 1906 that the problem of corruption in senatorial elections became a "national scandal" after 1890.[39] Senate investigations routinely found evidence of bribery, but strict rules made it difficult to punish offenders. Still, Montana Senator William A. Clark was induced to resign in 1899 after the revelation that his election had been won with cash-stuffed envelopes. In 1912 the Senate expelled Illinois Senator William Lorimer after a tumultuous two-year investigation of allegations that Lorimer had bribed state legislators in order to win his seat. Wisconsin Senator Isaac Stephenson narrowly avoided expulsion on corruption charges in the same year, mainly because the bribes that were paid to support his election were not given directly to state legislators.

The common belief was that senators themselves were prepared to invest large sums to purchase their seats in the Senate because they were certain of a generous return on their investment once they reached Washington.[40] There were complaints about the operation of a "third house" on Capitol Hill as well.[41] *Cosmopolitan Magazine* sent its sales soaring in 1906 when it published a series of articles by David Graham Phillips that purported to show how US senators had "sold out the people" to railroaders and financiers.[42] Phillips called it treason. His colleague Ernest Crosby said that politics in Washington had become a sham. "Wall Street is real and Washington is not," Crosby wrote. "Washington is a mere simulacrum, like the gilt pipes of an organ, only for show while the real tunes are played out of sight underneath."[43]

This idea—that democracy had become a fraud—pervaded popular thinking in the new century. Democratic presidential candidate William Jennings Bryan lamented that the United States was "merely a democracy in form—and a plutocracy in fact."[44] The journalist John Calvin Reed agreed that the American people were only "nominally and seemingly self-governing"; in reality, they were governed by private corporations.[45] Illinois Senator Robert L. Owen Jr. said it was like a new form of slavery, in which the American people were subjected to "government by the commercially strong."[46]

And foreign observers agreed with this diagnosis. "The American people," the Russian historian Moisey Ostrogorsky said in 1902, "have let the government slip from their hands." Ostrogorsky thought that American experience illustrated a larger problem: that democracy, in practice, could not sustain itself. The ordinary man is "proclaimed sovereign in the State . . . [but] wields only a shadow of the sovereignty which is laid at his feet . . . [H]e has, in reality, no power over the choice of the men who govern in his name."[47] An influential German sociologist agreed. American democracy, Robert Michels wrote in 1915, had been conquered by the "unrestricted power of capital." Again, this was seen as evidence of a larger truth about the frailty of democracy. "The notion of representation of popular interests . . . is an illusion," Michels concluded. Eventually, democracy was always supplanted by oligarchy.[48]

Signs of democratic failure were abundant in the United States by the early 1910s. One sign of disaffection was the decline in turnout for elections. In the northern states, 84 percent of the eligible electorate voted in presidential elections of 1884 to 1896; this dropped to 70 percent for the elections of 1904 to 1920.[49]

There was also a flight away from the two major parties. On average, new parties (Populists, Progressives, Socialists, and Prohibitionists) took 8 percent of the popular vote in presidential elections between 1892 and 1920. Meanwhile industrial workers became better organized—union membership quadrupled between 1896 and 1914—and more radicalized.[50] State governments strengthened their militias as conflicts between employers and workers became larger and more threatening.[51] Railroad strikes in Chicago became so violent that the War Department built a new camp outside the city so that it could restore order more quickly. A federal inquiry into labor-management relations led by Missouri lawyer Frank B. Walsh concluded in 1916 that frustration over the "unjust distribution of wealth and income" could soon "rise into active revolt or, if forcibly repressed, sink into sullen hatred."[52]

In fact, the Walsh inquiry was one of the instruments that American democracy used to repair itself after the turn of the century. It reflected the general enthusiasm for exposing corruption and maladministration that seized the country at this time. The exposure of misconduct was held to be the first step toward rehabilitation: as James Bryce himself said, sunlight was the best way to kill "those noxious germs which are hatched where politics congregate."[53] The expository impulse drove journalists like Steffens, Tarbell, Norris, and Phillips. But it was also incorporated into government practice through devices like the Pujo and Walsh investigations.[54]

The project of political reform had more important components. Populists pressed for the direct election of senators, and by 1900 it was part of the Democratic platform as well. By 1905, more than thirty states had passed resolutions calling for a constitutional amendment that would allow direct election.[55] In 1904, Oregon experimented with a statewide "advisory election" that was intended to bind the legislature's choice of senators, and other states followed: by 1912 most were selecting senators through some form of popular election. In 1911, Congress began the process of revising the Constitution to require direct election, and the proposed amendment was quickly ratified by states. The change came into force in 1913—a demonstration, according to New York governor William Sulzer, of the "rising tide of democracy."[56]

Oregon was one of those states that served as a testbed for the construction of a "new democracy" after 1890.[57] By 1910, Oregon citizens had the power to petition for referendums that would force state legislators to pass new laws or overturn laws already passed. Oregon also adopted a direct primary law that removed the power to nominate candidates from party conventions and put it in the hands of all party members in the state. The new system promised "the overthrow and expulsion of the party boss," one supporter said, "and to introduce democracy into the party system."[58] The law was not limited to candidates for state offices: it also applied to nominations for the House of Representatives in Washington, as well as the selection of delegates to national party conventions that chose presidential candidates. This innovation spread with extraordinary speed: by 1915, most states had adopted similar primary laws.[59]

At the same time, states were overhauling the mechanics of voting for national as well as local offices. Frustration with election fraud drove a countrywide movement to adopt the "Australian ballot": a system by which votes had to be cast with standardized ballots printed by state governments rather than parties, handed to voters only at the polling place. The Australian ballot was introduced in Kentucky in 1888 and by 1918 was being used in almost all states. States also took other measures to establish "quiet, order and cleanliness" at the polls.[60] Glass ballot boxes gave way to private voting booths, and campaigning was banned within the immediate vicinity of the polling place. Reformers hoped that the vote would be transformed into "a secret and sacred act."[61]

Congress itself joined in the movement for reform. In 1907, it followed the example of many state legislatures and prohibited corporations from making campaign contributions in federal elections. In 1910, it again followed state models by mandating the disclosure of information about campaign donations—another vote of confidence in the power of transparency, intended to "throw a glaring light on the corrupt alliance between business and politics."[62] Congress attempted to strengthen this law the following year, by adding spending limits on congressional campaigns. Congress also modified its own practices. In another concession to transparency, the Senate largely abandoned its practice of debating treaties and presidential nominations in secret sessions.[63] Corruption and incompetence, one reformer complained, were hidden in the "dark shadow of Senatorial secrecy."[64] Meanwhile there was a "revolution" in the House of Representatives, as Democrats and progressive Republicans combined in 1910 to limit the authority of Speaker Joe Cannon, who was said to wield power over bills and appointments "like an Eastern despot."[65]

All of the preceding changes were overtly political reforms. That is, they were adjustments to the rules of everyday politics, designed to remove power from moneyed interests and return it to the people. But the reform impulse was not strictly limited to the rules of the political game. It also extended to economic reforms that were designed to address the more fundamental problem, which was an imbalance of economic power. "If we want approximate political equality," the theologian Walter Rauschenbusch argued, "we must have approximate economic equality. If we attempt it otherwise, we shall be bucking against the law of gravitation."[66]

One goal of reform was to control the abuse of power by railroads. This was mainly a state concern until 1886, when a decision by the Supreme Court limited the power of state governments to regulate railroads whose activities crossed state lines. Congress responded in 1887 by establishing the Interstate Commerce Commission and giving it limited authority to control railroad prices. Initially, the Commission was hampered by modest powers, but as the pace of railroad consolidation quickened, Congress bolstered its authority three times—in 1903, 1906, and 1910. The Commission also had an unusual structure that was modeled on the design of some state regulatory bodies: its five commissioners had to be chosen from both political parties, were guaranteed six-year appointments, and were barred from holding any other job or any investment in railroads.[67] The aim was to drive special interests out of politics: the Commission would be independent of railroads and politicians who were bought by railroads.[68]

Congress also took action to curtail the emergence of monopolies in other parts of the economy. In 1890 it adopted the Sherman Anti-Trust Act, which allowed the Department of Justice to prosecute conspiracies to restrain trade. The statute was weakened by unfavorable court decisions, but still proved to be a powerful weapon against monopolies. One writer called it the most important law adopted since the Civil War, addressing a subject almost as weighty as the liberation of the slaves.[69] In 1903, Congress bolstered the law by creating a new Bureau of Corporations to investigate and publicize corporate abuses.[70] And then in 1914, it established a new Federal Trade Commission, "divorced from politics" like the Interstate Commerce Commission, to enforce a strengthened anti-trust law.[71] At roughly the same time, Congress took specific action against the "money trust." In 1913 it created the Federal Reserve System: a complicated structure of regional banks, overseen by a Washington-based board that was supposed to have independence like the two commissions. The new law, one of the Pujo commission investigators said, was a "triumph for popular government ... [over] the despotism of the great banks."[72]

The program of economic reform was rounded out by the establishment of a federal income tax. Throughout the nineteenth century, the cost of federal government was financed easily by tariffs on imported goods. In the 1890s, however, populists demanded a limitation of the tariff, the burden of which fell heavily on farmers and consumers, and the adoption of a graduated income tax instead. Senator William Borah, a progressive Republican, conceded that the lack of an income tax helped to maintain "an aristocracy of wealth and a democracy of paupers."[73] But the Supreme Court had ruled in 1895 that the federal government lacked authority under the Constitution to impose an income tax. In 1909, Congress began the process of amending the Constitution, and by 1913 the process of state ratification was completed. A graduated income tax—a "rough and ready sort of way of getting back at the predatory class"—was finally adopted in the form of the Revenue Act of 1913.[74]

There was another important way in which democracy was advanced as a result of the crisis of representation: the right to vote was granted to women across the United States. In 1888, James Bryce reported that some states allowed women to vote for school boards, and one state (Kansas) allowed them to vote in municipal elections too. But no state permitted women to vote in elections for state and federal offices, and proposals to amend state constitutions to extend the vote were "invariably rejected" by voters. The limited evidence from experiments with women's suffrage was unfavorable, Bryce reported. It was impossible to get "respectable" women out to vote except on "purely emotional questions," with the result that "women of the worst classes are those that most regularly go to the polls." Most women, Bryce said, were hostile to enfranchisement, and some were happy when their limited voting rights were rescinded.[75]

However, the situation changed quickly after 1888. In 1890, Wyoming was admitted to the union with full suffrage for women, and by 1900 three other western states had extended full voting rights as well. Eight states were added to the list by the outbreak of World War I, and another five within the next two years. Many other states granted limited suffrage for local elections.[76] In 1918, President Wilson urged Congress to approve a constitutional amendment allowing women to vote: Congress did so in June 1919, and the amendment was ratified by thirty-six states within fourteen months. The country had never seen so many people added to the pool of eligible voters at one time. Eighteen million people voted in the presidential election of 1916—but twenty-seven million voted in 1920.

The constitutional amendment was the "final victory" of a movement that had been campaigning for women's suffrage for seventy years.[77] The power of the movement improved considerably in 1890 when three rival suffrage groups agreed to merge into one, the National American Woman Suffrage Association. By 1910, NAWSA was a disciplined and well-funded organization with a national headquarters in New York, a press bureau dedicated to "suffrage propaganda," an expansive network of state and local affiliates, and a membership that would soon reach two million people.[78] It was a "strong machine," NAWSA leaders boasted in 1917, "run with the method of male politicians."[79]

Voting rights were determined mainly by state and local governments, and consequently there were hundreds of opportunities for suffragists to lobby for reform. Even small victories—such as the right to vote in a municipal or school board election—advanced the broader cause because it was difficult for parties to campaign against women's suffrage in one election without losing the support of women in other elections where they already had the right to vote. At the same time, these small experiments demonstrated to political leaders that the risk of political upheaval as a result of women's enfranchisement was low.[80] The extension of voting rights to women did not substantially alter the balance of power between major parties, economic classes, sections of the country, or races. NAWSA made clear that it had "no view . . . on the race question" or on the laws that were used in southern states to restrict the African American vote.[81]

American suffragists also gained strength because they were part of an international movement. Progress in other countries allowed them to cultivate a sense of national embarrassment at home. New Zealand gave full voting rights to women in 1893: "Domestic life," the American press reported, "has not been disturbed or even ruffled. . . . [W]omen have shown sound judgment."[82] When Australia followed in 1902, the suffragist Carrie Chapman Catt complained that the United States had "lost its place as the leading exponent of democracy . . . Australia and New Zealand have out-Americanized America."[83] Finland extended the franchise to women in 1906, Norway in 1907, Denmark in 1915, Canada and Russia in 1917, and Britain in February 1918. It was "unthinkable that the United States should lag behind Great Britain and Canada," Catt said. "Our national boast has been that nowhere in the world are women treated so well as in America."[84]

Suffragists also imported tactics from abroad. As the British suffrage movement became more militant in the prewar years, so did the American one. On the eve of Wilson's inauguration in March 1913, suffragists organized a demonstration in Washington "against the present political organization of society": it triggered a congressional inquiry after police failed to protect demonstrators from assaults by anti-suffragists.[85] When the United States entered World War I, suffragists established a regular picket at the White House, embarrassing the president as he received diplomats from allied countries. Soon after Russia extended the vote to women in March 1917, the Russian ambassador was greeted with a banner urging him to tell Wilson that the United States should "liberate its people" as well.[86] The picketers were arrested and then pardoned after going on a hunger strike. But they returned to the picket line and were arrested again after they burned the president in effigy. A leading suffragist protested: "President Wilson says that democracy consists in the right of those who submit to authority to have a voice in their own government, and American women are required to send their sons to die in Europe in order that democracy may obtain there. . . . It is a curious brand of democracy that the women of America are asked to sacrifice their sons for."[87]

As the war ground on, the suffrage movement became a serious problem for Wilson and other allied leaders. Before 1914, the question had mainly been whether the existing order could be maintained if voting rights were extended. Now the question was turned on its head: it was whether the existing order could be maintained if voting rights were not extended. Wilson addressed the problem directly when he urged Congress to endorse a constitutional amendment in September 1918:

> It is my duty to win the war and to ask you to remove every obstacle that stands in the way of winning it. . . . [A constitutional amendment is] clearly necessary to the successful prosecution of the war. . . . [T]he plain, struggling workaday folk . . . are looking to the great, powerful, famous democracy of the west to lead them to the new day for which they have so long waited: and they think, in their logical simplicity, that democracy means that women shall play their part in affairs alongside men and upon an equal footing with them. If we reject measures like this . . . they will cease to believe in us; they will cease to follow or to trust us.[88]

A constitutional amendment probably would have been adopted even if the United States had not entered the war, although not so quickly. The tendency in the states was toward reform, and the United States still would have been embarrassed as countries like Britain and Canada changed their laws. American involvement in the war simply brought matters to a head more quickly, as the imperatives of waging war dissolved remaining doubts about the risks of extending the vote to women.

So far, the story of the crisis of representation has been one of the rapid expansion of self-rule. The electorate was doubled by the enfranchisement of women, the popular vote was extended to the Senate and presidential races, some elections were run more professionally, and corporate power was better controlled. But there is another half to the story that is less benign. Other groups found their demands for inclusion in the American democracy repulsed. Laws were amended or broken, and violence was applied, with the aim of limiting the principle of self-rule. This was the experience of the five million adult African Americans who lived mainly in the Deep South at the turn of the century, and who constituted at least 40 percent of the voting-age population in six southern states.[89]

The promise of inclusion was contained in three amendments to the Constitution that were made at the end of the Civil War. The Thirteenth Amendment, adopted in 1865, abolished slavery in the United States. The Fourteenth, adopted in 1868, affirmed the citizenship of former slaves and attempted to protect their right to vote.[90] And the Fifteenth Amendment, adopted in 1870, stated more definitely that the right to vote could not be denied because of "race, color, or previous condition of servitude." In the immediate aftermath of the war, these constitutional provisions had meaning only because of the willingness of the federal government to deploy federal troops to enforce their terms. By 1877, over six hundred African Americans had been elected to state legislatures; they maintained steady control of the South Carolina legislature, while Louisiana had an African American governor.[91] There were seven African Americans in the Forty-Fourth Congress, which met between 1875 and 1877: six in the House of Representatives, and one in the Senate.[92]

Circumstances changed dramatically after the late 1870s. White power had been challenged but not broken. Throughout most of the South, whites were still the majority and held most elected offices, and in Washington, white southerners retained enough influence to block the continued use of federal power to protect African American voting rights.[93] One result of federal withdrawal was a resurgence in violence against African Americans. The South descended into a state of "armed guerilla warfare," as white mobs and secret societies like the Ku Klux Klan terrorized the African American population.[94] In Louisiana, the practice of voting-day intimidation was known as bulldozing—a word derived from the practice of giving an uncooperative slave "a 'bull-dose' of the cowhide on his naked back."[95] All of this was compounded by outright fraud in the casting and counting of ballots.[96]

Soon, though, techniques for suppressing the African American vote became more sophisticated. Southern states amended their constitutions and election laws to create new barriers to voting. This reduced the need for arbitrary violence, or at least covered violence with a thin patina of legality. The state of Mississippi set the precedent, revising its constitution in 1890 to require evidence that voters could read and comprehend its text. Other states soon followed, also adding requirements that voters own minimum amounts of property, pay poll taxes, maintain residence in fixed locations, and pass literacy tests. Such restrictions were not usually applied to the descendants of people who were eligible to vote before the adoption of the Fourteenth Amendment—that is, whites.[97]

"The colored race," one newspaper explained in 1900, "is no longer kept from the polls by sheer force of powder and lead."[98] Senator Benjamin Tillman, a former governor of South Carolina, described the strategy of southern states during a Senate debate in 1900:

> The colored race, even when it has been educated to a limited degree, is still unfit for suffrage, for the simple reason that the negroes do not possess that moral character and that moral fiber which are necessary for good citizenship.... South Carolina has disenfranchised all of the colored race that it could under the thirteenth, fourteenth, and fifteenth amendments. We have done our level best; we have scratched our heads to find out how we could eliminate the last one of them.... We stuffed ballot boxes. We shot them. We are not ashamed of it.... With that system—force, tissue ballots, and so forth—we got tired ourselves. So we called a constitutional convention, and we eliminated, as I said, all of the colored people whom we could.[99]

Tillman himself embodied the paradoxes of the time. In the North, he was celebrated as an enemy of "millionaires and pluto-crats" and anyone else who privileged "the moneyed few against the interests of the masses."[100] He was the main sponsor of the 1907 Act that banned corporate contributions to political cam-paigns. But Tillman was also one of the architects of the system of rule in the South that was widely condemned as a "white oli-garchy," and which depended, in his own state of South Carolina, on the wholesale exclusion from democratic politics of most of the adult population.[101] Throughout the South, the historian and activist W. E. B. Dubois wrote, "The disfranchisement of Negroes became nearly complete. In no other civilized and modern land has so great a group of people ... been allowed so small a voice in their own government."[102] One northern professor condemned southern practices as "a bare-faced stultification of the intent and claim of American democracy."[103]

In Washington, meanwhile, it proved impossible to build support for federal action against states that were violating constitutional guarantees. In 1890, Massachusetts Representative Henry Cabot Lodge introduced a bill to allow federal supervision of congressional elections and possibly the deployment of the army to protect voting rights. President Benjamin Harrison, a Republican, supported the bill, and Republicans had a majority in both houses of Congress. But even under these favorable conditions, Lodge's bill failed to become law—not only because of parliamentary maneuvering by the Democratic minority but also because of the diffidence of many Republicans. Some were prepared to barter with Democrats for support on other measures such as the tariff, while others privately shared their prejudices about African American voters.[104] "The African," a prominent Massachusetts Republican explained to James Bryce, "does not assimilate, and as far as the body politic is concerned, cannot be absorbed. [He is] an alien mass on the stomach of the defunct Confederacy."[105] Lodge's bill would be the last significant attempt in Congress to protect voting rights for decades.

The threat of violence made it difficult for African Americans to organize and protest, as other disempowered groups—farmers, industrial workers, white women—could do. For some, it almost quashed the ambition to agitate for enfranchisement. One of the country's best-known African American leaders, Booker

T. Washington, explicitly disavowed any interest in campaigning for voting rights, believing that this was a futile and dangerous project, given the weight of white power. In a famous 1895 speech, Washington urged African Americans to "stop emphasizing the political side" and concentrate instead on self-improvement through education and commerce. "Agitation of questions of social equality is the extremist folly," Washington warned: it was "more important that the negro should be prepared for voting than that he should vote."[106]

For the next twenty years, African American leaders wrestled with the question of reform strategies. In 1903 W. E. B. Du Bois directly challenged Washington's position, insisting that social progress was impossible so long as African Americans were "deprived of political rights [and] made a servile caste."[107] In 1905, Du Bois and like-minded activists met in Buffalo, New York, and published a manifesto urging African Americans to "protest emphatically against the curtailment of their political rights."[108] Du Bois became the first editor of *The Crisis*, a journal published in New York that promised to stand for "the highest ideals of American democracy." Its first issue, published in 1910, began with an assault on the voter suppression rules of the Arkansas constitution.[109] Du Bois was one of several African American and white activists who established the National Association for the Advancement of Colored People (NAACP) in New York in 1910, with the aim of making direct challenges to discriminatory laws. The NAACP quickly became established as the leading advocate of African American rights. By the time of Booker T. Washington's death in 1915, his policy of accommodation to white power had been largely eclipsed; even Washington himself had begun to harbor doubts about it.[110]

This movement was new and fragile, and the political establishment in Washington remained obdurate. Two Republican presidents, Theodore Roosevelt and William Howard Taft, gave only tepid support to the African American cause. As a matter of practical politics, their calculations were straightforward. The system of electoral suppression in the South was so effective that there were no votes to be won by advocating for civil rights in that region, while in northern states African Americans accounted for less than 2 percent of the population. In 1912, many African American activists abandoned the Republican Party and endorsed Woodrow Wilson. "Woodrow Wilson is a cultivated scholar," W. E. B. Du Bois said. "He will not advance the cause of oligarchy in the South.... He will not dismiss black men from office, and he will remember that the Negro in the United States has a right to be heard."[111]

Wilson was a thorough disappointment. Within a year, Du Bois conceded that southern oligarchs were "in the saddle" in Washington. Wilson stood by as members of his Cabinet fired African American employees and segregated federal offices. He declined to veto a law banning interracial marriage in the District of Columbia and showed the *Birth of the Nation*, a movie celebrating the Ku Klux Klan, in the White House. When war came, Wilson approved segregation in the army and condoned the denial of command to black officers. When a wave of race riots broke out across the North and South at the end of the war, Wilson refused to use federal troops to protect African Americans: his attorney general blamed the unrest on communist agitators within the African American community.[112] In Paris, meanwhile, Japanese diplomats pressed for the inclusion of a commitment to racial equality in the Versailles treaty. Wilson rebuffed the effort,

saying that he preferred to have discussion of "racial prejudices
... forced as much as possible into the background."[113] At home,
federal investigators looked for evidence that Japanese agents
might also be stoking African American radicalism.[114]

Du Bois and his colleagues approached the 1920 election
with deep frustration—feeling abandoned by Republicans and
"shamelessly betrayed" by Wilson and the Democrats.[115] And
they were right: this was an abject failure of presidential leadership.[116] The main effect of Wilson's administration had been
to put a federal imprimatur on the techniques for suppressing
African American voters that had been developed in southern
states over the preceding three decades. There were, however,
two reasons for hope. The first was the emergence of a movement
led by the NAACP that was dedicated to "arousing and strengthening the will to struggle."[117] In 1915, NAACP lawyers struck a
first blow against the white oligarchy when the Supreme Court
agreed that some aspects of southern election law violated the
Fifteenth Amendment.[118] The second was the beginning of the
great migration of African Americans to northern states—what
Isabel Wilkerson has called a pursuit of "political asylum" within
the United States itself.[119] By mid-century, African Americans
were a substantial voting bloc in many northern cities—a fact
that would eventually alter the dynamics of politics in the nation's
capital as well.

African Americans were not the only major group whose
demands for political inclusion were repulsed between 1890 and
1920. There was a similar response to the large number of people
who wanted to join the American democracy through immigration in the early twentieth century. In these three decades,

attitudes toward immigration shifted substantially, and laws were amended so that American democracy would not be "diluted" by the "unrestricted inpour" of people who were alleged to be ignorant of, or hostile to, democratic institutions.[120]

For most of the nineteenth century, federal restrictions on immigration were very loose. In fact, it was not clear before 1875 that the task of regulating the entry of immigrants belonged to the federal rather than state governments.[121] Record-keeping about the number and type of immigrants entering the United States was poor, precisely because there was no central authority responsible for keeping the count. Until the early 1890s, when a federal immigration bureau was established, immigrants never met a federal officer when they landed at an American port. Federal law, such as it was, was applied by state officials.[122] Once immigrants had landed, it was also easy to obtain citizenship and the right to vote. The naturalization law of 1802 required only that immigrants maintain residence for five years, swear allegiance to the Constitution, and renounce their previous citizenship.[123] Twenty-two states even allowed non-citizens to vote if they declared their intention to acquire citizenship.[124]

There was one glaring exception to the general liberality of federal law, which also anticipated the debate that would preoccupy the whole country after 1890. This had to do with the immigration of Chinese laborers to the West Coast. About 100,000 had been brought to the United States by the 1880s. Fear about the eventual enfranchisement of this population was intense. Chinese immigrants, a congressional committee said, were "an indigestible mass in the community, distinct in language, pagan in religion, [and] inferior in mental and moral qualities": the "safety of the State" demanded that they should never be allowed to vote.[125] In 1882, Congress prohibited the further immigration of Chinese laborers and denied citizenship to those who had already arrived.[126]

Broader hostility toward immigration began to rise because of changes in the number and type of immigrants after 1890, as well as in the patterns of settlement within the United States. Before 1890, most immigrants came from northwestern Europe—Britain, Ireland, Germany, and Scandinavia—as well as Canada, and often settled into farming in frontier states. After 1890, immigrants were more likely to come from Italy, Greece, Eastern Europe, or Russia. They also arrived in larger numbers, especially after the turn of the century: roughly 800,000 a year between 1900 and 1909, compared to 370,000 a year in the previous decade. And these new arrivals were more likely to settle into industrial work in the major cities of the Northeast and Midwest. By 1910, at least one-third of the population of New York City, Chicago, Philadelphia, and Boston was foreign-born.[127] By contrast, most native-born Americans still lived in towns with fewer than 2,500 people.[128]

The distance between native-born Americans and new immigrants was therefore physical as well as cultural, and this made it easier to blame immigrants for all the challenges of turn-of-the-century American life. Rapidly growing cities inevitably encounter problems of disease, disorder, and congestion, but because these cities were also populated by new arrivals, these urban problems tended to be interpreted as immigration problems. Similarly, the rapid expansion of a loosely regulated industrial economy inevitably generated conflicts between capitalists and workers, but because those workers were disproportionately new arrivals, labor unrest could also be construed as another problem of immigration. The radicalization of politics—the spread of "foreign creeds" such as anarchism, socialism, and communism—became an immigration problem as well. When President William McKinley was assassinated by the son of Polish immigrants in 1901, one Boston minister immediately laid "a large portion of the blame at the door of those who have approved promiscuous and unrestrained immigration."[129] Congress quickly passed a law banning the immigration of people affiliated with radical organizations.[130]

Above all, immigrants were blamed for the debasement of party politics. Political machines—those tight rings of bosses, wirepullers, and spoilsmen—were held to be the wellspring of political corruption, and those machines were most firmly established in big cities, where they were said to prey on ignorant but enfranchised immigrants. A "tap-root" of machine power, the sociologist Edward A. Ross said, "is the simple-minded foreigner ... [W]ithout them no lasting vicious political control has shown itself in any of our cities."[131] The urban machine "uses the foreigner to keep in power," another writer agreed. "Foreigners constitute an asset of the established political machine, neutralizing the antimachine ballots of an equal number of indignant American voters."[132] Henry Cabot Lodge, the Massachusetts legislator who had pushed for federal protection of African American voting rights in the South, also agreed that American politics was being ruined by the influx of "a mass of unfit voters ... drawn from the lowest and most backward populations of Europe ... [who] become the tools of the worst and most dangerous political managers."[133] A contributor to *Atlantic Monthly*, John H. Denison, warned that foreigners had "dispossessed us of the control of our great cities," and worse was to come. "They are to be our rulers.... We have given these people [power] to destroy the tree of liberty."[134]

In 1907, Congress established a commission to investigate the immigration problem, chaired by Republican Senator William P. Dillingham. Dillingham was already an advocate for stricter immigration controls, and the commission's forty-volume report, released in 1911, attempted to make a thorough case for restriction. This included an anthropological survey of all the "races and peoples" now landing in the United States. Slavs, for example, were "backward in western ideas, appliances, and forms of government . . . inequable or changeable in mood and in effort . . . [and prone to] fanaticism in religion [and] carelessness as to the business virtues of punctuality and honesty."[135] These "new immigrants," as the Commission called them, were "far less intelligent than the old," motivated by "different ideals," and slower to assimilate: the overall result was that they were "responsible for many social and political problems."[136]

By 1911, a movement to restrict the political power of immigrants was already well under way. In many states, for example, there were challenges to the long-standing practice of allowing aliens to vote if they had declared their intention to acquire citizenship. Even states like Oregon, that were otherwise in the vanguard of progressive reforms, abandoned the practice. It was "manifestly wrong," one Oregon official said in 1914, to allow voting by "illiterate aliens, unable to read or write, unable to speak our language, and unfamiliar with the purposes and ideals of our government."[137] By 1918, the practice of alien voting had been almost entirely eliminated, and the very last alien to vote in a presidential election probably did so in Arkansas in 1924.[138]

Meanwhile the federal government became stricter in determining which immigrants would receive citizenship after they had landed in the United States. In 1906 Congress amended

the naturalization law to require more evidence of good character and continuous residence in the United States, and denied
the possibility of citizenship to anyone who could not speak the
English language, espoused radical beliefs, or was affiliated with
radical organizations.[139] The Russian revolution of 1917 heightened anxiety about radical influences in the United States, and
in that year federal authorities also authorized the deportation of
radical aliens.[140] It was then possible to strip suspected radicals
of citizenship and deport them as aliens—as the Department of
Justice did with Emma Goldman and other radicals at the end of
World War I.[141]

But the most important response to the immigration problem
consisted of efforts to staunch the flow of immigrants into the
United States. In 1907, just as the Dillingham Commission was
beginning its work, Congress had broadened the discretion of
immigration officials to deny entry to people who had "mental or
physical defects," radical affiliations, or signs of "moral turpitude,"
or who seemed unlikely to support themselves.[142] The Dillingham
Commission itself advocated for much tighter restrictions on the
"quality and quantity" of immigration, such as literacy tests and
limits on "the number of each race arriving in each year."[143] The
advent of war briefly diminished the pressure for restrictions,
because it reduced the flow of people across the Atlantic: by 1916,
the number of immigrants was one-quarter of what it had been
a decade earlier. Still, Congress did impose a literacy test, as the
Dillingham Commission had proposed, in 1917.

President Wilson described this as a "radical change in the
policy of the nation."[144] Even bigger changes came as immigration rebounded at the end of the war. In 1921, Congress
adopted a quota system, just as the Dillingham Commission had

suggested. The new law capped the number of new arrivals of any nationality at 3 percent of the number of foreign-born persons of that nationality living in the United States at the time of the 1910 census. The 1921 law was passed as emergency legislation, but this quota system was maintained and tightened by Congress in 1924.[145] Between 1921 and 1939, annual immigration into the United States was only one-quarter of what it had been between 1900 and 1914. If prewar flows had been maintained, there would have been twelve million more foreign-born residents of the United States by the end of the 1930s—roughly equal to the total population of New York State.[146]

The United States called itself a democracy, in which people were allowed to rule themselves. But the nation's commitment to the ideal of self-rule was tested again as it wrestled with the question of what to do with territories acquired after the Spanish-American War. One Spanish colony, Cuba, was granted independence by the Treaty of Paris, which ended the war in 1898. But several other territories—Puerto Rico, Guam, and the Philippines—were simply surrendered to the United States. The most populous of these territories was the Philippines. There were more than seven million people living in the Philippine islands—equal to the number of people living in the most populous state of the union (New York), and the number of African Americans living in southern states.

American policy toward the Philippines was fraught with contradictions. The official policy was that Filipinos ought to enjoy the same right of self-government that had been granted to white male Americans.[147] This could have been accomplished by incorporating the Philippines as a state within the union. But no one seriously contemplated the possibility that this distant and

"Asiatic" land could be absorbed within the American polity.[148] Court cases soon made clear that Filipinos did not enjoy all of the rights granted to persons within the continental United States under the Constitution.[149] "You deal with the Filipinos just as we deal with the negroes," South Carolina Senator Benjamin Tillman taunted a northern colleague in 1900, "only you treat them a heap worse."[150]

The other way of bestowing the "blessings of liberty" would have been to grant independence to the Philippines. In fact, a revolt against Spanish rule was already under way in the Philippines at the outbreak of the Spanish-American War, and during the war itself, Filipino rebels declared their right to be "free and independent."[151] But Americans were equally hesitant about granting immediate freedom to the Philippines. Some said that the islands were simply unready, its population too diverse and backward, for independence. Others recognized the "immense value" of the islands in controlling the flow of commerce in the southern Pacific Ocean, and worried that a weak Philippine state might soon be absorbed by the rival Japanese or British Empires.[152] Meanwhile the War Department, responsible for administration of the Philippines after the Treaty of Paris, argued that most Filipinos actually preferred the establishment of a government "under the supremacy of the United States."[153] The reliability of this last claim was tested by the revival of rebellion. The War Department sent two hundred thousand American soldiers to the Philippines to fight in a brutal guerilla war between 1899 and 1902.[154] A quarter-million Filipinos may have died in the conflict.[155]

The US Congress did promise that a legislative assembly would be elected by popular vote as soon as order had been

established in the Philippines, and the body was finally con-
vened in 1907. But this was hardly a triumph for self-rule.
Voting was limited to males who were at least 26 years old, able
to pass a literacy test, and willing to acknowledge the "authority and sovereignty of the United States." Parts of the archi-
pelago that lacked "a sufficient proportion of civilized people"
were entirely excluded from the election.[156] The assembly
had no power to make law affecting parts of the Philippines
that were "inhabited by non-Christian tribes"; otherwise, the
assembly shared law-making authority with a second body,
the Philippine Commission, that was appointed by the US
president.[157] The US Congress also reserved the right to annul
any laws approved by Philippine legislators, while power over
the executive branch of the Philippine government was kept
in the hands of a governor also appointed by the US president.

These arrangements were slightly modified by a second
law approved by Congress in 1916. The new law replaced the
Commission with an elected Senate and extended voting rights
to males who owned property or paid taxes. But "supreme executive authority," including command of the armed forces, still
remained in the hands of a governor general appointed by the
US president. The governor general could veto any expenditure
proposed by legislators, while the president could veto any law at
all. The 1916 law was called the Autonomy Act, but this was false
advertising. "The problem," an advisor to President McKinley
had explained years earlier,

is to reconcile American sovereignty with Philippine
autonomy. . . . So long as the United States retains sovereignty
over the Philippine Islands . . . [its] control of the central or

general government must be absolute and indisputable.... We invite the Filipinos to co-operate with Americans in the administration of general affairs.... But the United States ... must remain the predominant partner.[158]

Throughout the 1910s, Congress refused to say when the United States would give up sovereignty over the islands.[159] American diplomats went to peace negotiations at the end of World War I insisting on the right of every nation to determine its own institutions, but Congress still did not set a timetable for Philippine autonomy until 1934. Briefly delayed by another war, independence was only achieved in 1946.[160]

A distinctive feature of American politics in the late 1880s, James Bryce observed, was "the absence of violent passions."[161] Nobody would have said this in 1920, about a country that had been rent by party polarization, strikes, race riots, suffragist protests, and colonial rebellion. Granted, the country was not engaged in actual civil war, but politics in the American democracy was undoubtedly hot. And much of the heat was generated by disagreement over whether American government could honestly be described as a system of rule by the people—and more fundamentally, who "the people" really were. This three-decade argument resulted in a substantial renovation of the American system of government, in both positive and malignant ways. By 1920, millions more people were voting in elections that were, in most states, administered more professionally. Parties and legislatures did their business more openly. Private economic power was controlled more tightly, as was the flow of immigration. In the South, however, the white establishment built a system for suppressing the African American population through law as well as violence, while overseas, the War Department developed new skills in guerilla warfare and colonial administration.

"When an American thinks about government building," the political scientist Samuel Huntington wrote in 1968, "he directs himself not to the creation of authority and the accumulation of power but rather to the limitation and the division of power."[162] As we have seen, this was only partly true during the crisis of representation. Certainly, reforms such as the enfranchisement of women and the direct election of senators were aimed mainly at the "limitation and division of power." But power was also "accumulated" in agencies like the Interstate Commerce Commission, the Federal Trade Commission, and the Federal Reserve, in the new Bureau of Immigration and the War Department, and in the hands of a southern white elite. The crisis of representation was not just concerned with the refinement of institutions that made self-rule possible. It was also concerned with restricting who was entitled to participate in self-rule, and this latter aspect was concerned with the concentration, rather than the diffusion, of political power.

In the first decade of the twentieth century, Americans often talked about "the race question," "the immigration question," and the "Filipino question." In some respects the three questions differed. Strictly, the country had no obligation at all toward immigrants who had not yet embarked for the United States. Filipinos, by contrast, were subject to American rule whether they liked it or not.[163] African Americans, meanwhile, were not only subject to American rule but also had rights that had been acknowledged in constitutional amendments. These were important distinctions that might have justified different treatment for these three groups. In practice, though, these distinctions were overlooked. All three of these "questions" seemed to raise the same issue: whether political power should be shared when there seemed to be a significant risk that this would upset the existing order and threaten the well-being of the already enfranchised. The immediate decision, in all three cases, was that power should not be shared. Self-rule was refined for some and denied to others.

Whatever the aims, the changes that were made to the architecture of American democracy in these three decades were substantial. Indeed, the changeability of political institutions was taken for granted by writers at the time. "America changes so fast," James Bryce said in 1888, "that every few years a new crop of books is needed to describe the new face which things have put on.... In a country so full of change and movement as America new questions are always coming up, and must be answered. New troubles surround a government, and a way must be found to escape from them."[164] In his popular 1898 book on American democracy, the political scientist Frederick Cleveland also described a system in which "customs, laws and institutions" were constantly adjusted to suit "shifting social and economic conditions." Cleveland called this the "law of change."[165] "The history of our political institutions," the historian Frederick Turner agreed in 1920, "is a history of the evolution and adaptation of organs in response to changed environment, a history of the origin of new political species."[166] Of course, the process of evolution did not stop in 1920. Political institutions were altered again in the next thirty years, as Americans grappled with a new question: Did popular control of government really matter, if government itself lacked the capacity to influence events at home or overseas?

Fig. 3.1 Convair B36D long-range bomber, 1949.
(US Air Force photo)

Mastery

The supreme test of the power of the people to conduct government for themselves is at hand.

> —CHARLES A. BEARD, "The Evolution of Democracy," 1919

Can a democratic form of government suffice in times of emergency?

> —JAMES M. COX, *Macon (GA) Leader*, October 10, 1936

One wonders to what extent an essentially anarchical people like ourselves can be persuaded to save democracy by giving power to even a democratically controlled administrative state.

> —J. LINUS GLANVILLE, *Annals of the American Academy of Political and Social Science*, 1940

The Consolidated Vultee Aircraft Corporation delivered the first combat-ready B-36 giant bomber to the US Air Force in June 1948 (fig. 3.1). The delivery was not difficult because the US government had instructed Consolidated Vultee to build its mile-long plant beside the runway at Carswell Air Force Base in Fort

Worth, Texas. The newspapers said that the B-36 was a leviathan, the biggest warplane ever built. ("Unless the Russians have built a bigger one," cautioned the *Idaho Statesman*.[1]) It occupied almost the area of a football field. Each of its six propellers had a diameter of nineteen feet, the length of the original Wright Flyer, and its bomb bay had the space of four railroad freight cars. It could fly 12,000 miles without refueling.

The B-36 could carry 72,000 pounds of bombs, but it seemed unlikely that it ever would. "We are more interested now in a 10,000-pound bomb," said Major General Roger Ramey, Commander of the Eighth Air Force.[2] That was the weight of the Mark III nuclear bomb. A precursor of the Mark III had been used at Nagasaki in 1945, where it may have killed 70,000 people.[3] The United States had conducted a highly publicized test of the Mark III at Bikini Atoll in the South Pacific in 1946. The bomb exploded with "the flash and heat of 10,000 suns," sending a peach-colored atomic cloud ten miles into the atmosphere.[4] The shock waves were measured in London, on the other side of the planet.

A B-36 carrying a Mark III bomb was a weapon of extraordinary lethality. Still, it seemed small next to the bureaucracy that brought it to life. The Manhattan Project, which had produced the first atomic bomb, was "the most staggering example of scientific collaboration in all history," employing a million workers.[5] Consolidated Vultee had become a major aircraft manufacturer because of contracts to build Liberator bombers during World War II. The B-36 fleet was operated by Strategic Air Command, or SAC, whose forty thousand personnel were charged with coordinating a "knock-out blow" against the Soviet Union.[6] SAC was contained within the US Air Force, with one-third of a million active duty personnel, and the Air Force itself was contained within the Department of Defense, which consumed almost one-tenth of the nation's entire annual income. The federal government levied the income taxes to pay for it all, conscripted men for military service, restricted trade so that Consolidated Vultee and other defense contractors had access to raw materials, and regulated the terms on which it hired its labor.

All of this was new. Only a few years before, there had been no Department of Defense, no US Air Force, no Strategic Air Command, no atomic bomb, no broadly based income tax, and no conscription. When the head of SAC, General Curtis LeMay, was born in 1906, the very idea of powered flight was a novelty. Few Americans at that time believed that the United States should play any significant role on the world stage, and many doubted that it could. Whatever its virtues might be, American democracy was held to be incapable of vigorous, purposeful action. American politicians, James Bryce explained in 1914, "resign themselves to a conscious impotence":

Clouds arise, blot out the sun overhead, and burst in a tempest; the tempest passes, and leaves the blue above bright as before, but at the same moment other clouds are already beginning to peer over the horizon. ... [N]ew problems begin to show themselves, and the civil powers, Presidents, and Cabinets, and State governments, and Houses of Congress, seem to have as little to do with all of these changes, as little ability to foresee or avert or resist them, as the farmer, who sees approaching the tornado which will uproot his crop, has power to stay its devastating course.[7]

So much had changed in thirty years, and this change was exemplified by the new B-36, its dull magnesium skin growing hot in the Texas sun. Once resigned to "overruling providence," American politicians were now determined to become masters of the world around them. In a sense, the United States had become the tornado. Its new giant bomber could carry an atomic weapon to any inhabited part of the earth. "The mammoth B-36," the United Press explained in October 1948, "can put the world in its bombsights."[8]

The roll-out of the B-36 in 1948 was a small part of a much larger project that had absorbed the attention of American democracy for the preceding three decades.[9] Today, political scientists would say that this was a project aimed at building "state capacity"—that is, the institutions through which governments actually exercise power, either at home or abroad.[10] Of course, this is not the language that was used at the time. Instead, reformers sometimes talked about building a "positive state" that could act with "power, initiative, and vision."[11] Or about building an "efficient democracy" that was "adapted to the realization of our national purpose and responsive to the will of our people."[12] Or about the need to improve "administrative techniques" so that government could properly address social and economic problems.[13]

However it was described, this massive project was intended to address a problem that became more pressing as the nation took steps to resolve the crisis of representation. That crisis was marked by a struggle for control of the state—and more precisely, for broader public control of the state. The struggle proceeded on the assumption that control of the state mattered, that real power rested there, that government could alter the conditions of everyday life through the actions of its bureaucrats and soldiers.

Today we take the power of the federal government for granted. In 2015, it employed 3.5 million people, while millions more worked for government contractors. No modern civics textbook is complete without a description of this large and influential bureaucracy. But circumstances were different a century ago. James Bryce wrote a two-thousand-page study of American government without giving any direct attention to bureaucracy, simply because there was not much to discuss. "That which Europeans call the machinery of government," Bryce explained, "is in America conspicuous chiefly by its absence."[14]

The absence of any such machinery meant that the campaign to extend democracy yielded a hollow victory. People were told "that the conquest of political power meant that they would be masters of the state," the political scientist Harold Laski observed in 1933. "But they found ... that to have won formal political power was not to have gained the mastery that they sought." Laski thought that this was true in many democracies, and that it explained the pervasive malaise at that time. However, the gap between expectations and capacities was especially wide in the United States. "The American democracy," Laski said, "is more remote from mastery in its own house than those of any country upon the European continent."[15]

In a simpler time, the fact that American government lacked machinery for exercising power might not have mattered very much. But the turn of the century was not a simple time. Americans were conscious of the fact that the country was being reshaped by powerful social and economic forces over which they had little control. The population grew by one-third between 1900 and 1914, as the result of barely regulated immigration. American cities—which James Bryce had condemned in 1888 as the "one conspicuous failure of the United States"—had doubled in size by 1908.[16] Twenty-five miles of railroad were built every day in the United States between 1900 and 1914—enough, in total, to circle the Earth five times. The industrial workforce doubled between 1890 and 1910.[17]

The transformation of the United States in the early years of the twentieth century is similar to the change that China has experienced since the process of economic liberalization began in the late 1970s. Massive migration, urbanization, industrialization, new communication technologies—today all of these developments threaten the stability of the Chinese political system, unless the nation's leaders can find effective ways of governing a fast-moving and complex society. Some people wonder whether the Chinese state can adapt quickly enough to master these powerful social forces.[18] This is exactly the question that was posed in the United States a century ago.

Of course, there is one important difference in circumstances. China today is an authoritarian state. Few people question its capacity to act decisively. But the United States began its transformation as a democracy in which authority was widely diffused. Even in 1888, James Bryce had observed how hard it was to get anything done in the United States. "There is an excessive friction in the American system," Bryce said. "Power is so subdivided that it is hard at a given moment to concentrate it for prompt and effective action."[19] By 1910, the feature that so clearly distinguished American democracy also seemed to be its greatest weakness.

Anxieties about the competence of democratic systems were often expressed. "America today is in a somber, soul-questioning mood," said Walter Weyl, the young co-editor of the *New Republic*, in a 1914 book. "Occasionally the unacknowledged thought arises: 'Is democracy after all a failure?'" The United States was evolving into "a complex, closely knit industrial system," with a host of problems that demanded "a definite constructive program" of government action. But the old political machinery of American democracy was unequal to the task. Government responded to the needs of the people, Weyl conceded—but "ineffectually, like a clumsy, ancient engine which utilizes only one or two percent of the power applied to it." For Weyl, a "radical revision" of the Constitution was necessary for American democracy to endure.[20]

Weyl's fears were shared by his friend Walter Lippmann. "The modern world is brain-splitting in its complexity," Lippmann wrote in his 1914 book *Drift and Mastery*. "[It is] strange . . . terrifying, alluring, and incomprehensibly big." For most people daily life was dictated by "brute forces" over which they had no control. Lippmann believed that this was a world that could only be managed by careful planning and administration, guided by experts with specialized knowledge of social and economic affairs. But Lippmann saw that American politics was held back by disdain for large-scale bureaucracy, mechanisms for enforced coordination, and the pretensions of experts. "Democracy has a load to carry," he concluded. "Its future is so uncertain that no one can feel any assurance in the face of it."[21]

Sometimes the anxieties of American reformers were so profound that they could only be expressed through fantasy. Shortly after the election of 1912, a New York publishing house released *Philip Dru: Administrator*, a novel by an anonymous author that seethed with frustration about the fecklessness of American democracy. Its protagonist is a "lithe young Kentuckian," a graduate of West Point, and expert in the "large questions of State." Despairing about the inability of American government to address the nation's woes, Dru leads an armed rebellion and becomes a benevolent dictator. He reforms the civil service, quintuples the size of the army, and establishes a British-style parliamentary system. After government has been made "vastly more efficient," Dru quietly retires, sailing from San Francisco "into a shimmering sea."[22] Eventually it was revealed that the author was Edward M. House, a close advisor to President Woodrow Wilson.

Americans were not alone in having doubts about the performance of democratic systems. Walter Lippmann was heavily influenced by the work of a British reformer, Graham Wallas, whose book *The Great Society* was published in 1914. Wallas argued that industrialization and urbanization had created a "vast and complex society" whose inner workings were a mystery. Moreover, any hope that this complex machine could regulate itself had dissipated. "We are afraid of the blind forces to which we used so willingly to surrender ourselves," Wallas said. But democratic government in its current form seemed unable to control these forces. Not only was modern society without a plan to shape its destiny, it was "without the machinery to make a collective plan possible." It was conceivable, Wallas thought, that representative democracy might not survive at all.[23]

There was similar pessimism in France. The parliamentary system that was established after the Franco-Prussian War of 1870 struggled to overcome deep ideological divisions. (The nation, a political scientist explained in 1905, "is divided as follows: Royalists, Imperialists, Bonapartists, Catholic Conservatives, Progressist Republicans, Nationalists, Radicals, Socialist Radicals, Reformatory Socialists, Revolutionary Socialists, and Anarchists."[24]) In the end, few were satisfied with its performance. The radical intellectual Georges Sorel said that parliamentary democracy was nothing more than rule by a "stupid and timorous" bourgeoisie, and that progress required a violent overthrow of the existing order.[25] At the same time, the conservative Charles Maurras demanded a restoration of the monarchy. Democracy, he believed, was undermining the nation's moral order and its ability to stand firmly against Germany and other great powers. "Democracy rots everything," Maurras said. "[It] is the most pernicious and the most disastrous epidemic that could possibly fall upon a people."[26]

The advent of World War I aggravated anxieties about the weaknesses of democracy. Propagandists for the German autocracy described it as a modern-day Sparta: virile, disciplined, and unconquerable.[27] All German males were expected to spend the first two years of adulthood in military training; the German army of 1.7 million men was also better organized and better equipped than its continental rivals.[28] "Can democracy stand against it?" a German writer asked in 1915. "Infirm of purpose, jealous, grudging, timid, changeable, unthorough, unready, without foresight, obscure in its aims ... [I]s it conceivable that such an undisciplined chaos can prevail against the Hohenzollern Empire?"[29] Some British and French observers were asking the same question. One said that democracy was proving to be a system dedicated to "the worship and cultivation ... of incompetence and inefficiency."[30]

Three more years would pass before the United States entered the war in 1917. As those three years passed, and the likelihood of military engagement increased, fears about reliability of American democracy were voiced as well. The Harvard historian Albert Bushnell Hart warned that the United States would be ruined if it did not take preparedness more seriously: "for either some centralized monarch will descend upon us . . . or else the American people will rise and create a dictator who may save them from destruction."[31] Democracy had become "slack and slovenly," another writer said, and so made itself vulnerable to Prussianism.[32] The president of the University of Virginia worried that American democracy was unequal to "the German genius for administration . . . Debate, political agitation, bold popular expression, are not the methods of smooth precision and relentless order."[33]

The looming war triggered an argument about the capacities of democracy that would persist for thirty years. For example, the fears of 1915–1916 were revived again on the eve of World War II. "Can a democracy fight a successful war?" a midwestern editorialist asked in June 1940. "The apparent difficulty of the democracies lies in slowness to take the emergency measures. This shows up as a major defect, when the democracies are pitted in conflict against a system which has sacrificed all other considerations to efficiency."[34] The rival system at that time was fascism, a "new technique of dictatorship" that seemed able to focus the "will and energy of a people" with unprecedented skill.[35] And anxieties about democracy resurfaced in the late 1940s, with the advent of the Cold War. The rival at that time was the Soviet Union, which was perceived to be a highly centralized regime that was ruled with "iron discipline" by the Communist Party.[36] Soviet leaders seemed to have the "capacity for endurance": they could make their plans secretly and execute them deliberately. American leaders, by contrast, had to manage "highly volatile psychological factors such as the stubborn particularisms of free people, a fact rendered doubly complex by the nature of the institutions and the social structures of the American people themselves."[37]

In 1916, the problem was not merely that the United States was a democracy. Britain and France were also democracies, but they were also unitary states with centuries of practice in fighting wars, often against each other. But circumstances in the United States were different. There was a long-standing aversion to the idea of a large standing army. The American people loved their navy, President Howard Taft conceded in 1909, but "it has always been easy to awaken prejudices against the possible aggressions of a regular army and a professional soldiery."[38] The idea of a large *federal* army was also noxious: many Americans preferred to fight wars by assembling state militias, despite the problems of coordination and unevenness in training that this practice created. Added to this was a distaste for compulsory military service—a "form of slavery"[39]—which had been a standard practice even in peacetime Europe. And finally there was the aversion, as old as the nation itself, to entanglement in European affairs.[40] The policy of American democracy was to "mind its own business and let the business of other people alone."[41]

All of this had been regarded as well-settled features of American democracy: but everything changed after the declaration of war on Germany in April 1917. In just twenty months, a poorly equipped army of 130,000 men was transformed into a force of 3.7 million. This was accomplished through an extraordinary project of administrative engineering.[42] Congress authorized the set-up of a conscription system that would operate, with some interruptions, for most of the next half-century, eventually drawing eighteen million men into military service. It also gave President Wilson broad authority to reorganize federal agencies, which he used to overhaul the structure of military command and logistics. The War Department extended its control over state militias. A powerful War Industries Board guided war production and wielded the power to seize industries that refused to cooperate, while a new Railroad Administration actually nationalized the country's railroads to ensure the steady flow of men and supplies. Other new agencies guided workers to essential factory jobs, mediated management–union conflicts, and requisitioned, built, and manned ships to carry the army to France. This massive exercise turned the tide of the conflict in Europe. As late as March 1918, many people still believed that Germany might win the war.[43] Eight months later, however, Kaiser Wilhelm abdicated.

The end of the war brought hope that the United States could return to its old ways, and the apparatus that was built up in 1917–1918 was rapidly disassembled. Economic controls were removed, railroads and shipping lines were returned to private ownership, and the army was reduced so that it was not much larger in 1922 than it had been in 1916. But the promise of a return to normalcy, as President Warren G. Harding called it, could not be kept. With the United States' entry into World War II in December 1941, the whole apparatus was reconstructed on a vastly larger scale. By 1945, there were twelve million Americans in uniform, and another 2.6 million civilians working on defense functions for the federal government; the new defense headquarters, the Pentagon, was hailed on its completion in 1943 as the world's largest office building. Federal expenditure on defense accounted for 40 percent of the nation's total annual income. Once again, federal agencies guided war production, labor relations, and the flow of strategic materials, and took control of the nation's railroads and merchant shipping.

In many ways, the apparatus that had been roughly constructed during World War I was refined during World War II. A new Office of Price Administration relied on a network of five thousand local boards to enforce price and rent controls, avoiding a reprise of the high inflation of 1917–1920.[44] The federal government also developed more sophisticated ways of working with industry and universities to develop new military technologies, including nuclear weapons.[45] A new organization, the Office of Strategic Services, was established for overseas intelligence gathering and clandestine work, while the Federal Bureau of Investigation expanded its domestic counter-intelligence capabilities.[46]

Although most economic controls were again removed after 1945, the expanded military and intelligence establishment survived. The United States was quickly preoccupied with a new threat, as the Soviet Union consolidated its control over Eastern European nations, threatened Greece and Turkey, and attempted a blockade of Berlin.[47] An Ohio newspaper lamented the advent of "war without end ... It's now evident that the war was not over in 1945 any more than it was over in 1918. Nothing has changed but the enemy."[48] The new status quo was affirmed by the National Security Act of 1947, which consolidated the three military departments—Navy, Army, and a new Department of the Air Force—within an umbrella Department of Defense; again reorganized the military's general staff; converted the Office of

Strategic Services into the Central Intelligence Agency; and created a new body, the National Security Council, to advise the President on foreign and defense policy.

Of course, the consolidation of this national security apparatus was not brought about easily. The drafters of the National Security Act worried about the erosion of civilian control over the armed forces and maintained the separate military departments within the Defense Department partly because it seemed easier to control them that way.[49] They also tried to limit the powers of the new Central Intelligence Agency so that it would not turn into an "American Gestapo."[50] At the same time, Congress reformed its committee system so that it could supervise the national security establishment and other parts of the federal bureaucracy more effectively.[51]

These measures did not quash worries about the emergence of an American "garrison state."[52] Indeed, fears about the power of the defense establishment were affirmed by President Dwight Eisenhower in his farewell address in January 1961. The United States, Eisenhower said, had built a "huge industrial and military machine ... [whose] influence—economic, political, even spiritual—is felt in every city, every Statehouse, every office of the Federal government." Eisenhower recognized the "imperative need" for this machine but warned that it should be watched closely so that it did not endanger democratic processes and civil liberties.[53]

The American democracy would spend the next half century wrestling with the problem that Eisenhower had identified. At no point, however, did the American people seriously contemplate the simplest solution: completely dismantling the country's new military capabilities. The United States would not go back to

1916. The "imperative need" for the national security apparatus was broadly acknowledged, notwithstanding the risks to democratic values that it posed. The country concentrated instead on finding ways of reconciling new security requirements with democratic norms.

Meanwhile another decades-old question faded away. Could American democracy organize itself for war, and especially for an enduring war? The very existence of Eisenhower's "military-industrial complex," constructed from almost nothing in the span of only thirty years, provided the answer. In the half century after 1947, the United States maintained an average annual force of 2.4 million soldiers, sailors, and airmen.

There was another domain in which American democracy struggled to achieve mastery between 1917 and 1948: the economy. The system of loosely regulated capitalism that operated in the United States before World War I was prone to wild swings in performance, producing bursts of tremendous growth that were followed by paroxysm and collapse. "Boom and slump, slump and boom; such is all financial and commercial history," stated a column *Everybody's Magazine* in 1904. "A panic every so many years; then recovery; then over-stimulation, and panic again. . . . Bury the dead, cart off the cripples!"[54] Champ Clark, the Missourian Speaker of the House of Representatives in 1919, had lived long enough to witness ten financial panics and four severe depressions.[55] He would observe a fifth depression—the "dizzy plunge" in industrial production that began in January 1920—before he died in March 1921.[56]

Yet another depression was triggered by the financial crash of 1929. The effects this time were much more severe. By 1933, industrial production and employment had declined by more than 30 percent, while prices received by farmers had been cut in half. Four thousand of the nation's banks suspended business in 1933 alone. And as the economy collapsed, disorder increased. By March 1930, the *New York Times* was already anguishing about rioting in major cities. A demonstration of 100,000 in Detroit that month was broken up by "running buses and street cars through the mobs."[57] In 1932, federal troops marched down Pennsylvania Avenue to clear the capital of a protest by destitute veterans. They were backed by cavalry, machine gunners, and tanks—"the most extensive use of troops in the capital since the Civil War."[58] More than a dozen states declared martial law or mobilized the National Guard over the next two years.[59] "The people of the United States," Supreme Court Justice Louis Brandeis said, "are now confronted with an emergency more serious than war."[60]

The question again was whether American democracy could achieve mastery over its circumstances. To "tame the economic demons," as Karl Popper put it, it was necessary to "construct institutions for the democratic control of economic power."[61] But there were people who despaired about democracy's capacity to undertake this task in a timely way. In February 1933, *Barron's* magazine expressed the mood:

> Of course we all realize that dictatorships and semi-dictatorships in peace time are quite contrary to the spirit of American institutions and all that. And yet . . . we return repeatedly to the thought that a mild species of dictatorship will help us over the roughest spots in the road ahead.[62]

Three weeks after Franklin Roosevelt's inauguration in March 1933, Metro-Goldwyn-Mayer released a movie titled *Gabriel over the White House*, in which a well-meaning President dissolves Congress, establishes himself as dictator, undertakes sweeping economic reforms, and suffers an aptly timed and fatal heart attack, so that democratic rule can be re-established. Columbia Pictures replied by releasing *Mussolini Speaks*, a documentary praising the accomplishments of Italy's Fascist ruler, on the same day. "Can President Roosevelt do for the United States what Mussolini has done for Italy?" Columbia's advertisement asked. "Everything he does is vibrant with force.... He acts with amazing speed."[63] *Fortune* magazine said that Mussolini provided a model of decisiveness in a world that was distinguished by "governmental wandering and uncertainty."[64] "If this country ever needed a Mussolini," agreed Republican Senator David Reed, "it needs one now."[65]

Roosevelt himself conceded that he was "deeply impressed by what [Mussolini] has accomplished."[66] In his inaugural address, Roosevelt warned that he would seek "broad Executive power to wage a war against the emergency, as great as the power that would be given to me if we were in fact invaded by a foreign foe."[67] The writer Edmund Wilson observed the machine guns defending the Capitol on inauguration day and thought that Roosevelt's speech gave "a suggestion . . . of a possible dictatorship."[68] A year later, Columbia University professor Lindsay Rogers wrote with admiration that Roosevelt actually had established a "presidential dictatorship": Roosevelt's own hands, Rogers said, "hold the reins very tightly . . . [W]e have a more totalitarian state than can be found anywhere save Russia."[69]

But Roosevelt had not in fact established a dictatorship. He did not dissolve Congress or suspend elections, and Congress passed the laws that authorized the major policies that constituted Roosevelt's New Deal. Admittedly, Congress showed a great deal of deference to the newly elected President: some New Deal laws were quickly drafted and broadly worded. This was justified as a sensible response to the needs of the moment. Roosevelt himself had made the case for pragmatism in a commencement address at Oglethorpe University in 1932: "The country demands bold, persistent experimentation.... The millions who are in want will not stand by silently forever while the things to satisfy their needs are within easy reach."[70] Congress had adopted an experimental attitude with regard to the delegation of power to the President, and the President intended to adopt the same attitude as he invented methods to revive the American economy.

At this point we should pause to acknowledge an anachronism. I have said that politicians in the 1920s and early 1930s struggled to gain control of the economy. This is not exactly true. At that time, politicians might have talked about business conditions, or trade and commerce, or national prosperity. In his 1932 address at Oglethorpe University, Roosevelt actually talked about ways of fixing "the economic machine." The notion of an economy—that is, of an integrated system of investment, production, trade, and consumption within national borders—was not yet established in everyday language (see fig. 3.2).[71] The first reference by a president to "the American economy" appears to have been made by Harry Truman in 1947. In fact, one of the most important inventions of this era was an idea, the concept of the economy—a "substantive entity" that could be measured and therefore mastered by government.[72]

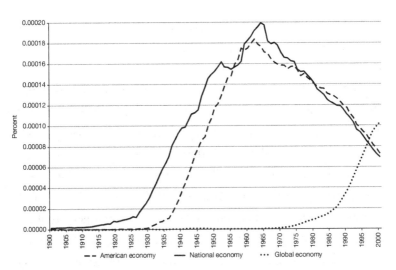

Fig. 3.2 Frequency with which three terms relating to the economy are mentioned in the collection of books published in the United States, 1900–2000, and subsequently digitized by Google.
SOURCE: Google Ngram Viewer.

Furthermore, measurement and regulation of the national economy could not be done without a build-up of new bureaucratic capacities within the federal government. After the depression of 1921, the Department of Commerce promised to do a better job of regularly publishing statistics on business conditions, "in a manner similar to weather reports."[73] But the federal government's ability to collect information about business and consumer activity was primitive. At the start of his presidency, President Franklin Roosevelt was hobbled by an "almost complete lack of reliable data" about economic activity.[74] After 1941, war planning intensified the pressure for better surveillance of economic affairs. By the end of the war, the federal government had more timely and extensive data on production, consumption, employment, and prices. It could even estimate the overall size of the economy and forecast its growth.[75] By the early 1950s, the routine release of federal data made "the state of the economy" a matter of general conversation.

At the same time, the federal government refined its capacity to control the economy. By the early 1930s, some economists argued that one way of encouraging economic recovery was to "prime the pump" through a debt-financed increase in federal government expenditure.[76] The federal budget thus became a tool for overall economic management. Of course, this was only possible if there was such a thing as the federal budget—that is, a unified plan for spending, taxing, and borrowing. But the concept of a unified federal budget was unknown before Congress, struggling with war finances and following innovations in some state governments, adopted the Budget and Accounting Act of 1921. ("Our legislators," one reformer said in 1915, "have until recently been as innocent of such an idea as an unborn babe."[77]) And the budget system that Roosevelt inherited still had major weaknesses. The small office responsible for preparing the national budget was not put under the direct control of the White House until 1939. A larger problem was the power of the Comptroller General, an independent officer appointed under the 1921 law, to veto the spending decisions of executive departments even after they had been authorized by Congress. The Comptroller General served a fifteen-year term, and in 1933 the office was held by John McCarl, a Republican appointed by Warren Harding who used his authority to stymie New Deal initiatives.[78]

"Priming the pump" by adjusting the federal budget also required other administrative capabilities. There had to be channels for getting money into the hands of businesses and citizens. In 1933, the federal government did not have much capacity to put unemployed people to work on public works projects, either directly or by giving aid to state and local governments.[79] It was not possible to increase unemployment insurance benefits or payments to indigent families and old people, simply because there were no systems for making such payments in the first place. Similarly, the expedient of sending checks directly to taxpayers (used by the Bush administration in 2001) was not available, because the overwhelming majority of Americans did not file income tax returns in 1933.[80] As a result, the main objective in the first years of Roosevelt's New Deal was to build the administrative apparatus that would allow the flow of federal money into the economy. The Roosevelt administration did this by inventing and reinventing an "alphabet soup" of agencies—such as the FERA, PWA, WPA, CCC, CWA, NYA, REA, and TVA—in a search for effective ways of executing public works, and by adopting the Social Security Act of 1935, which established the federal government's role in giving money to the poor and unemployed.[81]

The Federal Reserve System also had to be renovated if the federal government was to assume responsibility for overall management of the economy. Between 1836 and 1913 the United States had no central bank at all, largely because of fears that it would be captured by financial interests based in the Northeast. When the panic of 1907 exposed the need for some kind of coordinating mechanism for the banking system, Congress was careful to avoid creating a single central bank on the English or French model. Instead it divided responsibilities among twelve Federal Reserve banks, scattered across the country. The 1913 law also accommodated financial interests by limiting the power of those twelve banks to issue new currency, which might stoke inflation and erode the value of financial assets.

This constrained and decentralized system was unequal to the challenges of the economic emergency of the 1930s. In February 1932, Congress temporarily loosened the constraint on issuing currency, so that Federal Reserve banks could take action to stop the rapid deflation of prices.[82] But the system's effectiveness in using this new authority was hampered by disagreement among the twelve banks.[83] The result was a quick retreat from the principle of decentralization. The Banking Act of 1933 allowed a central committee of the Federal Reserve System to impose its decisions regarding the issuance of currency on all twelve banks. The Banking Act of 1935 again shifted power from the regional banks to the Washington-based Federal Reserve Board. Meanwhile Roosevelt was able to fill several vacancies on the Board with individuals who were sympathetic to his policies.[84] The overall result was a Federal Reserve System that was more centralized, more powerful in the field of monetary policy, and more likely to coordinate its actions with the Roosevelt administration, despite its formal independence from the executive.[85]

The project of mastering the American economy was not limited to the invention of better tools for setting fiscal and monetary policy. The Roosevelt administration also conducted experiments in the direct regulation of finance, production, and commerce. A new Securities and Exchange Commission was established to govern the issuance and trading of corporate stock. The Banking Act of 1933 expanded the power of the Federal Reserve and Treasury to control banks, and created a new agency, the Federal Deposit Insurance Corporation, to protect depositors against bank failures. The National Recovery Administration was founded to rationalize industrial production and limit "destructive competition" in the private sector.[86] A new National Labor Relations Board guaranteed the unionization rights of private-sector workers, while the Agricultural Adjustment Administration limited agricultural production and raised farmers' incomes. Other agencies were set up to revive the housing industry by insuring and buying mortgages, and promote rural electrification and construction of public highways.

As one political scientist observed, the 1930s brought "a new and revolutionary extension of the practice and theory of administration" within the federal government.[87] Another new phrase—"the federal bureaucracy"—entered the American vocabulary.[88] Along with bureaucratic expansion came an emphasis on the critical role of the president in setting policy and coordinating the work of federal agencies. Initially, the increase in presidential authority was defended as an emergency measure. By the late 1930s, however, it was regarded by many people as an essential component of an effective democracy. "The vast increase of the President's powers is a trend that must be encouraged for the sake of democratic government," wrote Pendleton Herring, a political scientist at Harvard University. "There is a great need for guidance and unity in the framing of national policy, and this can best be done through the Chief Executive."[89] A 1937 study by several leading scholars celebrated presidential power as the essential element of modern democracy. With this new device, it would be possible to rebut the claim that "democracy must fail because it can neither decide promptly nor act vigorously."[90]

Of course, the growth of bureaucratic and presidential power was deeply troubling for many Americans, and a large part of the 1930s and 1940s was occupied with the task of deciding what the limits of that power ought to be. Many early New Deal experiments did not survive. The National Recovery Administration, the main tool for coordinating industrial production, was dismantled in 1935, along with the Public Works Administration in 1943. The National Resources Planning Board, a high-profile instrument for coordinating executive action, was also abolished by Congress in 1943. Meanwhile Congress resisted attempts by the Roosevelt administration to eliminate entirely the formal independence of agencies like the Federal Reserve, the Federal Trade Commission, and the Civil Service Commission.[91] It dragged its heels in restricting the authority of the Comptroller General, and rebuffed administration proposals to consolidate New Deal policies by creating new federal departments of Public Works and Public Welfare. Congress also added new counterweights to executive power. The Administrative Procedure Act of 1946 required agencies to receive public comments on proposed regulations and publish many internal agency documents.[92] And Congress's reorganization of its committee system in the same year was intended to improve its oversight of domestic agencies, as well as the national security apparatus.[93]

Roosevelt himself stoked the controversy over executive power through a serious political misjudgment shortly after his reelection in November 1936. Emboldened by his overwhelming victory, Roosevelt released a report that proposed sweeping administrative reforms to consolidate his control over the executive branch. Immediately afterward, he called for reforms to the Supreme Court, which had repeatedly overturned New Deal legislation in the previous four years. The backlash was intense. Roosevelt was again accused of seeking dictatorial powers, but now for purely malignant purposes. In March 1938, Roosevelt felt obliged to assure the public that he had "no inclination ... [and] none of the qualifications" to be a dictator.[94] Still, Congress rejected many of his proposed reforms. Eight months later, in the mid-term elections of 1938, the Republican Party increased its share of seats in both houses of Congress.

But the results of the 1938 election hardly signaled a rejection of the idea of expanded executive power. Even after 1938, Roosevelt's Democrats held daunting majorities in the Senate and House of Representatives—as indeed they did throughout Roosevelt's twelve years as president. By 1946 it had become a settled fact that the president had primary responsibility for overseeing the management of economic affairs. Congress itself affirmed this in the Employment Act of 1946, which instructed the president to report annually on the condition of the American economy and the "economic program of the Federal government." The law also gave the president a new Council of Economic Advisers, a small planning body to oversee the substantial bureaucracy that had been created to gain mastery over the unruly free market.[95]

War and economic crisis were not the only problems that demanded an expansion of bureaucracy between 1917 and 1948. The federal government also struggled with disease, climate change, and technological advance. The global influenza pandemic of 1918–1919 began in a Kansas army camp and ultimately killed more than half a million Americans; influenza continued to be one of the top five causes of death in the United States until 1947.[96] And then there were the terrifying "summer plagues" of polio, which became a serious problem in the 1910s and persisted until the early 1950s, and whose victims included President Roosevelt himself.[97] Added to this was the advent of drought in the American Midwest—a problem identified at the time as one of "permanent climatic change" and considered by Roosevelt's advisors to be "one of the most serious peacetime problems in the nation's history."[98] And finally there was the rapid spread of innovations like the automobile, airplane, and radio. The mastery of all of these challenges also required the build-up of new governmental capacities—for basic research, administration of relief, construction of new infrastructure, and regulation of new industries.

By 1948, the architecture of American democracy had been dramatically transformed.[99] The main change was an extraordinary build-up in governmental capabilities. Not only were Americans committed to the idea of a more active federal government; they had, in the course of a generation, built the bureaucracy that was essential to make it a reality. The American citizenry now had the capacity to manage their own affairs. Harold Laski, the intellectual who had lamented in 1933 that the American polity was "remote from mastery in its own house," marveled at the transformation in his 1948 book, *The American Democracy*. "The era of the positive state," he wrote, "has arrived in America as decisively as in Europe." As late as 1914, James Bryce had painted a picture of American politicians who were "resigned to conscious impotence." Now, Laski observed, "there was no room for negativism in the White House any more than in Downing Street or in the Kremlin."[100]

Sometimes there is a tendency to think of this new "administrative state" as something that was imposed on American democracy, serving as a check on its tendencies toward disorganization and drift.[101] But this is a misreading of history. The administrative state was a creation of American democracy. The build-up of federal power was repeatedly endorsed by the American electorate, which wanted to give real meaning to the idea of self-rule. Moreover, this build-up was supported by American voters even though the redesigned federal government presented severe and persistent problems of presidential and bureaucratic accountability. The remedy for the crisis of mastery, in other words, was not a call for more participation and transparency. On the contrary, the project of expanding federal power actually made the task of democratic control more difficult. Everyone recognized this. But they proceeded with the project anyway.

In reality, American voters were pragmatic. They wanted control over events, and this meant a bigger and more powerful state, despite the risks. Indeed, the pragmatic spirit even involved the borrowing of ideas from non-democratic rivals. American politicians never seriously contemplated the establishment of a true dictatorship. But they played with the idea of the strong leader—and even used the language of dictatorship until the late 1930s, when the ugly trend of European politics had become clearer. American politicians and intellectuals were looking for ways of adapting the concept of the strong executive to American conditions, and extracting its benefits while avoiding its dangers. A truly risk-averse people, preoccupied with the "limitation and division of power," to use Samuel Huntington's words, would never have conducted this experiment.[102]

Fig. 4.1 College student Chuck McManis watches President Jimmy Carter's nationally televised "malaise" speech from a service station in Los Angeles on July 15, 1979.
(AP Photo/Mao)

Discipline

When Lord Bryce wrote his classic volumes, he thought America was setting a course of responsible liberty that would be the model for the world. . . . [Now] the outlook for liberty and democracy is bleak and depressing. . . . Has popular democracy gone too far?

—JAMES RESTON, *New York Times*, October 12, 1975

The political malaise of today is different in kind from others within the memory of contemporary politicians in the Western world. . . . The crisis is that institutions of government are overloaded.

—RICHARD ROSE, *European Studies Newsletter*,

December 1975

Can a democracy discipline itself? What is it that creates this sense of helplessness? . . . What we've got is these constant forces to increase expenditures, to increase nominal income, [and] to expand government programs.

—ALFRED KAHN, *Chairman, US Council on Wage and Price Stability, 1980, quoted in Theodore White*, America in Search of Itself

Jimmy Carter believed that something was wrong with American democracy in the 1970s and made the mistake of saying so. In July 1979 Carter withdrew to the presidential compound at Camp David, and for two weeks he summoned politicians, experts, businessmen, and theologians to discuss the sour mood of the country. On July 15, he returned to Washington and gave a televised address to the nation (fig. 4.1). The United States, Carter said, was seized by "paralysis and stagnation and drift." In Washington, government appeared to be "incapable of action . . . and pulled in every direction by hundreds of well-financed and powerful special interests." The American people themselves too often tended to "worship self-indulgence and consumption." Respect for government had collapsed, but so too had faith in the ability of citizens "to serve as the ultimate rulers and shapers" of the nation. This "crisis of confidence," Carter concluded, consti- tuted a "fundamental threat to American democracy."[1]

This quickly became known as the "malaise" speech, although Carter never used that word in it, and it is remembered as the moment in which Carter's presidency was doomed.[2] But Carter was criticized for an excess of candor rather than for being wrong in his diagnosis. Many people shared his fears about the condition of American politics. *New York Times* columnist James Reston also believed that democracy was in "serious trouble"—not just in the United States, but throughout the Western world. "We are living," Reston warned, "in a time of widespread doubt about the capacity of free societies to deal with the economic, political and philosophical problems of the age."[3] West German chancellor Willy Brandt thought that Western Europe might "slide under the surrounding sea of dictatorship" by the end of the century.[4] The British historian Arnold Toynbee said that Western politicians were simply afraid to tell voters that the era of continuous economic growth was over. In all developed countries, Toynbee said, a more austere way of life would have to be "imposed by a ruthless authoritarian government."[5]

In the United States, recent history offered many reasons for discontent. Since the mid-1960s the country had been rocked by controversy over the Vietnam War, a string of political assassinations, a constitutional crisis that ended in the resignation of President Richard Nixon, scandals over the abuse of intelligence and police powers, urban riots, and increases in crime and domestic terrorism.[6] But in the mid-1970s, it was the economy that weighed most heavily on the minds of Americans. It was no longer growing as it had in the two decades after World War II. In 1975 the unemployment rate was higher than at any point since the Great Depression; inexplicably, the inflation rate was also higher than at any point since World War II. And the federal budget, which had doubled between 1967 and 1975, was also badly imbalanced: one-fifth of federal spending was financed by borrowing. "The reality," the journalist Theodore White wrote, "is that no one, absolutely no one, can control the budget of the United States.... The moral mandate of the sixties and seventies locks expenditure into an ever-rising, irreversible escalation."[7]

But if American democracy was in crisis, as President Carter and others suggested, what sort of crisis was it? Certainly not a crisis of representation, as in the years before World War I. On the contrary, the preceding decade witnessed a substantial expansion in political participation by the American public. The passage of the Voting Rights Act of 1965 resulted in a marked increase in voting by African Americans, and in 1971 the Constitution was amended to lower the voting age from 21 to 18.[8] A national movement to promote political action by women had emerged and persuaded Congress to endorse a constitutional amendment prohibiting discrimination based on sex.[9] Activists were also becoming more effective in mobilizing public support on issues such as civil rights, the environment, and consumer protection.[10] Federal law had been modified to expand opportunities for public participation in agency decision-making and to check the influence of money in politics. In short, political power had never been so broadly diffused within the American democracy as it was in 1975.

Similarly, the United States was not experiencing a crisis of mastery, as it had in the three decades between 1917 and 1948. In that era, the obstacle to self-rule had been a lack of administrative tools to address public problems, compounded by the unwillingness of some political leaders to concede that government had any duty to solve those problems. But the two Democratic presidents of the 1960s—Kennedy and Johnson—were heirs of Roosevelt, deeply committed to the proposition that government should be a powerful instrument for societal transformation, at home and overseas.[11] By 1968 there were almost three-quarters of a million American soldiers fighting Communist expansion in Southeast Asia, while Johnson had launched an "all-out war on human poverty and unemployment" in the United States itself.[12] Congress established new health insurance programs for the poor and elderly; provided new aid for public education; expanded federal support for pensions, welfare, and urban development; and adopted laws prohibiting discrimination based on race and sex. The cumulative effect was "a dramatic transformation of American government."[13] Federal expenditures almost doubled between 1960 and 1968, while the federal payroll increased by 1.5 million people.[14]

Activist government was a bipartisan project. Richard Nixon, inaugurated as president in January 1969, was regarded at the time as a conservative Republican.[15] Still, it was Nixon who proposed a guaranteed income for all Americans, which would have been the biggest increase in welfare spending since Roosevelt.[16] Nixon also expanded the federal role in protecting civil rights and became known as the "father of affirmative action."[17] It was the Nixon administration that created the Environmental Protection Agency, the Occupational Safety and Health Administration, and the Consumer Product Safety Commission, and urged Congress to adopt the controversial Endangered Species Act.[18] And Nixon proved to be an inveterate tinkerer with the overall economy. In his five years as president, he experimented with "pump-priming" budget deficits, pressured the Federal Reserve to adjust interest rates, manipulated currency exchange rates, established wage and price controls, and imposed the first general increase in tariffs since the Smoot-Hawley Act of 1930.[19]

American democracy, as it stood in the early 1970s, ought to have been regarded as an efficient machine for satisfying public desires. The channels by which demands could be communicated to politicians had been cleared of obstructions, such as limitations on the right to vote. Furthermore, politicians had an expansive bureaucracy at hand that allowed them to respond to those demands—and if existing administrative capacity was not sufficient, politicians were eager to expand it. The result should have been an increase in public satisfaction with government. In fact, the outcome was the reverse. In 1958, according to one major survey, three-quarters of Americans believed that they could trust the national government most or all of the time. By 1972, only half expressed that level of trust; by 1978, not even one-third.[20]

What had gone wrong? Many observers believed that the United States and other advanced nations were actually suffering from a new form of crisis—one that was most likely to arise in a mature democracy in which problems of representation and mastery had largely been overcome. The underlying problem, these observers argued, was one of too much democracy. People had developed unreasonable expectations about what government could do for them; they had acquired new power to push their demands on their leaders—and leaders, lacking any method of regulating the pressure that was being placed upon them, had been overwhelmed.

This was not an entirely new argument. In 1956 the historian David Donald claimed that the American Civil War was a product of the extension of voting rights to all adult males: "universal democracy," he said, "made it difficult to deal with issues requiring subtle understanding and delicate handling."[21] A decade later, political scientist Samuel Huntington drew on Donald's work to state the proposition more generally. An "excess of democracy," Huntington suggested in his 1968 book *Political Order in Changing Societies*, could "erode the power of government" and its ability to deal with complex problems.[22]

Huntington soon had the opportunity to apply this idea to modern American politics. In 1973 an elite group of businessmen and intellectuals established a nongovernmental body, the Trilateral Commission, to study the shared problems of the developed world. The following year, the Commission retained

Huntington and two other scholars to examine the condition of government in those countries. Their report, *The Crisis of Democracy*, was published in June 1975. The three authors foresaw "a bleak future for democratic government" worldwide. Political leaders appeared to be incapable of meeting economic and social challenges, and trust in government was collapsing. Moreover, the troubles of the advanced countries seemed to arise "directly out of the functioning of democracy." Historically, the operation of these political systems had depended on "some measure of apathy and noninvolvement" among citizens. In the 1960s, however, barriers to involvement had been removed and old habits of "self-restraint" had faded away. The result was "an overload of demands on government, exceeding its capacity to respond." The problem was especially severe in the United States, where the "democratic surge" of the 1960s had produced a "deficit in governability" in the 1970s. The report concluded that the global crisis of democracy would only be resolved by restoring "a more equitable relationship between governmental authority and popular control."[23]

Oddly, *The Crisis of Democracy* was instantly disowned by the Trilateral Commission itself.[24] But the "overload thesis," as the argument came to be known, gained support on both sides of the Atlantic. In Britain, the journalist Samuel Brittan argued that democracy suffered from an "internal contradiction": it encouraged the build-up of "excessive expectations" that eventually undermined the stability of government.[25] A senior advisor to the Conservative Party held that modern democracies were simply victims of their own success in achieving mastery over the economy. The problem of excessive demands, he said, arose precisely because economic conditions were now seen to be "subject to the influence of government."[26] The political scientist Anthony King concluded that overload was likely to produce a "regime crisis" in Britain within a few years.[27]

The diagnosis by American conservatives was equally grim. James Q. Wilson, a colleague of Huntington's at Harvard University, lamented the collapse of mechanisms that had once encouraged moderation in demands upon government.[28] Another political scientist said that the country had been seized by "a psychosis of inflated expectations."[29] Aaron Wildavsky, a highly respected specialist on government budgeting, even suggested that citizens could be regarded as predators on the state.[30] Wildavsky complained that people were making demands on government that were impossible to satisfy, and that the result would be policy failure, public disillusionment, and a decline in public order.[31] In a popular 1976 book, the sociologist Daniel Bell agreed. Old norms of self-discipline and restraint were fading away, Bell said. The results were "a constant tendency for state expenditures to rise," persistent inflation, rising public anger, and increased political instability.[32]

Concern about the defects of democratic processes soon pervaded many areas of scholarly inquiry. In the field of economics, for example, a central concern was understanding the causes of the high inflation that afflicted the United States and other advanced countries after the late 1960s. Before 1970, inflation was generally regarded as a wartime problem: a sudden spike in military production intensified the competition for workers and resources, thus driving up wages and prices. In the postwar era, between 1948 and 1968, the average inflation rate was only about 2 percent in the United States.[33] But the pattern changed after 1968. The inflation rate exceeded 5 percent in 1969 and 10 percent in 1974. The average rate for the 1970s was roughly 8 percent, which meant that the purchasing power of a dollar was cut in half over that decade.

The diagnosis was that inflation arose and persisted because of a failure of political leadership. Total government expenditure increased sharply after the mid-1960s, because of the war in Southeast Asia and the "war on poverty" at home. As government-driven demand for goods and services increased, so did wages and prices. The federal government could have compensated for this added pressure on the economy by raising taxes. However, the White House and Congress knew that tax increases were politically unpopular. Similarly the Federal Reserve could have compensated by tightening credit, thereby slowing economic activity. But the White House pushed the Federal Reserve to keep interest rates low, especially in election years. The overall result was inflation, which was aggravated by unexpected spikes in the price of oil in 1973 and 1979.[34] By the end of the 1970s, the inflation problem could only be cured by severe measures—but many people doubted that American politicians had the courage to undertake them. No freely elected government, the journalist Theodore White said, would be prepared to undertake such "ruthless political surgery."[35]

Other advanced economies had similar troubles, although not always to the same degree. West Germany, for example, had a significantly lower inflation rate throughout the 1970s. But the West German central bank also had much stronger protection against political interference. This was a legacy of the German hyperinflation of the 1920s, which was said to have arisen because politicians prevented the central bank from taking firm measures to stop inflation. Indeed, the German intellectuals who helped to design their postwar government were generally cautious about allowing politicians too much control over many aspects of economic policy. Democracy, Wilhelm Röpke wrote, had to be "hedged in by limitations and safeguards"; institutions like the central bank had to be protected against assaults by the "hungry hordes of vested interests."[36]

The experience of the 1970s seemed to show the wisdom of the German approach, at least as far as the role of the central bank was concerned. In the early 1980s, two Canadian scholars examined the major economies and concluded that countries with central banks that were more independent of politicians also tended to have lower inflation rates.[37] A number of other studies soon appeared to support this finding. In 1993, for example, the Harvard economists Alberto Alesina and Lawrence Summers (who would become Treasury Secretary in the Clinton administration from 1999 to 2001) said that they had found "a near perfect negative correlation between inflation and central bank independence" among the advanced economies.[38] Economists went further, asserting that central bank independence was actually a cause of lower inflation, precisely because an autonomous bank was free to make the hard decisions that politicians avoided.

This was a significant retreat from the philosophy that prevailed between 1930 and the 1960s. In 1935, Franklin Roosevelt had pushed Congress to give him tighter authority over the Federal Reserve, on the premise that the president had responsibility for overall management of the economy, and that this responsibility could not be fulfilled without control over the central bank. Most other countries took a similar approach: after the

1930s, central banks in many countries were made "subservient to central government."[39] But politicians, it was now alleged, could not be trusted to wield this new power responsibly. Always acting with an eye on the next election, they allowed inflation to fester, or they pursued stop-and-start policies that created confusion about the long-term direction of government policy. The remedy was to take the central bank "outside the realm of party politics."[40] Autonomous central banks would be permitted to act "outside the normal pressures and requirements of democratic societies."[41]

Central banking was not the only area in which academics were beginning to take a more skeptical view of democracy. Economists also began to look at taxing and spending with a more jaundiced eye. At the University of Virginia, two academics—James Buchanan and Gordon Tullock—established a school of thought, known as Public Choice, that became highly influential in the 1970s. Their approach was built on two assumptions. The first was that individuals and groups engaged in the sphere of politics just as they did in the marketplace—that is, with the sole aim of advancing their own material interests. ("The basic behavioral postulate," one follower of Buchanan and Tullock said, "is that man is an egoistic, rational, utility maximizer."[42]) The second assumption was that the behavior of individuals and groups is shaped mainly by formal rules that define what they can or cannot do as they pursue their interests. The effect of combining these two assumptions was to produce a view of democracy as a simple and formal game, with nothing high-minded about it. "Policy outcomes," a student of Buchanan's later wrote, are "a more or less 'natural' product of people pursuing their interests through political processes, as this pursuit is shaped and constrained by constitutional rules. Undesirable or inefficient outcomes, then, call for constitutional remedy and not for exhortation to do better."[43]

Public Choice scholars argued that the game of democratic politics was set up to encourage the overproduction of public services. Politicians, for example, had an incentive to make large promises to win the next election. Bureaucrats in public agencies had an incentive to promote new programs so that they could increase their budgets and perquisites. Special interests had an incentive to lobby for programs whose costs could be loaded onto the shoulders of less-organized taxpayers. And voters in general had an incentive to press politicians for benefits whose costs could be transferred, by borrowing, to future generations. In sum, endless budget growth was the inevitable result of politicians, bureaucrats, and voters engaging in their "natural proclivities" within the democratic process.[44] This defect in democracy was held to be "inherent and universal."[45]

Unsurprisingly, Buchanan himself developed an early and intense antipathy toward the Keynesian approach to economic management that became dominant after World War II. Keynesian economists condoned borrowing by governments to "prime the pump" during periods of economic decline. The premise was that governments would repay these debts when the economy recovered. But Buchanan was doubtful that debts would ever be repaid. He believed that Keynesians, by dispelling the stigma that traditionally surrounded debt-financed expenditure, had created a new "bias toward extended public expenditure."[46]

There was an important inconsistency in Buchanan's assault on the Keynesian approach. Buchanan recognized that government deficits had not been a serious problem for the first 150 years of American history, because politicians and voters respected the "norm of budget balance." Buchanan said that this had been a widely shared "moral constraint" before World War II, "part of an accepted set of attitudes about how government should ... carry on its fiscal affairs."[47] Buchanan's lament about Keynesianism was that it caused a "shift in ideas on public debt ... There was no longer any reason for opposing deficit financing on basically moral grounds."[48] This emphasis on the decline of self-control after World War II was entirely consistent with other criticisms made against American democracy in the 1970s. But it was not consistent with the Public Choice axiom that self-interest, rather than morality, was the only relevant driver of human behavior. Nor was it consistent with the Public Choice view that democracy had a "*natural* tendency to generate budget deficits": as Buchanan conceded, the bulk of American history did not support this conclusion.[49]

Like other Public Choice scholars, Buchanan believed that the rules of the game were critically important, and his own remedy for the problem of debt-financed expenditure in the postwar period was straightforward: there should be an amendment to the Constitution that would force the federal government to balance its budget. The notion of a constitutional limitation on government borrowing was not new. Most American state governments operated under this sort of restriction.[50] However, no similar constraint had ever been imposed on the federal government. Buchanan regarded it as essential. "The structural flaw in our fiscal politics," he argued in 1997, "requires structural correction, that is, a constitutional constraint that will, effectively, change the basic rules for the fiscal game."[51]

By this time, economists had invented a name for legal constraints that forced governments to balance their budgets. They
were known as *fiscal rules*, and they were widely viewed as important tools for maintaining budget discipline within democratic
systems. The Public Choice diagnosis of democratic failure was
now generally accepted. In a 2007 paper, for example, European
researchers provided the now-standard account of the problem
with democracies:

> Post-war economic history provides evidence that fiscal
> authorities in industrialized countries may be prone to a
> "deficit-bias," which shows up in large and persistent deficits
> and growing public debts. . . . There is growing agreement
> that the sources of the deficit bias [is rooted in] the system
> of incentives and rewards that shape the behaviour of
> fiscal authorities. Governments, being unsure to be re-
> elected, are inherently short-sighted and do not fully
> take into account the longer term implications of deficits.
> Groups in the society that benefit from a particular type
> of government spending do not fully internalise the costs
> of this expenditure, since the financing is generally spread
> among a wide set of contributors through taxation. This
> "common pool problem" is at the source of overspending
> and the accumulation of deficits and debt over time.[52]

The surest way to fix the democratic disease of "deficit bias," these
economists agreed, was through the adoption of well-designed fiscal rules, like Buchanan's proposed constitutional amendment.[53]

In fact, it now seemed that any aspect of economic policy
that was set by a democratic system was liable to be corrupted

by the pressure of special interests. Before 1970, for example, there was a respectable body of opinion in the United States and other advanced economies that tariffs and other protectionist measures sometimes played an important role in promoting the development of key industries. Indeed, the United Kingdom and the United States had both relied on tariffs for this purpose, although as each economy gained dominance, its commitment to protectionism wavered.[54] As late as 1971, President Nixon still advocated the use of tariffs as a method of boosting the overall economy.[55] After the 1970s, though, scholarly attitudes toward protectionism changed. The idea that tariffs might serve the general welfare gave way to the view that they were mainly a device by which politicians catered to powerful lobbies. Groups that sought tariff protection were seen as "predators and parasites" who took advantage of politicians' "penchant for campaign gifts."[56] Free trade agreements were regarded as devices that prevented elected officials from succumbing to these unhealthy impulses.[57]

There was similar backtracking in the field of regulation. Throughout the first half of the twentieth century, it was generally accepted that regulatory agencies like the Interstate Commerce Commission or the Federal Trade Commission could play an important role in countering private power and protecting the public interest. After the 1960s, however, this idea was subjected to multiple assaults. Some critics emphasized the inefficiencies that were created as federal agencies imposed rules on the private sector that were supposed to enhance the general welfare.[58] Other critics went further, disputing whether it was even possible to define the public interest and asserting that the regulatory process had degenerated into yet another forum in which special interests wrangled for advantages.[59] And a third camp of critics argued that the aims of regulation had actually been turned upside down, because regulated industries were so much better at lobbying than their customers. Regulatory agencies, it was said, were usually "captured" by the very interests they were supposed to control.[60]

In all spheres of economic policymaking, it seemed, the grand ambitions of democratic governments had been undermined by the selfish maneuvering of politicians, voters, and special interests. A new term was coined to describe what groups were doing when they lobbied government for advantageous policies: *rent-seeking*. This term was the invention of Anne Krueger, an economist who later occupied senior roles at the World Bank and the International Monetary Fund.[61] A rent was defined as any favor conferred by a politician or bureaucrat.[62] The favor could come in many forms—such as welfare and pension payments, corporate subsidies, tax breaks, tariff protection, rules against competition from upstart firms, collective bargaining rights for unions, or minimum wage and anti-discrimination laws. Economists already considered many of these policies to be problematic because they interfered with the efficient operation of the market. But Krueger argued in 1974 that further losses were incurred because of the investment of resources in lobbying, bribery, and other activities that was necessary to obtain these favors in the first place. These investments are said to be "basically wasted."[63]

The concept of rent-seeking soon traveled from academia to journalism. The columnist George Will decried it as America's "national past-time," while another condemned it as "a basic defect" of democratic government.[64] This sort of talk had a powerful effect in delegitimizing any government action that happened to confer a benefit on particular individuals or groups. "The quest for personal advantage may be masked with the rhetoric of social advantage," one group of economists explained, "[but] the quests for income and wealth redistribution through public policy are comparable to the activities of thieves."[65] Before, advocates of lobbying argued that it served some socially useful purpose, because it conveyed information to decision-makers about constituent preferences and the feasibility of proposed policies. But lobbying was now construed as an entirely unproductive activity.[66] It was even corrupt—if not as a matter of law, then as a matter of principle. "Rent-seeking is unethical," one economist said, "in that people seek favors and privilege that allow them to benefit from someone else's productive effort."[67]

Krueger also introduced another idea—"the rent-seeking society."[68] This is a society in which rent-seeking is the dominant way of making a living: individuals and groups focus their energies on obtaining special treatment from government, rather than producing goods and services for the market. Another economist, Mancur Olson, amplified on the idea in a popular 1982 book, *The Rise and Decline of Nations*. Olson thought that he had identified a fatal weakness with long-established democracies like the United Kingdom and the United States. Long periods of stability, combined with the "democratic freedom to organize," allowed for the accretion of a large number of rent-seeking special-interest groups. These groups were like barnacles on the hull of the ship of state: they made it move more slowly and less nimbly. Olson called this a process of "institutional sclerosis." The long-term effect, he argued, was a sharp decline in the rate of economic growth.[69]

Another American writer, Jonathan Rauch, restated Olson's argument in the early 1990s. "People used to fear that democracy would dither fatally while dictators and totalitarians swept the field." Rauch said:

> That fear turned out to be mistaken. Now it appears that the vulnerabilities of democracy—at any rate, of the postwar style of democracy, with its professional activists and its large and fairly powerful government—are mundane and close to home. . . . [One vulnerability] is creeping special-interest gridlock: that is, progressive sclerosis. . . . Special-interest groups will always tend to accumulate over time; if shaken off, they will re-accumulate. . . . [The] whole accumulated mass becomes steadily less rational and less flexible.[70]

The transformation of a mature democracy into a rent-seeking society was said to have other costs as well. Respect for politicians and public institutions seemed to decline, while corruption increased, as the sordid race for government favors intensified.[71]

The indictment of American democracy that emerged out of the troubles of the 1970s was bleak and fatalistic. The complaint was not merely that the system had failed in the late 1960s and 1970s; it was also that advanced democracies like the United States should always be expected to fail in this way. The weaknesses of democratic politics that some people saw at that moment—the prevalence of selfishness, avarice, and shortsightedness—were held to be inherent weaknesses, which could be observed at any moment in history. Similarly the tendencies in policy that were observed at that time—such as the rapid expansion of government spending—were held to be universal tendencies, which operated at all times. Why did critics talk this way? Perhaps this was a product of the academic penchant for abstraction, or just the human habit of giving undue weight to immediate experience.

The prognosis was dark but also misguided. It underestimated the flexibility of the American system, and its ability to learn from the experience of policy failure. In fact, the crisis of the mid-1970s triggered a substantial change in the structure of American government, and in popular attitudes about the role of government. While critics persisted in their assertions about the "natural tendencies" of democracy, democracy itself was mutating in ways that made the assertions less tenable. The system was learning how to protect itself against the risk of democratic overload.

One important change was in the role of the central bank. After the 1970s many democracies gave formal independence to their central banks, so that they could pursue the hard measures that were sometimes necessary to prevent or curb inflation. The United Kingdom, for example, changed its national law so that the Bank of England had a mandate to maintain stability in prices. In the United States, the adjustment was one of actual practice, rather than law.[72] In July 1979, President Jimmy Carter appointed a new chairman of the Federal Reserve, Paul Volcker, who quickly began to fight inflation by raising interest rates sharply. Volcker later recalled that the economy "fell like a rock" in 1980, but Carter did not pressure the Federal Reserve to change policy. "There was no sharp reprimand," Volcker said. "There was no head-on fight."[73] Carter's successor, Ronald Reagan, also avoided attacks on the Federal Reserve, even as public anger over the economic downturn intensified. Reagan supported Volcker's reappointment as Federal Reserve chairman in 1983.[74]

By the late 1980s, the role of the Federal Reserve had been transformed. Two decades earlier, the Keynesian economist John Kenneth Galbraith argued that the central bank ought to be regarded as a "minor instrumentality of the state," like the federal printing bureau.[75] In Galbraith's view, power over economic policymaking belonged in the White House, while the role of the Federal Reserve was mainly to execute instructions from the president. After Volcker, no one viewed the central bank in this way. The chairman of the Federal Reserve, the journalist William Greider observed in 1989, now served as the "presiding patriarch for the American economy," with a single-minded concern for the preservation of sound money.[76] And the standing of the Federal Reserve increased even further under Alan Greenspan, who served as its chairman between 1987 and 2006. No politician, the journalist Bob Woodward said in 2001, dared to question Greenspan's judgment.[77] The Federal Reserve chairman had acquired "rock star status."[78]

The country's attitude toward fiscal policy also changed after the 1970s. Voter anger—often described as a nationwide "taxpayer revolt"—drove almost half of state governments to adopt new restrictions on taxing and spending in the 1970s.[79] (The most famous of these measures was California's Proposition 13, a constitutional restriction on property taxes that was endorsed by voters in a 1978 referendum.) Another product of voter frustration was the "no-tax pledge"—a promise by political candidates at all levels of government that they would not raise taxes after election.[80] Voter anger fueled a national movement as well, for a constitutional amendment that would compel the federal government to balance its budget except in times of national emergency. Between 1975 and 1979, twenty-nine state legislatures passed petitions urging Congress to adopt a balanced budget amendment.[81] Echoing Buchanan and others in the Public Choice school, advocates of the amendment argued that constitutional change was essential to restore "self-discipline" in Washington.[82]

The balanced-budget drive fell short of the thirty-four state petitions that were necessary to compel action by Congress. A second effort to amend the Constitution was mounted in 1982, beginning this time with votes in the House of Representatives and Senate. This effort also failed—but narrowly, when the House of Representatives endorsed the proposal with less than the necessary two-thirds majority.[83] Too many politicians and experts had deep reservations about the wisdom of a constitutional restriction on taxing and spending at the national level. This included some conservatives. Alan Greenspan, a strong critic of federal deficits, nevertheless said that no "responsible economist" could support a balanced budget amendment.[84]

Still, the movement brought legitimacy to the idea of adopting some legal constraint on fiscal policy. In 1985, Congress passed the Gramm-Rudman-Hollings Balanced Budget Act, which established a series of annual deficit targets, ending with a balanced budget in 1991.[85] If the president and Congress failed to agree on a budget that met a deficit target, the law required automatic spending reductions drawn equally from defense and some domestic programs.[86] The theory was that the automatic reductions would be so universally unappealing that the president and Congress would be driven to meet the deficit target. Senator Phil Gramm, one of the statute's sponsors, described it as a "binding constraint" that was necessary to achieve long-term budget discipline, and credited Buchanan with providing the "philosophical underpinning" for the law.[87] The Gramm-Rudman-Hollings Act was replaced by a new statute, the Budget Enforcement Act, in 1990.[88] It removed the binding deficit targets but established limits on some categories of federal spending for the five years, with the threat of automatic cuts if the limits were not respected. The key elements of the Budget Enforcement Act were extended twice in the 1990s and ultimately expired in 2002.[89] By then, the federal government had operated under some form of statutory fiscal rule for fifteen years.

After 2002, other laws also proved useful as devices for pursuing budget discipline. One of these was the statutory limit on total federal debt that has been set by Congress (with periodic adjustments) since 1939. If the borrowing limit is reached, the federal government must make major cuts in expenditure or default on existing debt.[90] Congress has always been cautious about raising the limit, so that further adjustments are constantly required. The renewal process was fraught with conflict in the decade after 2002—most notably in 2011 and 2013, when the Republican-controlled House of Representatives refused to raise the limit until the Obama administration made concessions on the federal budget.[91]

Another area in which Washington was said to be the victim of special interests was trade policy. The tariff schedule of the United States—the detailed statement of taxes that are levied on different types of imported products—was for decades viewed as a spider's nest of favors for powerful lobbies. In fact, tariff policy was often regarded as the best example of how sound policy could be corrupted by "pernicious lobbying."[92] In principle, free trade agreements that were negotiated with other nations could liberate the US government from special interests at home, by removing its capacity to manipulate tariff rates in their favor.[93] But for many observers it was difficult to see why domestic lobbies would allow this to happen. "The pressures supporting the tariff," the political scientist E. E. Schattschneider observed, "are overwhelming."[94]

And yet the 1970s triggered an acceleration of the process of trade liberalization. Congress invented a new "fast-track" procedure for approving trade agreements that limited its own capacity to alter deals that had been negotiated by the President.[95] The fast-track technique was used when the Reagan administration negotiated a free trade agreement with Canada, the United States' most important trading partner. The 1988 agreement bound the United States to remove most of its tariffs on Canadian imports within a decade. It also contained an important innovation: a promise that some disputes about the application of American trade law would be resolved by binational panels, rather than American courts.[96] The agreement was approved by Congress despite complaints that this promise undermined American sovereignty and compromised the "inherent and constitutional rights" of American citizens.[97] The same approach was taken in the North American Free Trade Agreement of 1992, which extended the 1988 treaty to include Mexico.[98] And in 1994 Congress approved American participation in the new World Trade Organization, a Geneva-based body that would oversee the implementation of free trade rules in over one hundred countries.[99]

The result of all these negotiations was that the tariff schedule ceased to be the focus for special interest lobbying that it had been in the earlier part of the twentieth century. In part this was because tariffs had been discounted as a legitimate tool for economic management. In 1910, the tax on dutiable imports was roughly 40 percent; in 2000, it was only 5 percent—and two-thirds of all imports entered the country without any tax at all.[100] More important, Congress had also limited its own ability to offer tariff protection. Its discretion was now disciplined by a web of international agreements.

The federal government also made important changes with respect to regulation, another field in which sound policy was said to be undermined by interest group politics. The Interstate Commerce Commission, the nation's first independent regulatory commission, once regarded as the most powerful agency in the federal government, was eliminated in 1995.[101] It had already lost many of its important functions: between 1976 and 1980, Congress substantially reduced the Commission's power over the railroad and trucking industry.[102] Federal controls over the airline industry were also reduced in the late 1970s, despite howls of protest by major airlines, and the body responsible for those controls—the Civil Aeronautics Board, a creation of the Roosevelt administration—was eliminated a few years later.[103] Rules governing the operation of the communications, energy, and financial services industries were eventually removed as well. In 1978 the Carter administration directed all federal agencies to scrutinize the burden of proposed regulations more closely, and Congress reinforced this obligation in two 1980 laws.[104]

This entire process became known as deregulation. The economist Alfred Kahn described it as a "revolution" within federal government.[105] The revolution was under way well before the inauguration of President Reagan, although his administration

spurred it on. Kahn, who in 1970 had published an extensive critique of traditional modes of regulation, later said that
he was surprised by the speed with which policies changed in
Washington.[106] The "Nirvana view of government," as other scholars of regulation called it, was in retreat within a decade, replaced
by a "greater willingness to allow markets to function without
interference."[107] The new market-friendly approach was evident
in Congress's 1990 amendments to the Clean Air Act, which used
a cap-and-trade system to address the problem of acid rain. And
sometimes, the federal government simply instructed industries
to regulate themselves. In 1998, for example, the Clinton administration passed off responsibility for oversight of the Internet to an
industry-run not-for-profit known as the Internet Corporation
for Assigned Names and Numbers (ICANN).[108]

The federal government also took steps to discipline another
special interest—the bureaucracy itself. The old idea of federal
employees as selfless servants of the public interest gave way in
the early 1970s to the notion of the "budget-maximizing bureaucrat," whose main goal was to increase salary, influence, and
freedom from supervision by elected officials.[109] The Reagan
administration dealt with this perceived problem crudely, by giving more power to carefully chosen political appointees in federal
departments, and by telling those appointees to treat career civil
servants almost as the enemy.[110] Soon, though, more sophisticated techniques for controlling the bureaucracy were developed.
In 1993, Congress instructed federal agencies to produce better
data on what their programs actually achieved.[111] Sometimes
agencies and employees were given stronger financial incentives
to achieve performance targets.[112] Increasingly, they were compelled to compete with private contractors for the right to provide

public services.[113] And all the while, the federal civil service was subject to intense budget pressure as Congress wrestled with the deficit. In 1998, the Clinton administration boasted that it had eliminated more than 350,000 employees in just six years.[114]

There are people who complain about "democratic overload" now, who see today's democratic malaise simply as a continuation of the troubles of the 1970s. In this view, Western democracies are still "sloppy and self-indulgent . . . [and] overloaded with obligations and distorted by special interests."[115] They believe that tendency toward unending governmental expansion and societal sclerosis persists, and none of the institutional reforms of the past thirty years have done much good.

There are critics, for example, who question the United States' commitment to the idea of central bank independence. Congress could have changed the law that determines the status of the Federal Reserve, to make clear that it had the freedom and duty to focus on fighting inflation. The European Union did this when it set up its European Central Bank in the 1990s. The 1992 Treaty of European Union specifies that the single most important goal of the ECB is maintaining price stability. By contrast, Congress carried on with a 1970s-era statute whose broad wording might allow the Federal Reserve to sacrifice long-term price stability for the sake of short-term growth. Congress ignored calls for the law to be made more precise, so that it was consistent with the European approach.[116] Indeed, some people thought that the Federal Reserve exploited the vagueness of American law after the global financial crisis of 2007–2008, by giving more priority to politically popular stimulus measures than to preventing inflation in the long run. The idea of Federal

Reserve independence, two critics concluded in 2013, "is more myth than reality."[117]

This criticism is both right and wrong. In one sense, Federal Reserve independence certainly is a myth. The central bank gained influence mainly because politicians like Jimmy Carter and Ronald Reagan made the choice not to interfere in its decision-making. The existing law does not provide as much protection against interference as it might. And even if Congress toughened the law to discourage interference, it would always have the power to change it back. For all these reasons, autonomy really is an illusion: ultimately, it depends on political support. Even Paul Volcker conceded that the Federal Reserve must operate "within the range of understanding of the public and the political system. You can't just go do something that is outside the bounds of what people can understand, because you won't be independent for very long if you do that."[118]

But all of these reservations must be weighed against our observation of political realities. As a practical matter, politicians have allowed the Federal Reserve more freedom to make hard decisions. Even when they had the capacity to intervene, they chose not to. And as time passed, the political costs associated with any attempt to intervene grew higher. A new norm of noninterference became established, and the Federal Reserve was in a better position to defend itself. These facts were probably more important than any guarantee about independence that could have been expressed in federal law. The Federal Reserve has acquired prestige and allies, mainly because it is perceived to be successful in its work. In the three decades after 1983, consumer prices barely rose more than they did in the ten years between 1970 and 1980.[119] Throughout the 1970s, a majority of Americans told pollsters that they regarded inflation as the nation's most important problem.[120] Some experts wondered whether the problem was fixable at all.[121] But now that problem is history: most Americans living today have no firsthand experience of high inflation.[122]

Present-day advocates of the overload thesis also see the past thirty years as a long story of failure to control taxing and spending. Once again, the complaint is not entirely baseless. The same treaty that established the European Central Bank also set firm rules on fiscal policy for many European countries: never a deficit larger than 3 percent of national income, and never a total debt larger than 60 percent of national income.[123] By contrast, politicians in the United States generally avoided such hard rules. Attempts to introduce a constitutional balanced-budget amendment failed repeatedly. The Gramm-Rudman-Hollings Act of 1985 was promoted as a "binding constraint" on the federal budget, but when it became clear two years later that its targets for deficit reduction could not be met, Congress simply adopted less demanding targets. Targets were adjusted again when the economy slowed down in 1990. In 1992 one newspaper condemned Washington for its "copious tinkering" with the law.[124] For the next decade, policymakers continued to invent ways of softening or evading the budget control law, which was finally abandoned in 2002.[125] Throughout the whole era, budget making was fractious and unsystematic, typified by last-minute dealmaking and ugly compromises.[126]

All of this might seem to suggest that the federal government was incapable of escaping the pattern of "endless growth in spending" that James Buchanan had identified in the late 1960s.[127] But the data does not support that conclusion. Admittedly, there was a perceptible upward trend in federal spending as a share of the national economy from the mid-1950s to the mid-1980s—that is, the time in which the Public Choice school became established (fig. 4.2). But the trend does not continue after that: on the contrary, the trend was slightly downward until the financial crisis of 2008. National debt continued to increase until the early 1990s, because tax revenues fell short of expenditures—but debt also declined after that time. In 2008, spending and debt levels were not much different than they had been in 1964. In short, the budget story of the last thirty years is not one of failure. It is the story of a system that struggled to contain expenditure growth—not easily, and often with setbacks—but in the long run, with considerable success.[128]

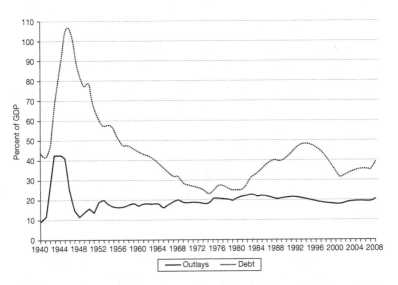

Fig. 4.2 Federal outlays and debt as a share of Gross Domestic Product, 1940 to 2008.
SOURCE: Historical budget tables, Office of Management and Budget.

The burden of expenditure control fell heavily on the federal bureaucracy. The academic literature of the 1960s and 1970s emphasized that federal civil servants were "budget maximizers," skilled in duping their political masters and protecting their own job security. Again, though, experience after 1980 did little to support that view. As politicians tried to protect entitlement programs like Social Security, Medicare, and Medicaid, they imposed severe restraints on programs in other areas, such as environmental protection, transportation, education, and diplomacy. In inflation-adjusted terms, spending on non-defense discretionary programs grew by only 1 percent a year between 1980 and 2008; by contrast, this kind of spending grew by about 6 percent a year between 1962 and 1980.[129] It is important to remember that both the economy and population grew faster than 1 percent a year in the latter part of the twentieth century. Thus, the share of the economy that was dedicated to such programs actually shrank: by 1990, it had returned to levels of the early 1960s, where it remained until 2008.[130] In fact, the civilian federal workforce that was inherited by President George W. Bush in 2001 was 15 percent smaller than that inherited by Dwight D. Eisenhower in 1953.[131] So much work had been transferred to government contractors that one expert argued it was time to "bring back the bureaucrats."[132]

A recurrent feature of complaints about present-day "democratic indiscipline" is the failure to acknowledge how much the world has changed since the 1970s. After the global financial crisis, for example, some people were alarmed by the softening in public support for free trade, and feared that the United States might return to "the tempting path of protectionism."[133] But any "protectionist impulse" that the country expressed in the immediate aftermath of the financial crisis was a faint echo of the pressures that had shaped trade policy before the 1970s.[134] The private-sector trade union movement, once a strong advocate of protection, has collapsed, while many American businesses have restructured themselves to fit the realities of a globalized economy. Today, tariff barriers are negligible. As a share of the economy, trade volume in 2014 was almost triple what it was in the late 1960s.[135]

Similarly, there are still complaints about the regulatory burden imposed by federal government. Unfortunately, there is no easy way to measure this burden. One common technique is to count the number of pages of regulations in force: this has increased steadily since 1975.[136] For some, this seems like a pattern of "non-stop" regulatory growth, and evidence that the problem of sclerosis—the "morbid hardening" of social and economic structures that Mancur Olsen said in 1982 was the curse of stable democracies—persists today.[137] But there are good reasons to view this measure skeptically, as well as the inference that is drawn from it.[138] A truly sclerotic society would not have overhauled its approach to the regulation of critical industries as quickly as the United States did after 1975—and it would not have tolerated the dramatic changes in social and economic structure that were triggered by deregulation.[139] The American economy of 2015 is larger, more complex, and more dynamic than it was forty years earlier. This alone might account for the growth in pages of regulation: even a market-friendly regulatory regime has to keep pace with rapidly changing social and economic realities.[140]

There is a different sort of critic who concedes that government has changed radically over the last forty years, and who also

concedes that many of these changes have succeeded in controlling the problem of democratic overload, but who doubts that
this says anything about the capacity of a mature democracy to
control its own impulses. For example, some people argue that all
of these reforms were imposed by capitalist elites, because capitalism itself could not thrive unless it "rid itself of social expectations" that were expressed through democratic politics.[141] In this
view, discipline was imposed on democracy. These are limitations
on popular sovereignty that were established against the wishes
of most voters, or at least without much regard for their wishes.

The people who make this sort of argument often regard themselves as friends of democracy, but the argument itself is not flattering to the concept of self-rule. The possibility that citizens
might have recognized the problem of overload by themselves,
and invented their own solutions for that problem, is discounted.
A comparable way of thinking was evident forty years earlier,
during the crisis of mastery: democracy was held to be incapable of performing major functions, until elites compelled
ordinary voters to accept the new realities of presidential and
bureaucratic power.

Of course, we cannot deny that many reforms of the post-1974
era were supported by business interests precisely because they
would profit from them. But American voters were not simply
victims of elite manipulation. Widespread public disenchantment
with the federal government was evident by the early 1970s: it pre-
ceded reform and was not manufactured to justify it.[142] Indeed,
some aspects of the post-1974 reform program—such as constitutional or statutory restrictions on taxing and spending—were the
product of authentic grassroots movements.[143] More broadly, the
whole program—including changes in Federal Reserve policies,

budget and trade deals, and deregulation initiatives—was openly debated, often sanctioned by new laws, and repeatedly ratified in elections. Critics can reasonably dispute whether voters were adequately informed in any one election about the likely effect of any one policy. But it is an entirely different thing to argue that over the whole of the period—four decades comprising sixteen national elections in which votes were cast 1.3 billion times— voters did not understand what they were doing.[144]

Of course, voters were often uneasy about the reforms that they eventually endorsed. There was a persistent tension between what appeared to be necessary and what conformed to old under-standings about how a democracy ought to work. As steps taken by the Federal Reserve began to cause economic pain after 1979, many asked why unelected officials should wield such "awesome power."[145] (The Federal Reserve, one writer said, had become a "monetary dictatorship."[146]) A constitutional amendment that required balanced budgets was also recognized as an attempt to limit "future democratic decisionmaking."[147] Trade agree-ments that established new mechanisms for resolving disputes between governments and corporations appeared to "subvert the democratic process" in two ways: because of the secretive way in which the new tribunals worked, and because the tribunals might try to override laws passed by Congress or state legislatures.[148] Similarly, deregulation seemed like a surrender by democracy of the right to oversee the market.[149] And privatization of public services often meant that organizations performing important functions were no longer subject to laws that were designed to promote transparency and public participation.[150]

The predicament that confronted American voters after the mid-1970s was not new. It was the same problem that arose as the federal government was built up during the 1930s and 1940s. At that time, the question was how to deal with the expansion of executive and bureaucratic power, which seemed essential in order to deal with economic and military crises, but which also threatened democratic control. New circumstances required an adaptation of old ideas about how democracy ought to work. That adaptation was accomplished: by 1948 the American people were living with a form of government that would have seemed completely alien in 1916. But the adjustment was accomplished in a certain way: by experimentation, adjustment, and the addition of counter-measures. A similar process was under way after 1975. Overall, American voters did not balk at institutional changes simply because they threatened settled ideas about popular sovereignty. But these innovations were not adopted with wholehearted enthusiasm either.

A good example may be the American approach to central banking. Ambivalence about the concept of central bank independence meant that the idea was never applied strictly, as it was with the European Central Bank. A woolier statutory mandate left open the possibility of policy reversal. Meanwhile the Federal Reserve itself developed internal controls that reduced the risk that its chairmen would wield power arbitrarily, while it responded to complaints about undue secretiveness by releasing more information about its decision-making.[151] Appearances by the chairman before Congress also became major events that promoted accountability. And chairmen themselves became adroit in making public tours to explain bank policy and "listen to ordinary Americans."[152]

None of these adjustments were planned in advance; they were worked out over years. The end result was that the practice of central banking after 1980 fell short of what some hard-money theorists might have preferred. There was no irreversible commitment to a policy of inflation-fighting by a truly autonomous central bank. But there was enough of a commitment to get the job done. Meanwhile the overall design of central banking had been made less threatening to democratic ideals and was more broadly supported for that reason. These more flexible arrangements also made it easier for the Federal Reserve to shift policy after the financial crisis of 2008. While the European Central Bank was hobbled with a restrictive mandate, the Federal Reserve shifted its focus from inflation-fighting to the short-term problem of preventing a dangerous slump in economic activity.[153]

The experience with central banking illustrates a more general point. Over the past forty years politicians and voters have tinkered with anti-democratic innovations, looking for ways of extracting the benefits that were associated with those innovations, while avoiding the harms that might be imposed if they were taken too far. In the field of fiscal policy, for example, the tactic was again to avoid rigid long-term commitments. A constitutionalized balanced-budget rule was avoided, in favor of more pliable statute-based rules. Balanced-budget laws still had some effect: they increased awareness of the need for fiscal discipline and raised the political price associated with any retreat from discipline. But the sovereignty of future Congresses was never seriously threatened, as experience showed. Politicians could adapt to new conditions, such as recessions, terror attacks, or financial crises. This flexibility frustrated observers who believed that Washington needed to make a more "credible commitment" to fiscal discipline.[154] As we have seen, though, significant progress was made in controlling the overall budget.

Overall, the approach to discipline was pragmatic. In the field of trade policy, politicians responded to complaints about the undemocratic nature of international bodies by establishing new rules to assure more open decision-making by those bodies.[155] The pace of trade liberalization also slowed as the marginal benefits associated with the elimination of trade barriers declined.[156] The commitment to deregulation also had its limits: although the substantial changes in regulatory approaches after 1975 cannot be denied, Congress also proved ready to reverse course and "re-regulate" in critical instances.[157] Privatization had similar boundaries. For example, Congress quickly abandoned anti-bureaucratic rhetoric and nationalized the business of airport security screening after the terror attacks of September 11, 2001, and during the financial crisis seven years later, it purchased major stakes in two automobile manufacturers and a multinational insurance company.[158]

None of this is meant to suggest that the balance between discipline and democracy was struck perfectly in the three decades after 1975. The process of adjustment to new realities was often messy. And there is no doubt that, overall, democratic practices were constrained after the mid-1970s. The country appeared to accept some version of the overload thesis. It developed a new way of talking about democratic politics that emphasized its frailties, such as its bias toward governmental expansion, its inconstancy in economic decision-making, or its vulnerability to special interests. In some ways, the country was actually reviving the "moral constraints" that had guided democratic politics before World War II, according to the Public Choice scholar James Buchanan. And the country was also redesigning the architecture of government in ways that expressed and reinforced those moral constraints.

But the project of containing democracy also had its boundaries. Some economists and political scientists might have called for hard and irreversible constraints on popular sovereignty, but actual reform was more tentative. During the free-trade debates of the early 1990s, Senator Bob Dole told critics that "the sovereignty issue is a red herring. If our rights are being trampled, we are going to be able to fix it."[159] Perhaps this was the essence of the matter. In any domain—central banking, fiscal controls, trade liberalization, deregulation, privatization—the principle of self-rule was never surrendered entirely, and so the possibility of reversal was always preserved. The institutional innovations of 1975–2008 were designed to meet the needs of a specific moment in history. If circumstances changed, institutions could be changed as well.

Fig. 5.1 More than 100,000 people march in New York City on September 21, 2014, as part of the People's Climate March, a worldwide mobilization calling on world leaders to commit to urgent action on climate change. (Kike Calvo via AP Images)

Anticipation

Virtually all [analysts] agree that the people of Western civilization knew what was happening to them but were unable to stop it. . . . [N]o planning was done, no precautions were taken, and the only management that finally ensued was disaster management.

—Naomi Oreskes and Erik Conway, *The Collapse of Western Civilization*, 2014

Liberal democracy has fundamental flaws. . . . In preparation for collapse, reform of governance must accept the primacy of science and develop mechanisms for urgent decision-making.

—David Shearman, *New Scientist*, May 2008

Orderly survival . . . may require, as in war, the suspension of democratic government for the duration of the emergency.

—James Lovelock, *The Vanishing Face of Gaia: A Final Warning*, 2009

The failure to take serious action on climate is a clear and absolute failure of democracy.

—STEPHEN LEAHY, Inter Press Service, January 4, 2013

Democratic crises do not arrive on the front step in clearly labeled boxes. Evidence of malaise emerges in bits and pieces, accompanied by debate about what each piece of evidence really means. It takes time to reach a rough agreement about what has gone wrong with American democracy and how the problems ought to be fixed. Almost twenty years passed between the first stirrings of the populist and progressive movements in the early 1890s and broad acceptance of their reform agendas in the 1910s; between the crash of 1929 and the consolidation of a new system of overall economic management under the Truman administration; and between the first signs of economic trouble in the early Nixon administration and the consolidation of Reaganism in the late 1980s.

It is difficult to pinpoint exactly when the United States' current bout of democratic malaise began. Many people think that it arose in the aftermath of the financial crisis of 2008.[1] If that is right, history tells us that there is no good reason to expect that we would have the diagnosis and remedy sorted out by 2016. A more reasonable expectation would be that the country would find itself in a phase of intense controversy, as people and parties struggle to win adherents to their particular view of what has gone wrong with American democracy. And this seems to be a reasonable description of the state of American politics today.

One camp in today's broad and rolling dispute has revived arguments that were heard a century ago. For people in this camp, the central question is once again whether the United States can properly be called a democracy at all. The writer Steve Fraser, for example, has argued that the country has degraded into a plutocracy, while Darrell West says—in a reprise of a classic Progressive Era theme—that one good way to counter the "power of the rich" would be to make government more transparent.[2] There are also people who lament the continued exclusion of African Americans from democratic politics because of felon disenfranchisement and voter identification laws.[3] And there are some who insist that American democracy is being subverted through the partisan exploitation of immigrant voters, and by terrorists who take advantage of weaknesses in the United States' immigration laws.[4]

Another camp revives arguments that were heard eighty years ago, during the crisis of mastery. The complaint here is not so much about voting and elections but the apparent inability of the government machinery to perform basic tasks. Yale University professor Peter Schuck argued in a 2014 book that there was a chasm between the federal government's ambitions and its ability to execute programs competently: federal policy failures, he said, were "large, recurrent and systemic."[5] Federal agencies, it seems to some, are incapable of defending the nation's borders, finding illegal immigrants, responding to natural disasters, collecting taxes impartially, delivering mail on time, maintaining airport security, providing healthcare to veterans, or even setting up a website so that people can sign up for health insurance under the 2010 Affordable Care Act. "The incompetence [in federal agencies] is staggering," the talk show host Joe Scarborough recently complained. "Our government is stuck in the 1960s."[6] There is a "gap between vision and action" in federal government, former Federal

Reserve chairman Paul Volcker agreed in 2015, one that makes "the fate of our great democracy . . . increasingly precarious."[7]

There is also a third camp that insists the country is still mired in a crisis of discipline. If the federal government is dysfunctional, this group says, it is because there is too much democracy, not too little. The system has been altered so that power is distributed more widely, but people have abused their newfound power to make unreasonable demands on government. The result is said to be chaos in Washington and endless governmental sprawl. For example, Elaine Kamarck of the Brookings Institution argues that Congress's ability to formulate sound policy has been undermined by three reforms, all of which were supposed to return power to the people: the primary system, campaign financing restrictions, and policies to make government more transparent.[8] Her colleague Jonathan Rauch has also attacked the "fixations on corruption and participation," arguing that a "decades-long war" on political insiders has compromised the workability of modern American democracy.[9] Jason Grumet agrees that American government is "more open, more transparent, and less functional than ever before."[10] And Charles Murray has recently argued that the nation still suffers from the "sclerosis" diagnosed by Mancur Olson in 1982. The last three decades, Murray says, have demonstrated that it is "impossible to contain [the public's] demand for government favors."[11]

We could say that these complaints about representation, mastery, and discipline are focused on the moment: that is, they are complaints about problems with American society whose effects are evident today. If we take action to remedy these problems, benefits might be realized immediately. But there is also a fourth camp of critics, comprising people who make a different argument about the weaknesses of today's democracy. People in the fourth camp focus on another class of problems that have a very long time lag: the potential harm is far in the future, assuming we do not take preventative action today. The fear is that American democracy is not competent in anticipating such long-term problems—and that the consequences of this neglect might be catastrophic.

Complaints about the incompetence of democracies in dealing with long-term problems are not entirely new. Democracy, a nineteenth-century critic said, "is always shortsighted and selfish ... 'Let the morrow provide for itself,' is always [its] most likely maxim."[12] This defect is said to arise partly because of the rules of the game, which give politicians strong incentives to fixate solely on the next election.[13] This shortsightedness is aggravated by human nature. Most people are anchored in the past: they acquire habits of thought early in life that are difficult to overturn, even as evidence of changing circumstances accumulates.[14] Research has also confirmed that people procrastinate, avoid actions that cause immediate discomfort, and discount problems that lie too far in the future.[15] At the same time, they tend to put self-interest ahead of the needs of strangers, including future generations.[16] And even calculations about self-interest are bounded by the realities of a limited lifespan. If humans lived as long as ocean quahog clams (that is, up to five hundred years), they might care more about the state of the world a century from now.[17]

Of course, we have already seen how American democracy has grappled successfully with some problems of long-term decision-making. People who worried about the lack of military preparedness before the two world wars explained it as a symptom of democracy's tendency toward a "short-sighted, careless and happy-go-lucky attitude," and a similar fear was expressed about the capacity of the American public to exercise the foresight and patience that were needed to fight a long Cold War against the Soviet Union.[18] But by the early 1950s the country had built a national security establishment that had a strong interest in ensuring that the country maintained military readiness. Today the defense establishment regularly conducts planning on long-run threats.[19] (Long-run planning is essential because of the time required to invent and deploy new technologies. For example, it took almost a quarter-century to deploy the Air Force's F-22 fighter.) And in the 1970s, high inflation was also explained as the product of shortsightedness: voters, it was said, fixated on the short-term pain of anti-inflation policies, and overlooked the long-term gains that would result from restoring stable prices. But the nation addressed this problem as well, by bolstering the autonomy of the Federal Reserve—a reform that is widely credited with restoring price stability by the end of the 1980s.

On the other hand, we could say that these two problems—military preparedness and inflation control—were not strong tests of the capacity of democracies to deal with future threats. In both cases, any harm that might be caused by present-day inaction was only a few years away. The politicians and voters who were asked to make hard decisions in 1939 or 1979 would themselves feel the consequences of their actions in 1945 or 1985, and it was relatively easy to envision what those consequences might look like. (It could also be argued that there was no problem of foresight associated with the Cold War at all: many people saw an immediate threat that the Soviet Union would "destroy us and our way of life by whatever means are available."[20]) A more difficult situation is one in which real sacrifices are required now, to avoid harms that will arise in two or three decades. Because these harms are more distant, they are harder to imagine, and in any case, they are less likely to be felt by the people who are being asked to make sacrifices. Preventative action becomes a matter of altruism rather than self-interest.

There are said to be four serious long-run problems confronting the United States today. One is the challenge of meeting the needs of an aging population. Another is the task of repairing infrastructure such as roads and utilities. A third is the rise of China and the erosion of the United States' status as the sole economic and military superpower. These are all substantial problems, but there is a fourth that dwarfs all of them in significance and complexity. Global warming may be an extreme test of democracy's ability to overcome its tendency toward shortsightedness. Indeed, some people think it might require us to abandon democracy entirely.

The problem of global warming came to public attention almost forty years ago. In 1979 the World Meteorological Organization gathered three hundred scientists in Geneva to assess the state of climate research. The meeting was dominated by concern about the risk of severe climate change.[21] For two centuries, the world had been burning an ever-increasing amount of fossil fuels— coal, oil, and gas—and releasing ever-increasing amounts of carbon dioxide into the atmosphere.[22] Research suggested that the build-up of carbon dioxide was impairing the release of heat radiation from the planet into space, and causing an increase in the temperature of the atmosphere itself. This became known as the greenhouse effect, and carbon dioxide became known as one of the main "greenhouse gases." Still, computer simulations of the potential consequences of global warming were imperfect at that time, and consequently warnings of disaster were widely discounted. The *Wall Street Journal* told its readers that the real threat was global cooling and the advent of a new ice age.[23] In any case, all the major countries were preoccupied with other problems: the Western nations with inflation, the Soviet Union with its invasion of Afghanistan, and China with the transition away from Maoist state planning.

Our knowledge about global warming improved with time. In 1988, the United Nations endorsed the creation of an Intergovernmental Panel on Climate Change (IPCC), which became the main body responsible for assessing the state of scientific knowledge on the risk of global warming and its possible consequences. In its first report, issued in 1990, the IPCC confirmed that human activity was contributing to climate change and predicted that the global mean temperature would likely increase by three degrees Celsius over pre-industrial levels by 2100. The IPCC conceded that climate models were still crude. Still, the central point was clear: there was an absolute limit to the total amount of greenhouse gases that could be added to the atmosphere without danger, and every day the world came a little closer to reaching that limit.[24]

After another quarter-century of research, uncertainty about the causes and effects of global warming has been substantially reduced. In 2014 the IPCC warned that the global mean temperature is likely to increase by four degrees Celsius by 2100 if current trends do not change. The anticipated effects of this much warming are dire. A large fraction of the planet's species would become extinct, and supplies of food and fresh water would be jeopardized around the planet. This might trigger mass migrations and wars over scarce resources. Changes in environment and the collapse of public institutions in poorer countries could also encourage the emergence of pandemics. North America in particular is expected to face an increased risk of droughts and wildfires, intense storms that cause the breakdown of essential services, flooding of coastal cities because of rising sea levels, and more heat-related deaths.[25]

Since 1990 the United States has taken some steps toward reducing emissions of carbon dioxide and other greenhouse gases. The federal government has tightened fuel economy standards for cars and trucks as well as efficiency standards for appliances, proposed rules to limit emissions from electric power plants, provided financial support for development of wind and solar power, and supported research on climate change. A few state governments have gone further: California, for example, has an ambitious program to limit greenhouse gas emissions from major industries.[26] The United States also played a role in developing international agreements on global warming. It signed the 1992 United Nations Convention on Climate Change, under which countries agreed to stabilize atmospheric levels of greenhouse gases; the 1997 Kyoto Protocol, which obliged the advanced countries to reduce emissions by specified amounts; and the 2009 Copenhagen Accord, which recognized climate change as "one of the greatest challenges of our time" and accepted the scientific consensus that global temperature should not be allowed to increase by more than two degrees Celsius.[27]

Still, the United States has often balked at taking strong action to avert global warming. In 1990 President George H. W. Bush warned that strict emission controls might jeopardize economic growth.[28] At the time, the country was entering a brief recession.

Congress also refused to ratify the Kyoto Protocol after it had been signed by President Clinton in 1997. In 2001, with the American economy again in recession, President George W. Bush disavowed the Protocol entirely, warning that it would cause "lay-offs of workers and price increases for consumers" while impos-ing no restrictions on China and other developing countries.[29] In 2010, Congress refused to adopt legislation that would impose national emission limits, undermining promises that the Obama administration made under the Copenhagen Accord; support for the proposed law had softened as the economy slowed down again after the financial crisis of 2008.[30] Political leaders also dis-missed the idea of imposing taxes to discourage the consumption of coal, oil, and natural gas.[31] Meanwhile, the Obama administra-tion approved the expansion of offshore oil drilling, as well as coal mining and natural gas extraction on federal lands. ("Today," President Obama boasted in 2015, "America is number one in oil and gas."[32])

In fact, the overall effect of American government policy over the past quarter-century has been to accelerate the pace at which the world is approaching the climatic danger point. US produc-tion of fossil fuels increased by 18 percent between 1990 and 2015, while consumption increased by 11 percent.[33] As part of the 1997 Kyoto Protocol, the Clinton administration promised that the United States would reduce its annual greenhouse gas emissions by 7 percent from 1990 levels by 2012.[34] But annual emissions actually increased by about 4 percent between 1990 and 2012.[35]

"Our democratic process is painfully slow," President Obama conceded in 2015. "You wish the political system could process an issue like this just based on obscure data and science, but, unfortunately, our system doesn't process things that way."[36] Some critics have argued that Congress and federal agencies have simply been captured by powerful corporations with an interest in extracting and burning fossil fuels.[37] But inaction cannot be blamed on special interests alone. Public indifference has also played a role. Gallup Polls taken over the last quarter-century show that the proportion of the population that worries about global warming has not shifted substantially, while the proportion that claims not to worry about it all has actually increased (fig. 5.2).[38] There are hopeful signs: for example, younger Americans are much more likely to regard global warming as a serious problem.[39] In general, though, the public has focused on more immediate concerns, such as the economy, terrorism, immigration, and healthcare.[40] "People have to see it and feel

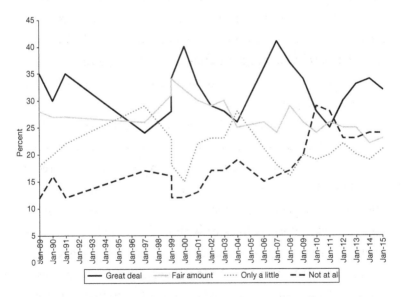

Fig. 5.2 Gallup Polls, 1989-2015: "How much do you personally worry about global warming?"

it and breathe it," President Obama said in 2015. "The average American right now, even if they've gotten past climate denial, is still much more concerned about gas prices, getting back and forth from work, than they are about the climate changing."[41]

The United States is certainly not the only advanced democracy that has been slow to address global warming. Most of the established democracies failed to meet the targets for reduction of greenhouse gas emissions that they accepted under the Kyoto Protocol.[42] Canada withdrew entirely from the Protocol in 2011 and continued with the exploitation of the Alberta tar sands, that country's single largest source of greenhouse gases. Australia abandoned a tax on greenhouse gas emissions in 2014 and promoted the mining of coal for export to Asia instead. The continued burning of coal, Australian Prime Minister Tony Abbott said in 2014, was "good for humanity [and] good for prosperity."[43] Japan increased its dependence on fossil fuels after the Fukushima nuclear disaster of 2011. Germany's progress in reducing emissions has also slowed, after public protests led to the shutdown of nuclear power plants and more reliance on plants that burn highly polluting brown coal.

The developed countries, the respected analyst Nicholas Stern observed in 2015, have displayed "a politics of doubt, dithering, and delay."[44] The world, he says, is far short of achieving reductions in emissions that would give even a 50/50 chance of meeting the two-degree target that was agreed on in 2009. "Overall progress," says Stern, is "recklessly slow."[45] The IPCC also warned in its 2014 report that achievement of the two-degree target requires "an urgent and fundamental departure from business as usual."[46] Pope Francis expressed the same frustration in his 2015 encyclical on climate change. The advanced nations, Francis said, are plagued by "a politics concerned with immediate results" that neglects future generations and the world's poor. This period, he warned, "may well be remembered as one of the most irresponsible in history."[47]

Under such circumstances, it is probably not surprising that many experts have expressed reservations about the capacity of democratic systems to deal competently with long-run threats like global warming. In 2014 the distinguished political scientist John Dunn argued that our faith in democracy was "utterly misplaced" and that the world risked "biological disaster" because of the failure of citizens in democratic states to overcome their "deep-seated preferences for short-term comfort and convenience."[48] Another prominent political scientist, David Runciman, has offered a similar assessment. Democracies, he said in 2013, face the risk of "systemic failure" because of their inability to wake up to threats such as climate change.[49] Runciman argued later that politics in the Western democracies was "stuck in a rut: petty, insular, narrow-minded, uninspiring."[50]

Skepticism about the ability of democracies to deal with major environmental threats was first raised over forty years ago, after the Club of Rome issued its report *The Limits to Growth*, which warned about the certainty of societal collapse by 2070 if there was no change in population growth and the economic system.[51] The economist Robert Heilbroner doubted that the United States and other advanced democracies would heed the warning and concluded in 1974 that "centralization of power" was the only means by which civilization could survive.[52] In an award-winning book published in 1977, the environmentalist William Ophuls agreed that management of the environmental crisis would eventually require some form of "elite rule." The average person, he suggested, was not competent to participate in the governance of a "steady-state society."[53] In 1984 the philosopher Hans Jonas also speculated about the advantages of a "well-intentioned, well-informed tyranny" in dealing with an ecological crisis. "Such a tyranny," Jonas argued, would be "better than total ruin."[54]

This way of thinking became known as "green authoritarianism," and it has been reinvigorated by evidence of apparent democratic failure in the face of global warming.[55] The central question, one political scientist wrote in 2010, "is whether democracy can be sustained ... given the unprecedented and unforgiving nature of the challenges we collectively face."[56] The machinery of democracy, designed for the "languid rhythms" of decision-making in the twentieth century, is said to be unfit for the environmental challenges of the twenty-first century.[57] One imagined possibility is that democratic governments will collapse in the face of crisis and be replaced by quasi-military "green juntas."[58] Or Western democracies might plan for an orderly transfer of power to "a few executive agencies manned by capable and uncorrupt elites."[59] Two Australian scholars, David Shearman and Joseph Smith, have argued for the establishment of a "Platonic form of authoritarianism based upon the rule of experts" whose training is carefully designed to inculcate "scientifically correct knowledge." Democracy, they argue, will prove to be "just a moment in human history": in the future, government should be "based upon a supreme office of the biosphere [comprising] specially trained philosopher/ ecologists ... [who] will rule themselves or advise an authoritarian government."[60]

This may seem like a flight of imagination, but Shearman and Smith argue that Singapore demonstrates the viability of their model. Singapore, they say, is a stable and prosperous society, largely free of political discord, and governed by a self-renewing technocratic elite.[61] China has also been presented as an example of green authoritarianism.[62] In 2009, *New York Times* columnist Thomas Friedman suggested that China's authoritarian system was doing a better job of addressing the problem of global warming because it allowed a "reasonably enlightened group of people" to impose the measures necessary to avert a crisis.[63]

The green critique of democracy has two aspects. One is retrospective: it condemns democracy for creating the risk of complete environmental collapse. And the second is prospective: it questions whether democracy is capable of managing that risk competently in the years ahead. Both aspects of the green critique are misguided. The blame for our current predicament does not rest only on the shoulders of democracy, and democracy seems more likely than authoritarian alternatives to produce a viable way of managing the risk of environmental collapse.

First, consider the question of blame. Did democracy lead us to the predicament that the IPCC described in its 1990 report? Not exactly. There are two other features of modern life that have probably played a more important role in generating today's environmental crisis: one is the organization of the world into a system of states, and the other is our mode of economic activity, which we can call carbon-powered capitalism.[64]

First, a word about the system of states. There are roughly two hundred states in the world today, each one of them independent, with the right to govern a defined territory. It may seem perfectly natural that global society is structured in this way, but there is nothing natural about it.[65] Before the mid-seventeenth century, politics was a more muddled affair. In Europe, nations did not have well-marked borders, and national governments did not assert the exclusive right to govern within those borders. Social and economic affairs across the continent were integrated by the Catholic Church, by the intermarriage of royal families, and by alliances among traders and financiers. These interconnections weakened after the mid-1600s, and by the nineteenth century it was generally understood that the building block of political organization was the state: an entity that had the exclusive right to rule within its borders.[66] In the twentieth century, the concept of the nation-state was globalized: colonial empires were broken up, more borders were drawn, and the number of independent states quadrupled.

This "world of states" became established before the spread of democracy in the modern era, and well before the world became aware of the problem of global warming.[67] It complicates the task of taking decisive action to avert radical climate change for several reasons. The first is the reality of competition between states. Within this system, there is no supreme authority that is capable of guaranteeing that any one state will be protected from attacks by other states, or that it will have access to global markets and a fair share of the world's resources.[68] Each state must fend for itself: it must build armed forces to defend its own territory and trade routes, make defensive alliances, and negotiate for access to markets that are controlled by other states. The pressure on states is intense, because their neighbors are also racing to consolidate power.[69] To succeed in this competition, every state must maintain a thriving national economy. An expanding economy means that there will be more tax dollars available to build military forces and recruit allies with aid and other inducements.[70]

Consumers and businesses will also have more to spend, which gives other states a stronger incentive to negotiate trade agreements. In short, the security of states within the international order hinges critically on the condition of the national economy. No state, democratic or authoritarian, will be eager to do anything that impairs the capacity of its economy to generate wealth.

States are also insecure in a second way. A state may assert the right to govern territory, but this does not mean that it has the actual capacity to govern. Some poor states have very limited capabilities: they struggle to maintain law and order, and lack the bureaucracy that is necessary to monitor and regulate the movement of people, money, and trade. And even in advanced societies, the capacity to govern is bounded. Eventually, people resist the taxes that are needed to expand bureaucratic capabilities, refuse to divulge information to authorities about their business and private affairs, ignore laws if they think that noncompliance can be hidden, and change their behavior to sidestep the letter of the law. If government agencies attempt to eliminate regulatory loopholes and crack down on noncompliance, the result may be public protests or a backlash on election day. Even authoritarian regimes confront the reality that their power is limited. Chinese officials also struggle to control evasion of regulations and tax laws, and keep a careful count of demonstrations, strikes, and other "mass incidents" that indicate dissatisfaction with the regime.[71]

Every state attempts to bolster its limited capabilities by cultivating political legitimacy—that is, the sense that government has earned the right to rule and therefore ought to be obeyed. Legitimacy makes "[state] power more effective by lowering the costs of enforcement and raising the efficiency of the state."[72]

Historically, states have tried to bolster their legitimacy in several ways. Two familiar methods are providing guarantees against arbitrary state action—that is, establishing the rule of law—and also allowing citizens to select their rulers through democratic procedures.[73] But there are also other strategies for building legitimacy, which tend to complicate the task of grappling with climate change.

One strategy is building a strong sense of national identity and patriotism. The aim is to erase old loyalties, which often cross national borders, and to build up a new loyalty to the territory in which people actually live. The distinction between citizens and aliens—that is, between insiders and outsiders—is sharpened, and the sense of obligation that insiders might feel toward outsiders is diminished. This can be justified on the grounds that outsiders have their own state and can fend for themselves. States that succeed in building a strong sense of national identity find it easier to enforce laws and mobilize resources when there are conflicts with other states. But those states may also find it harder to justify action on climate change, because insiders are being asked to make sacrifices on behalf of outsiders. Our obligations, it is understood, largely stop at the border.[74]

States have another technique for maintaining legitimacy. They can build public support by improving the financial well-being of citizens, either by providing opportunities for advancement in the private economy, or by delivering income or services directly to citizens. Even in democracies, politicians understand the close connection between citizens' trust in government and their perceptions of their economic prospects.[75] They also understand the value of government programs such as pensions or social services in bolstering public support for government.

But this gives politicians another strong reason for being leery of policies that might jeopardize economic growth: either because slow growth will diminish opportunities in the private sector, or undermine the ability to finance government programs. Leaders in non-democratic states are even more cautious about growth-dampening policies, because they cannot fall back on alternate foundations for legitimacy, such as democratic procedures and guarantees about the rule of law.[76]

The second feature of modern life that has helped to create the problem of global warming is the mode of economic organization that became dominant across the globe over the course of two centuries. This is the model of carbon-powered capitalism. It is a system in which private investors, rather than governments, make most of the important decisions about the allocation of capital, and in which the rules that restrict the movement of capital, commodities, and goods and services are lightly drawn. This system requires the input of massive amounts of energy before it can work: to extract raw materials, produce and transport goods, and even to consume goods and services. For the last two hundred and fifty years, that energy has been obtained mainly in the form of coal, oil, and gas. (In the United States today, two-thirds of the electricity supply is also derived by burning fossil fuels.[77]) These forms of energy have been used excessively because they have been priced too cheaply: that is to say, the market price has never reflected the full cost that is imposed on society by their extraction and use. We have always been conscious of some of side-effects of our dependence on fossil fuels—such as the spoliation of the environment through coal mining and oil extraction, deadly urban smog, and non-environmental effects such as the maltreatment of coal miners or corruption in resource-rich states.[78] But not until recently did we understand the long-term damage that is done to the climate by burning fossil fuels. In this respect, the mispricing of fossil fuels was inadvert: we simply did not know about the full costs associated with the use of those fuels.[79]

The history of the last quarter-millennium has been dominated by the rapid expansion of carbon-powered capitalism out of its birthplace in Western Europe. In one country after another, laws that inhibited the expansion of capitalism—by controlling prices or limiting the movement of capital, labor, commodities, and goods—were overturned. Factories became more numerous, larger, and more complex. Transportation technologies for carrying raw materials to factories, and finished products to consumers, also became more sophisticated. The reach of markets expanded so that, by the end of the twentieth century, capitalism could be regarded as a truly global phenomenon.[80] The demand for energy grew as well. Entrepreneurs who promoted new ways of using the energy derived from fossil fuels—Robert Fulton, Henry Ford, the Wright Brothers, Steve Jobs[81]—were celebrated. So were the inventors and businessmen who found new ways of extracting and distributing coal, oil, and natural gas.

Ordinary people in many countries were usually pleased by the twin benefits provided by this system: rapid economic growth as well as innovation in goods and services. But the influence of ordinary people should not be overstated: democracy was not yet established when the capitalist takeoff began.[82] More important, it was in the interest of states themselves to encourage this mode of economic development. This was a straightforward matter of survival in the competition among states. A robust fossil-fueled economy generated the tax revenues needed to raise large armies and navies, as well as the technological innovations that made it possible to build powerful weapons. Statesmen were acutely aware of the close connection between fossil fuels and national power. "Without coal," a nineteenth-century British writer said, "our steam power would be annihilated, and with that, our prosperity as a nation, and our supremacy.... The future historian of the revolution of empires would date the decline and fall of the vast dominion of Britain from the period when her supplies of mineral fuels were exhausted, and her last coal-fields worked out."[83] American writers made the same argument eighty years later, during World War II. "We are threatened with a permanent oil shortage within two years if we do not have miraculous success in discovering new wells," one warned. "We know of no substitute for oil.... It will be an unhappy day for us if we discover, at war's end, that our democracy has an exhausted arsenal to support it. We cannot be a great nation if we are forced to join the have-nots."[84]

An unfortunate irony of history is that the system of carbon-powered capitalism conquered the globe just when we were becoming aware of the long-term damage caused by burning fossil fuels. Consider the thirteen years between the First World Climate Conference in 1979 and the publication of the 1990 IPCC report that concluded with certainty that human activity was causing global warming. In that period, the major industrial democracies—led by the Reagan and Thatcher governments—backed away from state planning and economic regulation. There was a similar turn toward market-friendly policies in the developing world.[85] At the same time, the Eastern Bloc collapsed, and then the Soviet Union itself. And most important, China committed itself to a market-friendly model of economic development.[86] Premier Zhu Rongji, echoing the rhetoric of British and American statesmen in the nineteenth century, boasted that China would make itself "the factory of the world."[87] China, Francis Fukuyama wrote in 1989, put itself on the path toward "bourgeois consumerism."[88]

Altogether, these events were said to herald the final triumph of capitalism.[89] They also transformed the global economy. World production and consumption has increased threefold since the 1970s. Trade routes and production chains have lengthened. In the developing world, cities that serve as the new homes of industry have expanded their population by more than two billion people. This larger and more complex system burns 70 percent more coal and oil, and more than twice the volume of natural gas.[90] China's energy consumption alone has increased sevenfold, not least because of the extraordinary growth in the number of diesel- and gasoline-burning vehicles on Chinese roads: from fewer than two million in 1980 to 126 million in 2013.[91] More fuel-burning also means larger emissions of greenhouse gases. According to the International Energy Agency, global emissions from fuel combustion doubled from 1973 to 2013.[92] But the possibility of reforming the global economy to reduce emissions has also become more difficult, precisely because the system is now so much larger and complex. Over the span of four decades, billions of people—business people, consumers, and governments—have invested heavily in the system of carbon-powered capitalism.

Developed countries are in trouble, and not simply because citizens and politicians in democracies tend to be shortsighted.

Over two centuries, the Western world unwittingly constructed a system of states and markets that was engineered to produce a climatological disaster. Now radical change is necessary, and soon: Nicholas Stern has suggested that the world must undertake a "global energy-industrial revolution" in the span of only two or three decades.[93] Frustration with the democratic process—with its delays, compromises, and endless debates—is understandable. People who understand the dangers and the scale of the required response want immediate action. This is the allure of the authoritarian model, as it always has been: remember the appeal of Mussolini in 1933 (ch. 3).

But there is no good reason to believe that authoritarian states would manage the problem of global warming any better. David Shearman and Joseph Smith, the two academics who argue for a form of green authoritarianism, concede that "existing authoritarian societies . . . have had an appalling environmental record. . . . [All] existing authoritarian governments have a worse environmental record than all liberal democratic societies."[94] There are many reasons for this. Rulers in authoritarian systems are still human beings and suffer from the same cognitive limitations as rulers in democratic systems. Even though they may not be thrown out of office by elections, they can be ousted in other ways that can be even more unpredictable; knowing this, authoritarian rulers may still engage in shortsighted and corrupt behavior.[95] And even the best-intentioned authoritarian ruler is still burdened with the task of maintaining a state. They must worry about national defense, alliances with other states, internal order, and legitimacy. All of these tasks require a thriving economy that can generate healthy tax revenues. Even if authoritarian rulers are more decisive, this advantage could easily be applied to the objective of achieving faster carbon-powered economic growth rather than reducing greenhouse gas emissions.

China has sometimes been presented as the sort of system that has the capacity to act decisively on global warming, in contrast to the dithering of Western democracies.[96] In its most recent five-year plan, adopted in 2011, the Chinese government promised that it would "actively tackle global climate change" and achieve "massive reductions" in greenhouse gas emissions.[97] China rapidly increased its spending on wind and solar power, and by 2015 was responsible for almost one-third of total world investment in renewable energy projects.[98] It also attempted to discourage the burning of coal by power plants and heavy industry—although this effort has been compromised by the limited influence of the central government, even in an authoritarian system.[99]

A broader difficulty, though, is the central government's determination to maintain rapid economic growth. The 2011 plan also anticipated that the Chinese economy would grow by 40 percent in five years. The measures that the Chinese government has taken to promote renewable energy will not meet the needs of an economy growing at that pace, and the gap must be filled by burning more fossil fuels. For this reason, a critical part of Chinese foreign policy is preoccupied with the task of ensuring a steady supply of oil, coal, and gas from around the world. In fact, Chinese plans assume that greenhouse gas emissions will continue to increase until 2030.[100] Even if China executes its environmental programs successfully, annual carbon-dioxide emissions in 2030 may be 70 percent higher than they were in 2011, six times higher than in 1990, and double the combined emissions of Europe and the United States.[101] Nicholas Stern recently concluded that this growth in emissions would be "clearly incompatible" with the declared goal of limiting global warming to two degrees Celsius.[102]

The Chinese government could choose to grow more slowly, taking the time needed to build an economy that does not depend heavily on fossil fuels. But it has good reasons for not doing so. One is a sense of unfairness: Why should China not be allowed to match the wealth of developed countries as quickly as possible? Another is the determination to restore national pride after humiliation by Western nations in the nineteenth century. (A spokeswoman for the Chinese government said in 2015 that China would never forget "our lesson from history: those who fall behind will get bullied."[103]) In addition to this, there are compelling reasons of state. Rapid growth is the main strategy that Chinese leaders have used to maintain public support despite the restriction of human rights. "If we can continually raise the people's living standards," Zhu Rongji explained in 1992, "the people will support us."[104] An expanding economy also makes it possible to improve popular social service and pension programs, and build an elaborate internal security apparatus to monitor dissent and contain protests. At the same time, a larger economy allows more spending on national defense, so that China can wield more influence abroad. In 2015, China planned to spend more on the military than any country in the world other than the United States. It is believed that China spends comparable amounts on internal security and social programs.[105] Such expenditures would have been unimaginable a quarter-century ago, when the Chinese economy was one-tenth its present size.

Singapore is another country that is sometimes promoted as a model of decisiveness on global warming. Singapore is not an authoritarian regime like China; it has regular elections to a legislative body and gives its citizens more room to organize and express themselves. Still, the rules of the game are crafted to limit popular control of government and maintain a strong role for a highly trained bureaucracy.[106] The system has been described as a "highly authoritarian democracy."[107] This feature appears to give it the ability to execute long-term plans to deal with problems like global warming, and it is indeed the case that government policies have contributed to a bigger percentage reduction in greenhouse gas emissions over the last twenty years than what has been achieved by the United States and many other advanced democracies.[108]

But the Singaporean example must be treated cautiously. For most of its fifty-year history, the leaders of this city-state actually pursued a path like China's, which aimed to maintain public support through rapid carbon-powered growth. "The right to govern," one analyst recently explained, has long been predicated on the regime's "ability to deliver material benefits."[109] A 2007 study of public attitudes in Singapore observed that "There is a gap between [Singaporeans'] pro-democratic orientation and the perceived extent of democracy in Singapore. This gap is reconciled by their satisfaction with the Government's performance [in promoting economic development]."[110] In fact, the culture of consumerism is now so deeply entrenched that official websites describe shopping as a "national pastime."[111] As a result of this policy of rapid growth, Singapore's per-capita greenhouse gas emissions were higher by the 1990s than those of most other Asian countries and many cities in the advanced world.[112] For example, Singapore's per capita carbon-dioxide emissions were twice as high as in Los Angeles.

Although greenhouse gas emissions have recently been reduced in Singapore, the economic growth rate has also slowed, from an average of 8 percent between 1960 and 2000 to 5 percent after 2000. Appreciation for the long economic boom among older Singaporeans still contributes to a high level of support for the country's rulers. But complaints about the cost of living are increasing, particularly among younger citizens who have no firsthand knowledge of the long boom, and support for the government is weaker within this generation.[113] It is not clear, therefore, that Singapore's model of "authoritarian democracy" is viable in the long run. If high growth rates cannot be sustained, other methods might have to be found to suppress the popular demand for more control over Singapore's rulers.

In sum, there are no real-world models of governance by an "eco-elite" that has the power to take the preventative measures necessary to avert a climatological disaster.[114] So we are obliged to use our imagination. The ethicist Dennis Thompson has speculated about the advantages of a Tribunate that would have the power to overrule decisions by the President or Congress that unduly threaten the interests of future citizens.[115] A British analyst has argued for the establishment of a new body, the Guardians of the Future, that could initiate and veto legislation to protect "future people."[116] Similarly, several German writers have advocated for constitutional changes to create a fourth branch of government, perhaps in the form of an Ecological Council, with authority to act on behalf of future generations.[117]

A more familiar model might be something parallel to the Federal Reserve, which currently makes independent decisions on monetary policy in the United States. The Federal Reserve is a popular model for people who are frustrated with Washington politics. For example, it has already been suggested that there ought to be a similar independent agency to control taxing and spending, so that today's voters do not put large debt burdens on the shoulders of tomorrow's citizens.[118] After the terror attacks of 2001, analysts even suggested that a comparable agency could be created to manage homeland security. The proposed Federal Security System would have had independent power to force companies to adopt security measures, and to coordinate law enforcement agencies at all levels of government.[119] We might imagine an independent agency on this model—a "Green Fed"— that has the power to make or veto laws based on its judgment about long-term risks of climatic disaster.[120]

The obvious question that is raised by any of these proposals for governance by an "eco-elite" is how they could be adopted at all. If lawmakers are unwilling to approve more modest measures, how likely are they to surrender sweeping authority to a new Green Fed? And suppose that we get over this hurdle. There are other difficulties. The Federal Reserve itself has a relatively narrow assignment: it sets the interest rate and regulates a limited number of financial institutions. Our hypothetical Green Fed would have a much broader role. It would oversee a "new energy-industrial revolution" that would touch every corner of American life.[121] To enforce its policies, the Green Fed would depend on cooperation of a multitude of other agencies, businesses, and citizens, and it would need tools to force action when any of these other actors balked. The Green Fed would also need a large research and communications office to justify its policies, in response to the inevitable protests against its interventions in everyday life. (For an intimation of what those protests might look like, recall the demonstrations that seized European capitals after technocrats imposed austerity programs in the wake of the global financial crisis.) A reluctant population would have to be persuaded or compelled to obey the Green Fed's commands. A planning agency might quickly be transformed into a police and propaganda agency as well.

This imaginary Green Fed would also have a second kind of problem. Suppose that it is given a legal responsibility to protect the interests of future citizens. At first this seems like a mandate to take measures that protect the environment. But the hard reality is that the value of citizenship is closely tied to the power of the state relative to other states. In the extreme, if the state becomes so weak in relative terms that it is attacked and collapses, citizenship means nothing at all. So the Green Fed has a predicament. If other states refuse to take growth-dampening environmental measures, paying attention to the interests of future citizens might mean continuing to burn fossil fuels, so that relative economic and military power is maintained. The reality of competition between states does not disappear just because the internal structures of states are changed. In this way, the Green Fed might find itself turned reluctantly into an oil-burning Black Fed. Moreover, the kinds of decisions that the Green Fed would be required to make—that is, ugly compromises between high principles and everyday realities—would no longer seem like something that needs to be reserved for people with special scientific training. Instead, it would look like ordinary politics, the sort of thing that ought to be left to elected officials.[122]

The response to global warming involves four tasks. The first involves the improvement of our knowledge about the dimensions of the problem: for example, understanding how quickly the planet will heat up, and what the consequences will be. The second is building trust between states, so that no one country feels that it is putting itself at a disadvantage by taking global warming seriously. The third is crafting laws that are effective in inducing businesses and citizens to use alternative forms of energy and reduce consumption of fossil fuels. And the final task is shifting public opinion so that these laws are not ignored or evaded.

The problem with green authoritarianism is that it does not promise to handle any of these tasks particularly well. At first, we might admire the decisiveness of authoritarian regimes. But the actual power of rulers in authoritarian states is easily overestimated. The attitudes of millions of people cannot be changed by executive action, and so long as attitudes are unchanged, compliance with burdensome laws will be poor. An unwilling population will also be slow to volunteer their labor to produce better knowledge about global warming and invent new ways of reducing dependence on fossil fuels. And authoritarian regimes have no particular advantage in the realm of international affairs: just like democracies, they lack authority to force rival states to cooperate in any global plan for reducing greenhouse gas emissions.

Democratic systems may not handle any of these tasks as efficiently as we might like, but they arguably handle them more adeptly than their authoritarian rivals. The American public's attention to global warming may have waxed and waned over the last quarter-century, but awareness of the problem in the United States is still substantially higher than in China or Singapore, according to cross-national opinion polls.[123] Every kind of society wrestles with the power of vested interests, but open societies provide a space in which activists, researchers, and entrepreneurs can challenge orthodoxies and promote new ways of thinking about the world. (One illustration: the number of scholarly articles published annually on the subject of global warming increased tenfold between 1990 and 2010.[124]) An open and decentralized system of government also provides more room to experiment with new techniques of regulation. A good example is the invention and refinement of emissions-trading schemes by federal and state regulatory agencies in the United States over the last forty years.[125]

The openness that typifies democracies has not just encouraged learning at home. It has also fostered the same sort of invention and adaptation in international negotiations. Activists and researchers in the established democracies played an important role in shaping the climate change agreement that was signed in Paris in December 2015.[126] Granted, the Paris agreement is imperfect: the commitments about emission reduction that had been made by national governments by December 2015 were not sufficient to achieve the two-degree target that was set in 2009. But the Paris agreement does not repeat the errors of the Kyoto Protocol. It includes all of the major economies and avoids the hard limits on emissions that were likely to make the agreement unacceptable to many countries, including the United States. Instead it provides a mechanism for reporting on actual emissions, and targets for emission reduction, in a consistent and verifiable way. It is a device for building the trust and transparency that are essential to reach more demanding agreements in the future.[127]

Of course we would like these processes of learning and invention to proceed more quickly. But the pace of adjustment cannot simply be blamed on democracy. It is more the result of three bigger considerations: The scale of our investment in carbon-powered capitalism, the tensions inherent in a centuries-old system of states, and the unavoidable fact that a great mass of people is not easily ruled, even in authoritarian systems. It is relatively easy to deny people the right to vote, but much harder to eliminate their capacity to resist demands by the state that they feel are arbitrary and burdensome. One of the virtues of democracy is that it provides a way of channeling and taming resistance to rule that is more effective in the long run than the techniques used by authoritarian regimes. What is more, it provides a superior mechanism for promoting changes in knowledge and attitudes, so that the motivation to resist government policies diminishes over time. Whether the United States and other democracies will change quickly enough to avoid climatic disaster is unclear. But what does seem clear is that there is no other system that could make the adjustment more easily.

Adaptable Democracy

Lengthen your experience, and you would begin to notice differences in the constancy of things. . . . The more variability you would note, until at last you would say with Heraclitus that all things flow.

—WALTER LIPPMANN, *The Phantom Public*, 1925

The formation of states must be an experimental process. . . . And since conditions of action and inquiry and knowledge are always changing, the experiment must always be retried; the State must always be rediscovered.

—JOHN DEWEY, *The Public and Its Problems*, 1927

A public philosophy is something that every stable polity possesses. . . . [It] can and does change over generations.

—THEODORE LOWI, "The Public Philosophy: Interest-Group Liberalism," 1967

Democracy provides the institutional framework for the reform of political institutions. It makes possible the reform of institutions without using violence, and

thereby the use of reason in the designing of new institutions and the adjusting of old ones.

—KARL POPPER, *The Open Society and Its Enemies*, 1945

This book began with a recitation of grim warnings about the
state of democracy in general and American democracy in particular. It is worth remembering some of the language that has
been used to describe the current bout of democratic malaise.
There are some people who say that American democracy is
a sham, some who say that it is inept and dysfunctional, and
some who say that it is lazy, self-indulgent, and shortsighted.
There are even people who say that we are living in the "twilight of democracy" and that the future belongs to authoritarian states like China.

Not only is American democracy said to be in bad shape; the
complaint is that it is unlikely to get better anytime soon. The self-
healing capacities of the American system are alleged to be very
limited, for two reasons. The first alleged defect is that American
politicians and voters are not very creative when it comes to inventing remedies for democratic malaise. For example, they fixate on
reforms that tear down authority and give more power to ordinary
people, even when conditions actually require a concentration of
authority and dilution of democratic control. The second is that
political institutions are ossified and almost impossible to change.
In other words, it hardly matters whether reformers have clever
ideas for curing malaise, because the remedy can never be administered. The system is broken and almost impossible to fix.

A long view of history should give us better grounds for optimism. This is not the first time that the country has sunk into

malaise. It is, in fact, a recurrent feature of American politics, and perhaps of democratic politics more broadly. This does not mean that periods of malaise should be dismissed as inconsequential phenomena. On the contrary, every moment of malaise has been triggered by well-founded doubts about the integrity or performance of American democracy. But these dark moments of malaise have served as preludes to longer periods of ideological and institutional renewal. Out of each preceding "crisis of democracy" there has emerged a new understanding about the character and aims of American politics. The nation's public philosophy—the widely accepted principles that explain who is entitled to participate in government, what the aims of government should be, and the means by which those aims should be pursued—has been revised, and then revised again.[1] The institutions of government have also been renovated repeatedly. Throughout the twentieth century, citizens of the United States habitually referred to their system of government as "American democracy," which encouraged the thought that it was always the same thing. But the American democracy of 1900 was very different than the American democracy of 2000.

Moments of democratic malaise have also been marked by fears about the threat posed by authoritarian or semi-democratic rivals. In 1916, the problem with American democracy was that it lacked the efficiency of Hohenzollern Germany; in 1933, that it lacked the decisiveness of Mussolini's Italy; in the Cold War era, that it lacked the resoluteness of Soviet Russia. Of course, none of these regimes survive today. The habit of overestimating such rivals is encouraged by three factors. The first is the very fact that these are more-or-less closed systems, so that the weaknesses and tensions that must exist within any state are not easily observed. The second is the tendency, in moments of uncertainty, to emphasize evidence of external threats and discount contrary evidence.[2] And the third is the tendency to put undue weight on the short-run performance of rival systems.

Why do we judge rival systems based on short-run performance? In the late 1970s, the financial analyst Peter Miller suggested that investors often suffer from "retrospective myopia": that is, they assume that the future can be predicted based on the experience of the preceding few years alone.[3] Miller's theory was illustrated spectacularly by the pre-2008 housing boom, which was partly fueled by the widespread assumption that house prices would always increase as they had over the previous decade.[4] This habit of dwelling on the "remembered past" affects judgments about politics as well.[5] The historian Arthur Schlesinger suggested that for most people, history begins at the moment when "political consciousness" is awakened: that is, at the beginning of their adult life.[6] For the average American, that is a span of about twenty years. Indeed, some political scientists suggest that retrospective myopia among voters is even shorter than that.[7]

Retrospective myopia leads people to make judgments about the future based on the very short span of history that they have personally observed. It might be argued, for example, that the rapid expansion of governmental functions in the United States in the late 1960s and early 1970s was encouraged by the expectation that the American economy would continue to grow at the extraordinary but unusual rates that were witnessed in the 1950s and early 1960s. Similarly, theories about the pro-spending bias of democracies that became popular in the 1970s were heavily influenced by the unusual growth in government spending in the

1960s, while theories about the intrinsic inflationary tendencies of democracies that became popular in the 1980s were shaped by the experience of the 1970s. In other words, we have a habit of generating universal propositions about the character of democratic systems based on what we have recently seen. And we do the same with regard to authoritarian systems. China, for example, has enjoyed a two-decade run of extraordinary economic growth. For the majority of Americans that is the whole of their adult life. And so it is not hard to draw the conclusion that China must eventually rule the world.[8]

Pessimism about the condition of American democracy is also aggravated by the belief that its self-healing capacities are not particularly strong. This belief is founded on two assumptions. The first is the assumption that the system is not very creative when it comes to inventing remedies for weaknesses in existing political institutions. The second is the assumption that the system is ossified and slow to adopt innovations that would improve the integrity or performance of American democracy. We will examine these two assumptions in turn.

Why are Americans thought to be uncreative in their response to crisis? One view, as we noted in chapter 1, is that Americans have a blind spot when it comes to imagining how institutions might be adapted to deal with new conditions. They are good at inventing ways of dividing and checking authority, but not very good at concentrating authority, even when circumstances require it. "When an American thinks about the problem of government building," Samuel Huntington wrote in 1968, "he directs himself not to the creation of authority and the accumulation of power but rather to the limitation and the division of power."[9]

Or as Francis Fukuyama has recently observed: "The traditional American solution to perceived governmental dysfunction has been to try to expand democratic participation and transparency."[10] The Huntington thesis, as we might call it, plays on an old idea: that the American polity, born out of a revolution against authority, has never been particularly adept at rebuilding it.

The difficulty with the Huntingtonian thesis is that it is at odds with most of the experience of the last century. Certainly there have been moments in which the response to crisis was to expand democratic participation and transparency. Voting rights have been extended, new oversight bodies have been created to monitor federal agencies, procedural requirements have been established to assure fairness in bureaucratic decision-making, and laws have been adopted to improve government transparency. But we should not forget the other changes that we have reviewed in this book, which were very much concerned with accumulating power and limiting democratic control, and not always for benign purposes. This includes the disenfranchisement of African Americans in the decades following Reconstruction; measures to curb the influence of immigrants in the early twentieth century; the suppression of rebellion in the Philippines; mobilization for war and the construction of a vast military-industrial complex; the development of an apparatus for regulating the newly invented "national economy"; the creation of a strong presidency; the limitation of political control over trade and fiscal policy through devices such as fast-track authority, trade agreements, and fiscal rules; and the delegation of power over monetary policy to a Federal Reserve in the late 1970s. In November 2015, *Forbes* magazine listed Federal Reserve chairman Janet Yellen and President Barack Obama as two of the seven most powerful people on the planet: an odd accomplishment for a political system that is said to be allergic to the concentration of authority.[11]

When we take all of this history into account, it is difficult to see how pro-democratic reforms could be construed as "the traditional American solution to perceived governmental dysfunction." It might even be argued that, for the last century, the typical solution to governmental dysfunction has been to invent new institutions that actually complicate the task of democratic oversight—sometimes inadvertently, and sometimes deliberately. Indeed, many pro-democratic reforms introduced over the last century were partly or wholly reactions to earlier reform projects that were aimed at building up state power. As we have seen, the movement to extend voting rights to women gained momentum during World War I, as Woodrow Wilson and other politicians sought to buttress popular support for their newly constructed war machine. Similarly, the voting age was lowered a half century later to quell opposition to American engagement in Vietnam. The adoption of the Administrative Procedure Act of 1946, which laid down procedural requirements for bureaucratic decision-making, was an attempt to assuage anger about the expansion of the federal bureaucracy over the preceding fifteen years. Similarly, the strengthening of the Freedom of Information Act and other oversight laws in the 1970s was a response to the expansion of presidential power and the growth of federal surveillance activities. The story of the last century is more accurately described as one in which power has been consolidated to meet new challenges, and then regulated in an attempt to preserve democratic control.

Another way of describing the experience of the last century is to say that it has been guided by pragmatism in the design of institutions.[12] Old ideas have been set aside quickly if the moment required it. A good example: Americans had an aversion to any sort of large standing army in 1900, but they had one of the most powerful military forces in the world in 1960. The system has even played with ideas that at first seemed alien to American democracy. No one seriously contemplated the establishment of a Mussolini-style dictatorship in the United States in the early 1930s. But politicians and voters certainly toyed with the idea of the powerful executive, looking for ways of extracting some of the perceived advantages of that model, without undercutting the idea of democratic accountability. Similarly, American policymakers played with the idea of the independent central bank in the 1980s and 1990s, seeking to extract some of the purported advantages of an independent body without wholly compromising popular control. The process of experimenting with alien ideas is always messy and unsatisfactory. The Federal Reserve, for example, does not have the purity of design that characterizes the European Central Bank. It has a vaguer mandate and a more confused relationship with elected politicians. This is equally frustrating to both diehard advocates of a hard currency and proponents of strong democratic control. But the arrangement seems to work, at least for the moment, and that is what pragmatists care about most.

A critical feature of the pragmatic approach to institutional design is its recognition of the contingency of any particular reform prescription. Reforms are accepted because they appear to work under certain circumstances, but circumstances may change, and if reforms no longer seem to achieve the intended purpose, they are likely to be abandoned. As we look back on the history of American government, we see a landscape that is strewn with old administrative equipment that has been unsentimentally abandoned when it ceased to be useful. One example is the Interstate Commerce Commission—a powerful federal institution before World War I, "next to the Supreme Court in importance," that no longer existed at the end of the twentieth century.[13]

Admittedly, reformers themselves often fail to recognize that institutional changes are always provisional. Rather, they have a habit of regarding reforms as permanent fixes to eternal problems. In 1910, for example, it was held as an immutable truth that public servants would exploit any opportunity to abuse their power for personal or partisan advantage, just as it was held in 1980 that democratic systems had an intrinsic bias toward deficits and high inflation.[14] In both instances this was overstatement: there may have been good evidence of such problems at the time, but the evidence that the problem was timeless was less compelling. Still, reformers demanded a rock-hard check against the abuses they had identified—in today's language, a "credible long-term commitment" to their preferred policies. But rigid long-term commitments are antithetical to the pragmatic approach, and have generally been avoided—because conditions may change, and old reforms may have to be abandoned.

Pragmatism about institutional design is only one of the features that enable American democracy to respond creatively to crisis. Another often-noted feature is the federal system itself. "It is one of the happy incidents of the federal system," Justice Louis Brandeis wrote in 1932, "that a single courageous State may, if its citizens choose, serve as a laboratory; and try novel social and economic experiments without risk to the rest of the country."[15] Brandeis saw experimentation by states as a valuable way of "remolding institutions to meet changing needs." States demonstrated how railroads could be regulated in the late nineteenth century, how the franchise could be expanded in the early twentieth century, how executive authority could be built up in the 1920s and 1930s, and how fiscal constraints could be imposed in the 1970s. Today, states are experimenting with techniques for regulating greenhouse gas emissions. Of course, there are many other examples, not all of them progressive. Still, the freedom that is available to states means that there is a steady supply of ideas about the renovation of federal institutions as well.

So important are these two features—pragmatism and political decentralization—that Chinese authorities have sought to replicate them. Deng Xiaoping, China's paramount leader from 1978 to 1992, was famous for his pragmatic defense of the nation's turn toward capitalism: "I support whatever type [of production] can increase output. . . . Yellow or white, a cat that catches mice is a good cat."[16] Deng also encouraged "vigorous" experimentation with new techniques of social and economic development by provincial and local leaders. Since 1978, one sympathetic scholar has recently observed, China has adopted a "pragmatic, experimental and 'trial-and-error' approach to its reform . . . Beijing tends to encourage various local experiments throughout the reform process, and then extend elsewhere whatever is successful in the experiments."[17] It has been argued that Deng merely revived a way of thinking that was broadly accepted by many Communist Party leaders of the revolutionary period. It was heavily influenced by the American pragmatist John Dewey, who lectured in China in 1919–1921, and became entrenched in Chinese communist philosophy during long years of guerilla warfare, but was forgotten during the latter part of Mao's rule as the party leadership became more doctrinaire and intolerant of deviations in policy.[18]

Still, there are critical differences between the American and Chinese approaches to experimentation. In the United States, state and local officials often undertake experiments in policy without regard to the preferences of officials in the federal government, and sometimes with open disdain for federal policy. In China, by contrast, the system of experimentation is a creation of central authorities. Lower-level officials engage in experiments to meet objectives that are defined by Beijing, with the hope that success will improve chances for promotion by Beijing to more senior positions. In other words, the creative potential of the system is bounded, and it also creates strong incentives for lower-level officials to misrepresent the results of their experiments.[19] Moreover the survival of the entire "trial-and-error" system depends on the forbearance of central authorities—a weakness illustrated by the collapse of the system during Mao's later years. Indeed, the tenure of China's current paramount leader, Xi Jinping, has been marked by a re-concentration of power at the center of government, a revived emphasis on ideological consistency, and a decline in tolerance for experimentation by provincial and local officials.[20]

Obviously there are also other differences that distinguish the American and Chinese approaches to experimentation. One of the virtues of democracy is its ability to make the evaluation of institutional experiments a task for the whole of society, and not just for higher-level government officials. A well-functioning democracy is a powerful machine for inventing and testing solutions to public problems. But this requires a free media, independent watchdog organizations, easy access to information held by government agencies, and space for the articulation and testing of new ideas.[21] It also requires a powerful mechanism—such as periodic elections—that will compel officials to pay attention to emerging evidence about the inadequacy of current policies. The Chinese government, by contrast, continues to insist on party control of the media; strictly limits access to information about the work of governmental agencies; censors discussions of sensitive topics such as pollution, food safety, and disaster response; punishes dissent when it threatens to undermine respect for the Communist Party and its policies; and rejects the "Western" idea of general elections.[22] Overall, the capacity of Chinese society to learn and adapt has been crippled by the effort to maintain party control.

Fatalism about the future of democracy is also encouraged by the widely held perception that public institutions do not change easily, if at all. If this is true, then creativity in inventing solutions to government failure hardly matters, because the solutions cannot be adopted. But there is no good reason for accepting this belief at face value.

As we noted at the end of chapter 2, people have not always believed that public institutions are ossified. On the contrary, the more common attitude throughout much of American history was that the institutions through which the United States was governed were malleable. They could and did change in response to new conditions. The life experience of the typical American of the early nineteenth century, the writer Algie Simons said in 1911, made it impossible to believe in "the unchangeableness of social institutions."[23] The historian George Bancroft made the point more poetically in his 1885 history of the US Constitution. "American society," he wrote, "is composed of separate, free and constantly moving atoms, ever in reciprocal action, advancing, receding, crossing, struggling against each other and with each other; so that the institutions and laws of the country rise out of the masses of individual thought, which, like the waters of the ocean, are rolling evermore."[24] A few years later, the writer George Cary Eggleston took a similar view about the adaptability of American government. "Institutions grow as trees do," Eggleston explained. "They grow in such ways as best fit them to their environment. . . . Under different conditions institutions take varying forms in adaptation to varying needs."[25] The observation that public institutions had often changed in the past gave hope to reformers, because it meant that campaigns for further improvement had a good chance of success.

However, belief in the malleability of public institutions seems to have declined significantly over the last thirty years. This change may have been encouraged by a growing body of scholarship that specializes in the study of governmental institutions and the processes by which they change. This academic movement is known as the "new institutionalism."[26] People working within this movement often disagree on the reasons why institutions emerge and change. But there is broad agreement on the proposition that the pace of institutional change is generally slow. "No matter what the analytic perspective," the political scientist Sven Steinmo has observed about the new institutionalism, "one of the features noted about institutions . . . is that [they] do not change easily."[27] John L. Campbell, writing in the *Oxford Handbook of Comparative Institutional Analysis*, has also affirmed the prevailing view that institutions "typically do not change rapidly—they are sticky [and] resistant to change."[28] One particularly influential strand within this literature, known as historical institutionalism, places special emphasis on the rigidity of public institutions.[29] Within this camp, the proposition that institutions change slowly is taken as a matter of "common sense."[30]

But the proposition that governmental institutions change slowly is anything but common sense. There is no body of scientific research that has established the truth of this idea. In fact, the statement that "institutions change slowly" cannot be proved or disproved purely through empirical analysis.[31] Slowness is a matter of judgment. When we say something changes slowly, we are making a comparison—perhaps to the rate at which something else changes, or more likely to some assumption about the rate at which something ought to change. The question that is not explicitly answered by scholars who emphasize the slowness of institutional change is this: Slow compared to what?[32]

To answer this question, we should look at the way in which the problem of institutional rigidity is often explained. In 1984, one political scientist suggested that the new institutionalism was distinguished by the view that "institutional structures do not respond in any rapid and fluid way to alterations in the domestic or international environment."[33] At the same time, two prominent advocates of the approach, James March and Johan Olsen, suggested that history might be "inefficient" because institutions failed to evolve rapidly to accommodate "current environmental conditions."[34] Later, March and Olsen suggested that institutions could be said to change slowly because "the rate of change is inconsistent with the rate of change in the environment to which the institution is adapting."[35] In a similar vein, other scholars have recently said that the "finding . . . [of] institutional inertia" is justified because "institutions fail to adapt even when the need for adaptation is, or should be, apparent."[36] "Human institutions are 'sticky,'" Francis Fukuyama explained in 2011, because "institutions that are created to meet one set of conditions often survive even when those conditions change or disappear."[37]

All of these explanations share a common feature. They involve a judgment that "environmental conditions" have changed, and that institutions ought to adjust to those new conditions. In other words, the stopwatch that is used to measure the speed of institutional adjustment starts once the "need for adaptation" becomes apparent. But apparent to whom? Presumably it is the experts themselves. Climate change provides a recent example of this mode of reasoning at work. Scientific research shows the emergence of a new challenge; institutions do not react; and reformers ask—to borrow the title of a recent book by Nicholas Stern—*Why Are We Waiting?*[38] The same logic operates in other domains. Experts identify a new social problem, or a defect in the economy, or an emerging security threat. A "need for reform" is identified, but institutions do not respond to this need with sufficient speed.

Of course, this raises another question: What is sufficient speed? Obviously, we cannot expect institutions to change overnight. Some period of time must be allowed for adjustment. But how much time are experts prepared to allow? We have to speculate. A working hypothesis is that experts suffer from the same sort of retrospective myopia that seems to afflict the population at large. Figure 6.1 represents a rough effort to judge how far back in the past American political scientists are likely to look as they conduct their own research: it suggests that this group is also preoccupied with the preceding fifteen or twenty years.[39] In other words, experts also seem to give undue weight to their own "remembered past." Perhaps they are also inclined to say that the

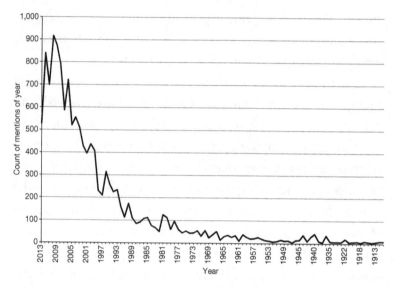

Fig. 6.1 Frequency with which years prior to 2014 are mentioned in research articles in *American Political Science Review* 108 (2014).

pace of institutional adaptation is too slow if they do not see significant institutional change within that period.

We can put all of this together and articulate the standard by which the pace of institutional adaptation appears to be judged: institutions change slowly if they do not respond within ten or twenty years after the identification of a "need for reform" by experts. Of course, when we state it this plainly, we can see how problematic the standard is. For example, it seems a little anti-democratic. Why should experts determine whether the "need for reform" has arisen? There is no purely technical way of deciding that a social problem exists: while it certainly hinges on facts, it also involves a value judgment that certain conditions are undesirable and ought to be changed.[40] Moreover, there are many problems that a society might choose to address at any moment in time, and ranking one problem over another also involves a decision about values and priorities. The premise of democracy is that citizens, not experts, decide what the priorities of the country should be. But if we start the stopwatch for gauging the pace of institutional adaptation only when the existence of a problem is broadly acknowledged by citizens, then we are much less likely to conclude that institutions change slowly.

And even if we accept the premise that the stopwatch ought to start when experts recognize a problem, we run into a second difficulty. Why would we expect institutions to change within ten or twenty years? This is a completely arbitrary timeframe, dictated by human biology, not by anything we know about the character of institutions. There is no particular reason why the scale of institutional time should be the same as the scale of human time. Why not use a window of fifty or a hundred years to gauge the pace of institutional adaptation? If we did that, institutional change might not seem so slow after all.[41]

By now we can see that the proposition that "institutions change slowly" is anything but common sense. Indeed, it can be difficult to reconcile the proposition with common sense. Consider how the world changed in the thirty-year period from 1986 to 2016. At the start of 1986, there were a quarter-million US troops in Germany, ready for an attack by the Soviet Union. NASA was preparing for a dramatic expansion of its space program, involving a space shuttle launch every twenty days. Homosexual acts were criminalized in much of the country, homosexuals were not permitted to serve in the military, and same-sex couples were denied the benefits of marriage. No one worried about surveillance of the Internet, which was still unknown to most Americans. Similarly, "homeland security" was an unknown phrase, airline passenger screening was a simple process that was managed by the airlines themselves, and a national healthcare program seemed like a pipe dream.[42] We could go on. In many ways, the architecture of government has changed substantially in the span of our "remembered past." Why, then, do we insist on the blanket proposition that institutions change slowly?

And, of course, the proposition becomes even more untenable if we abandon the arbitrary timeframe of a few decades. Suppose we look at the span of history since the publication of James Bryce's influential book, *The American Commonwealth*, in 1888. At that time, the large majority of Americans adults could not vote and the national government did little at home or abroad. "In America," Bryce wrote confidently, "there is less need and less desire than in Europe for a perennial stream of federal legislation. People are contented if things go on fairly well as they are. Political philosophers perceive some improvements which federal statutes might effect, but the mass of the nation does not complain."[43] By 1920, such complacency had been shattered. The country was seized with debate over voting rights, the Senate was popularly elected, the federal government was busy regulating railroads and other trusts, and two million US troops had just returned from Europe. Attitudes about the proper role of the federal government—and also the institutions of government—had been upended in the span of a generation.

This was followed by another transformation over the next thirty years. In 1920, the White House staff was still negligible: the president was supported by only two or three secretaries.[44] There was no such thing as a federal budget, the national government asserted no overall responsibility for management of the economy, and the biggest federal department was still the

Post Office. By 1950, however, everyone understood that there was a national economy, and they agreed that President Truman, now supported by a battery of new agencies, was responsible for attending to its health. At the same time, the country was wrestling with the reality of a vast and apparently permanent military establishment—a new "garrison state."[45]

And, of course, there was another transformation in public philosophy after the 1970s. The self-confidence that typified political discourse in the 1960s and encouraged federal activism in domestic and foreign policy faded away. Americans adopted a new and more skeptical manner of talking about public policy, emphasizing the ways in which "great expectations in Washington" are frequently dashed in practice, and how politicians, bureaucrats, interest groups, and voters pursue narrow self-interest rather than the public welfare.[46] Over the course of a generation, federal institutions were again altered, to limit the capacity for all of these so-called "rent-seekers" to exploit government—for example, by restricting the power of elected officials to influence fiscal and monetary policy, domestic regulation, and tariffs. The shift in attitudes and policies over this period was dramatic. Richard Nixon was considered by some to be a conservative Republican in 1968, but much of his record as president in 1969–1974 would be suited to a liberal Democrat in 2016.

A body of scholarship that dwells on the rigidity and stickiness of institutions seems to miss the larger truth that emerges from the history of the last century: change, not stasis, is the reality of American government. It is certainly true that some parts of government have not changed as quickly as others, and that the overall pace of change has often frustrated well-meaning reformers, and even that delay has sometimes imposed significant social costs. Overall, though, observers in the first half of the twentieth century had it right: the system is constantly under renovation, with features being added, altered, or removed. The broad lesson of history is that it is imprudent to make any statement with finality about the goals and design of American democracy. And there is a practical implication to all this. There is hope for reform today: important features of the system can be altered in the future, just as they have been altered in the past. Even the orthodoxies of the past thirty years—open borders, free trade, deregulation, small government, low marginal tax rates—may be subject to reconsideration, as the presidential race of 2016 showed.

To be clear, a defense of democracy does not imply a defense of every policy that has been pursued by a regime calling itself a democracy. Advanced democracies make mistakes all the time, and because they can be long-lived regimes, the catalog of mistakes for which they are responsible is large and constantly growing. Sometimes democracies choose the wrong response to a new problem, and sometimes they fail to adjust once-sensible policies promptly when conditions have changed. And sometimes they make mistakes because they have failed, in some important respects, to behave as democracies ought to behave.

Today, for example, the United States is criticized for its decision to invade Iraq as part of the "Global War on Terrorism" that was launched in response to the terror attacks of September 2001. The invasion was an ill-conceived and poorly executed debacle, which may have led to the death of two hundred thousand people and the displacement of another three million.[47] It is a testament to the virtues of an open society that the errors associated with the invasion of Iraq were so quickly exposed and broadly acknowledged. Opinion polls since 2006 have shown that a solid majority of Americans consider the invasion to have been an error.[48] The lessons of the Iraq War also shaped the foreign policy of the Obama administration after 2008.[49] Still, it would have been preferable if the mistake had never been made. It gives critics reason to ask: If this is the sort of thing that democracy does, who wants it?[50]

The answer is that the invasion happened not because the United States is a democracy, but rather because, at a crucial moment, it failed to fully act like one. A healthy democracy takes time to deliberate, scrutinizes demands for action carefully, and acts on the best available evidence. The United States did not do this before the invasion of March 2003. Instead, the country rushed to war: legislators, journalists, and citizens showed too much deference toward an executive that had an exaggerated sense of its own competence.[51] An excuse that was offered later was that the nation had been traumatized by the terror attacks of September 11, 2001. The United States became "another nation" after the attacks, the *Christian Science Monitor* observed: an "undercurrent of fear" discouraged people from thinking carefully about the country's options.[52] Many wanted strong leadership and decisive action, and the Bush administration—conscious of its own weakness after the disputed 2000 election and missteps in the months before September 2001—exploited that desire. The proportion of the American public that regarded George W. Bush as a strong leader was never higher than it was in the few months preceding the invasion of Iraq.[53]

At the time, many people said the 2001 terror attacks had plunged the United States into "a new normal." This quickly became a buzzword that was often invoked to describe substantial shifts in the structure of everyday life.[54] The financial crisis of 2008 was also said to have created another "new normal" that involved a "fundamental restructuring of the economic order."[55] By 2012 the phrase was so commonplace that NBC launched a new sitcom, *The New Normal*, "a heartwarming comedy about a blended family of a gay couple and the woman who becomes a surrogate to help them start a family."[56] The title tempted fate. The first episode of the sitcom was preempted by Hurricane Sandy, an event that was said to be the portent of yet another "new normal" of extreme weather caused by global warming.[57] The sitcom was canceled in 2013. *The New Normal* was old news in less than a year.

This preoccupation with normalcy has been with us for a long time. Warren G. Harding, the Republican candidate for president in 1920, called for a "return to normalcy" after the upheaval of World War I. The nation needed to "steady down," Harding said, and get back to a state of "serenity and equipoise."[58] At the time, a Michigan pastor objected to the premise: "There is no stable normalcy in the past to which we can go back."[59] And the search for any kind of normalcy after 1920 would indeed prove to be futile. Everyday life was constantly disturbed over the next century—by wars and protest movements, economic transformations and financial crises, technological innovation and obsolescence, climatic changes and natural disasters, migrations, disease, and shifting fertility rates. The pastor from Michigan was right: normalcy was a chimera in 1920, and it still is today. The normal condition of modern life is flux, and the central concern of the American political system is the constant adaptation of institutions and policies to accommodate altered circumstances.

The difficulty is that this process of adaptation is always pervaded with uncertainty. At first, we are never sure how seriously we should take a change in circumstances, or what the appropriate response ought to be. This uncertainty creates a tension that can be difficult to manage. On one hand, the resolution of uncertainty requires patience and open-mindedness. We need time to sift evidence about emerging problems, invent possible responses, and experiment to see which responses are likely to be most effective. On the other hand, though, uncertainty produces feelings of dread of what the future might hold, and an impulse to relieve that dread through immediate and bold action.[60] The extent to which decision-making is affected by dread depends on the kind of change that confronts the decision-maker. Some changes—shifts in the structure of the economy, migration patterns, or fertility rates—happen so slowly in comparison to a human lifespan that they are unlikely to provoke anxiety. But other changes—like the 9/11 attacks—are sudden and dramatic. In such moments, as the writer Elaine Scarry has observed, there is a powerful "seduction to stop thinking."[61] And too often there are politicians who seek advantage by exploiting the temptation in such moments to forgo deliberation and yield to a strong leader. The result can be mistakes like the invasion of Iraq.

Perhaps feelings of anxiety and dread also arise in those historical moments when a long-established way of thinking about government and society—the prevailing public philosophy, as Lippmann and Lowi called it—is in the final phases of its collapse. Today, for example, political debate is pervaded with a sense that many of the ideas that have ordered our thinking about politics for the last three decades are exhausted. At the same time there is no clear sense of what the new public philosophy should be. This is a liminal moment, in which neither problems nor solutions are clearly defined. Demands for vigorous government action and the reassertion of national power are oddly mixed with deep reservations about the ability of politicians and bureaucrats to wield power competently. Polls taken over the last two years have shown that Americans are "deeply uncertain" about the nation's future.[62] As the presidential race of 2016 showed, there is a temptation in such moments to seize on rough but viscerally satisfying solutions: to pull down the pillars of the establishment, seal the borders, engage in mass deportations, bar entry to strangers, abandon longtime allies, bomb enemies "into oblivion," torture suspected terrorists, and assassinate their relatives.[63] At the same time there is a longing for the strong leader who can rise above the disorderliness of ordinary democratic politics and "get things done," and an evident supply of politicians ready to exploit that longing.[64]

Fatalism about the democratic process—about its capacity to respond creatively to changing circumstances—may contribute to this longing for the strong leader. This is another reason why we should be concerned about all of the writing on democratic malaise that has been accumulating for the past several years. If we take the long view, there is more room for optimism about American democracy. There have been many periods in American history where settled ideas about the role of government have been thrown into doubt. The task of forging a new public philosophy is not easy, and it takes years. The first steps in that process are especially confused and difficult. But these first steps cannot be avoided, and we should resist the temptation to make broader judgments about democracy in this difficult moment. Democracy does not work neatly, but it does work. And in the long run, as Karl Popper said, it is the only sure way of ensuring that rulers pay attention to the interests of the people they rule.

CHAPTER 1

1. Karl R. Popper, *All Life Is Problem Solving* (New York: Routledge, 1999),
   94 and 334. Here I have adapted Popper's short definition of democracy: "the right of the people to judge and to dismiss their government."
   Definitions of democracy vary in complexity. James Bryce emphasizes
   the formal aspect of selection and dismissal: democracy is "nothing
   more or less than the rule of the whole people expressing their sovereign will by their votes": James Bryce, *Modern Democracies*, 2 vols.
   (New York: Macmillan, 1921), 1:viii. Phillippe Schmitter and Terry
   Lynn Karl pitch their definition more broadly, emphasizing the never-
   ending competition for public support: "Modern political democracy is
   a system of governance in which rulers are held accountable for their
   actions in the public realm by citizens, acting indirectly through the
   competition and cooperation of their elected representatives": Philippe
   C. Schmitter and Terry Lynn Karl, "What Democracy Is . . . And Is Not,"
   Journal of Democracy 2, no. 3 (1991): 75–88, 76. Other scholars have
   even more comprehensive views of what democracy requires, emphasizing the arrangements that are needed to protect public debate (such
   as guarantees of free expression, access to official information, and a
   healthy media and civil society) and the capacity for political mobilization. For example, see Robert A. Dahl, *Democracy and Its Critics*
   (New Haven, CT: Yale University Press, 1989), 221; David Beetham,
   Democracy: A Beginner's Guide (Oxford: Oneworld, 2005), 6.
2. John Keane, *The Life and Death of Democracy* (New York: W. W. Norton,
   2009), 78–84.
3. Freedom House, *Freedom in the World 2000* (Washington, DC: Freedom
   House, 2000). Fifty-nine countries attained scores of eight or higher
   in the Polity IV assessment for 2000. The Polity Project develops

quantitative measures of the "authority characteristics of states." See http://www.systemicpeace.org/polityproject.html.

4. Commission on Global Governance, *Our Global Neighborhood: The Report of the Commission on Global Governance* (New York: Oxford University Press, 1995), ch. 2.

5. Marc F. Plattner and Larry Diamond, "Democracy's Future," *Journal of Democracy* 6, no. 1 (1995): 3–5, 4.

6. For an overview, see Joshua Kurlantzick, *Democracy in Retreat* (New Haven, CT: Yale University Press, 2013), 18–21.

7. Gallup Poll, "Trust in Government," http://www.gallup.com/poll/5392/trust-government.aspx.

8. Peter Mair, *Ruling the Void: The Hollowing of Western Democracy* (New York: Verso, 2013), ch. 1.

9. Article 21.

10. World Bank, *Anticorruption in Transition* (Washington, DC: World Bank, 2000), 3.

11. Wolfgang Streeck, *Buying Time: The Delayed Crisis of Democratic Capitalism* (London: Verso, 2014), 177; Gavin Hewitt, *The Lost Continent* (London: Hodder & Stoughton, 2013).

12. Vladimir Putin, *Speech at the Russian Federation National Awards Presentation Ceremony* (Moscow: The Kremlin, June 12, 2015); Karen Dawisha, *Putin's Kleptocracy* (New York: Simon & Schuster, 2014), 8. See also Andranik Migranyan, "What Is Putinism?," *Russia in Global Affairs* 17, no. 2 (2004): 28–44.

13. Prayut Chan-o-cha, *National Broadcast* (Bangkok: Secretariat of the Prime Minister, May 22, 2015); Christian Caryl, "Can Thailand Move Beyond the Coup?," November 22, 2014, http://foreignpolicy.com/2014/11/22/can-thailand-move-beyond-the-coup/. See also Bertil Lintner, "The Battle for Thailand," *Foreign Affairs* 88, no. 4 (2009): 108–118.

14. Ioan Grillo, *El Narco: Inside Mexico's Criminal Insurgency* (New York: Bloomsbury Press, 2011); Ioan Grillo, "Mexico's Deadly Narco-Politics," *New York Times*, October 9, 2014.

15. Simon Johnson, "The Quiet Coup," *The Atlantic*, May 2009. See also Simon Johnson and James Kwak, *13 Bankers* (New York: Pantheon Books, 2010).

16. Joseph E. Stiglitz, *The Price of Inequality* (New York: W. W. Norton, 2012), 136.

17. Paul Krugman, "Oligarchy, American Style," *New York Times*, November 3, 2011.

18. Walter Lippmann, *Drift and Mastery* (New York: M. Kennerley, 1914).

19. Rodolfo Sarsfield and Fabián Echegaray, "Opening the Black Box: How Satisfaction with Democracy and Its Perceived Efficacy Affect Regime Preference in Latin America," *International Journal of Public Opinion Research* 18, no. 2 (2006): 153–173, 169.

20. Kurlantzick, *Democracy in Retreat*, 171.

21. Moisés Naim, "Latin America: The Second Stage of Reform," *Journal of Democracy* 5, no. 4 (1994): 32–48; Nicolas van de Walle, "Crisis and Opportunity in Africa," *Journal of Democracy* 6, no. 2 (1995): 128–141; Michael Bratton and Eric C. C. Chang, "State Building and Democratization in Sub-Saharan Africa: Forwards, Backwards, or Together?," *Comparative Political Studies* 39, no. 9 (2006): 1059–1083; Thomas Carothers, "Democracy Assistance: Political vs. Developmental?," *Journal of Democracy* 20, no. 1 (2009): 5–19.

22. Gideon Rachman, "The West Has Lost Intellectual Self-Confidence," *Financial Times*, January 5, 2015.

23. Anthony King and Ivor Crewe, *Blunders of Our Governments* (London: Oneworld Publications, 2013).

24. Larry Diamond, "Facing Up to the Democratic Recession," *Journal of Democracy* 26, no. 1 (2015): 141–155, 152.

25. Thomas L. Friedman and Michael Mandelbaum, *That Used to Be Us* (New York: Farrar, Straus and Giroux, 2011), 251; Thomas E. Mann and Norman J. Ornstein, *It's Even Worse Than It Looks* (New York: Basic Books, 2013), xvii.

26. Donald F. Kettl, *The Next Government of the United States* (New York: W. W. Norton, 2009), ch. 1.

27. Peter H. Schuck, *Why Government Fails So Often* (Princeton, NJ: Princeton University Press, 2014), 372 and 412.

28. Francis Fukuyama, *Political Order and Political Decay: From the Industrial Revolution to the Globalization of Democracy* (New York: Farrar, Straus and Giroux, 2014), 449 and 465. See also Francis Fukuyama, "America in Decay," *Foreign Affairs* 93, no. 5 (2014): 3–26.

29. Philip Coggan, *The Last Vote* (London: Penguin, 2013), 221.

30. Matthew Flinders, "Explaining Democratic Disaffection," *Governance* 27, no. 1 (2014): 1–8, 5.

31. John J. DiIulio, *Bring Back the Bureaucrats* (West Conshohocken, PA: Templeton Press, 2014), 7.

32. John Micklethwait and Adrian Wooldridge, *The Fourth Revolution* (New York: Penguin Press, 2014), 11, 222, 251.

33. Niall Ferguson, *The Great Degeneration* (New York: Penguin Press, 2013), ch. 1.

34. Richard V. Reeves, *Ulysses Goes to Washington: Political Myopia and Policy Commitment Devices* (Washington, DC: Brookings Institution, 2015), 20–21.

35. Peter G. Peterson, "Gray Dawn," *Foreign Affairs* 78 (1999): 42–55, 55.

36. Ian Buruma, "China's Dark Triumph," *Los Angeles Times*, January 13, 2008. "Across much of Asia—notably in Singapore but also in Malaysia and Vietnam—democracy is disparaged by officials as a Western imposition to which Asians are not suited": *Harper's Magazine*, June 2015, p. 50.

37. Jacob von Uexkull, *The State of the World* (Hamburg, Germany: World Future Council, 2007).

38. John Dunn, *Breaking Democracy's Spell* (New Haven, CT: Yale University Press, 2014), ch. 4.

39. David J. C. Shearman and Joseph Wayne Smith, *The Climate Change Challenge and the Failure of Democracy* (Westport, CT: Praeger, 2007). See also David J. C. Shearman, "Democracy and Climate Change: A Story of Failure," OpenDemocracy.net, November 7, 2007, https://www.opendemocracy.net/article/democracy_and_climate_change_a_story_of_failure.

40. Samuel P. Huntington, *Political Order in Changing Societies* (New Haven, CT: Yale University Press, 1968), 7. Similarly, Charles Anderson observed in 1971 that most Americans "accept as a matter of course that the principal problem of institution-building is the limitation of government power": *Statecraft: An Introduction to Political Choice and Judgment* (New York: Wiley, 1977), 193.

41. Fukuyama, "America in Decay." Elsewhere, Fukuyama has observed: "The state, that is, the functioning of executive branches and their bureaucracies, has received relatively little attention in contemporary political science. ... [E]veryone is interested in studying political institutions that limit or check power—democratic accountability and rule of law—but very few people pay attention to the institution that accumulates and uses power, the state": Francis Fukuyama, "What Is Governance?," *Governance* 26, no. 3 (2013): 347–368, 347.

42. David Frum, "The Transparency Trap," *The Atlantic*, August 13, 2014.

43. Richard Pildes, "Romanticizing Democracy, Political Fragmentation, and the Decline of American Government," *Yale Law Journal* 124, no. 3 (2014): 876–881, 817.

44. R. A. W. Rhodes, Sarah A. Binder, and Bert A. Rockman, eds., *The Oxford Handbook of Political Institutions* (Oxford: Oxford University Press, 2006), xv.

45. J. G. March and Johan P. Olsen, "Elaborating the 'New Institutionalism,'" in *The Oxford Handbook of Political Institutions*, ed. R. A. W. Rhodes, Sarah A. Binder, and Bert Rockman (New York: Oxford University Press, 2006), 3–22, 12.

46. Tariq Ali, "The New World Disorder," *London Review of Books*, April 9, 2015, 19–22, 19.

47. W. J. Breen, *Labor Market Politics and the Great War* (Kent, OH: Kent State University Press, 1997), xiii.

48. Martin Jacques, *When China Rules the World* (New York: Penguin Press, 2009), 620.

49. Wei-Wei Zhang, *The China Wave: Rise of a Civilizational State* (Hackensack, NJ: World Century, 2012), 169.

50. Freedom House, *Country Report: Singapore* (Washington, DC: Freedom House, 2013), available from https://freedomhouse.org/report/freedom-world/2013/singapore. Its 2014 assessment was more flattering.

51. Kishore Mahbubani, "What Is Governance?," March 26, 2013, available from http://governancejournal.net/2013/03/26/mahbubani/.

52. Graham T. Allison, "The Lee Kuan Yew Conundrum," *The Atlantic*, March 30, 2015, http://www.theatlantic.com/international/archive/2015/03/lee-kuan-yew-conundrum-democracy-singapore/388955/. Also: "Lee is the founding father of what might be termed 'the Asian alternative' . . . a different way of doing things that most Westerners associate with mighty China but that is to be found at its most advanced in tiny Singapore. . . . [T]he rest of the world can learn a lot from the Asian alternative": Micklethwait and Wooldridge, *The Fourth Revolution*, 133.

53. Slavoj Žižek, "Capitalism Has Broken Free of the Shackles of Democracy," *Financial Times*, February 1, 2015.

54. World Bank data, http://data.worldbank.org/indicator/NY.GDP.MKTP.CD.

55. United Nations data, http://esa.un.org/unpd/wup/CD-ROM/.

56. Zhang, *The China Wave: Rise of a Civilizational State*, chs. 4 and 5.

57. OECD, *Government at a Glance 2013* (Paris: OECD, 2013), 25–26.

58. Zhang, *The China Wave: Rise of a Civilizational State*, 63, 135, 152.

59. Kurlantzick, *Democracy in Retreat*, 10 and 200.

60. See, e.g., Donald K. Emmerson's sharp critique of the work by Kishore Mahbubani: Donald K. Emmerson, "Kishore's World," *Journal of Democracy* 24, no. 3 (2013): 166–174, 172.

61. The authors also praise reforms in Denmark, Norway, Sweden, and Finland. "The Chinese are right to be looking to the Nordic world as well as Singapore for enlightenment": Micklethwait and Wooldridge, *The Fourth Revolution*, 144, 166, and 246.

62. Michel Crozier, Samuel P. Huntington, and Joji Watanuki, *The Crisis of Democracy* (New York: New York University Press, 1975), 2.

63. Richard E. B. Simeon, "The 'Overload Thesis' and Canadian Government," *Canadian Public Policy* 2, no. 4 (1976): 541–552, 541.

64. James Reston, "The Crisis of Democracy," *New York Times*, March 3, 1974.

65. Samuel P. Huntington, "Democracy's Third Wave," *Journal of Democracy* 2, no. 2 (1991): 12–34.

66. Harold Laski, *Democracy in Crisis* (Chapel Hill: University of North Carolina Press, 1933), 47 and 55.

67. Wolfgang Schivelbusch, *Three New Deals* (New York: Metropolitan Books, 2006), 31.

68. Victor Zarnowitz, *Business Cycles* (Chicago: University of Chicago Press, 1996), table 7.4.

69. Walter Edward Weyl, *The New Democracy* (New York: Macmillan, 1914), 1–4.

70. H. G. Wells, *Social Forces in England and America* (New York: Harper, 1914), 293–294.

71. Woodrow Wilson, "The Study of Administration," *Political Science Quarterly* 2, no. 2 (1887): 197–222, 220; Edward Mandell House, *Philip Dru, Administrator: A Story of Tomorrow* (New York: B. W. Huebsch, 1912).

72. "Women Share Honors with Sterner Sex," *Ann Arbor (MI) Daily Times News*, February 12, 1919, 8.

73. David Runciman, *The Confidence Trap* (Princeton, NJ: Princeton University Press, 2013), xviii and xix. Similarly, Stephen Salkever has written: "For well over one hundred years the best social theorists ... have agreed ... that a fundamental instability or incoherence is built into" liberal democracy: Stephen Salkever, "The Crisis of Liberal Democracy," in *The Crisis of Liberal Democracy*, ed. Kenneth L. Deutsch and Walter Soffer (Albany: State University of New York Press, 1987), 245–268, 245. Runciman also observes that democracies have a habit of

comparing themselves unfavorably to authoritarian systems. However my analysis differs from Runciman's in several respects. First, I believe that democracies can distinguish between serious and "fake crises," as he calls them. Second, I consider that serious crises often vary in character and are important because they lead to significant changes in ideology and institutions. Finally, I do not believe that the cumulative effect of past crises is to build over-confidence about the future. My review of Runciman's book is found here: Alasdair Roberts, "The Confidence Trap: A History of Democracy in Crisis from World War I to the Present," *Acta Politica* 50, no. 2 (2015): 242–245.

74. For an elaboration of this argument, see David Coen and Alasdair Roberts, "A New Age of Uncertainty," *Governance* 25, no. 1 (2012): 5–9.

75. On the other hand, my periodization is not entirely original. For example, Alexander Keyssar suggests that the period between 1890 and 1920 was one in which there was unusual ferment over the right to vote: Alexander Keyssar, *The Right to Vote* (New York: Basic Books, 2009), 111, 136, 197, 223, and 230. Similarly Walter Nugent, in his study of progressivism, observes that the United States became a "vastly different" country between 1901 and 1921: Walter T. K. Nugent, *Progressivism* (New York: Oxford University Press, 2010), 124. Meanwhile, Barry Dean Karl is one of several authors who have identified the period 1915–1945 as one in which "the major transformations of our modern history took place": Barry Dean Karl, *The Uneasy State: The United States from 1915 to 1945* (Chicago: University of Chicago Press, 1983), 14. And many authors have described an "age of neoliberalism" beginning in the 1970s. For example: David Harvey, *A Brief History of Neoliberalism* (New York: Oxford University Press, 2005). There is also some similarity between my periodization and that proposed by Arthur Schlesinger Jr., although I do not suggest, as Schlesinger does, that American politics is typified by cycles: Arthur M. Schlesinger, *The Cycles of American History* (Boston, MA: Houghton Mifflin, 1986), ch. 2.

76. This is another way of saying that "crises of democracy" are social constructions: Joseph Schneider, "Social Problems Theory: The Constructionist View," *Annual Review of Sociology* 11 (1985): 209–229.

77. Ali, "The New World Disorder," 19.

78. Frum, "The Transparency Trap."

CHAPTER 2

1. Edmund S. Ions, *James Bryce and American Democracy, 1870–1922* (London: Macmillan, 1968), 16.

2. "Prof. Bryce at the University," *Baltimore (MD) Sun*, October 21, 1890, 4.

3. Ions, *James Bryce and American Democracy, 1870–1922*, 16.

4. Ibid., 130; "Prof. Bryce's 'American Commonwealth,'" *Boston (MA) Herald*, 1888, 12.

5. Ions, *James Bryce and American Democracy, 1870–1922*, 130.

6. "English Diplomat Discussed by Dr. Anderson," *Macon (GA) Telegraph and News*, April 16, 1933, 3.

7. James Bryce, *The American Commonwealth*, 3 vols. (London: Macmillan, 1888), 3:24–33.

8. Ibid., 2:217, 2:352, 2:440, 2:619, 2:621, 3:292.

9. James Bryce, *Modern Democracies*, 2 vols. (New York: Macmillan, 1921), 1:20.

10. On November 11, 1912, Wilson wrote to Bryce to express "deep appreciation of your generous letter." Bryce Papers, University of Oxford, MSS Bryce 233, fol. 31.

11. "Why the Progressives," *Springfield (MA) Union*, September 12, 1912, 8.

12. Voting Machine. Langrill, W., assignee. Patent US860675A. 23 July 1907.

13. A thorough history of the right to vote in the United States is provided by Alexander Keyssar, *The Right to Vote* (New York: Basic Books, 2009). My approach differs from Keyssar's in four respects. First, I am interested in other institutional reforms that promoted self-rule and not simply the extension of the right to vote. Second, Keyssar's analysis relies on a periodization that runs from 1850 to about 1920, while I think that it is possible to discern distinctive patterns within the shorter period of 1890 to 1920. Indeed, Keyssar's book itself tends to support this view: ibid., 111, 136, 197. Third, Keyssar does not examine the problem of enfranchisement in the territories acquired after the Spanish-American War. And fourth, Keyssar's view is that the overall trend in this longer period was "toward a narrowing of the franchise . . . a piecemeal rolling back of gains achieved in earlier decades": ibid., 80. I believe this is an excessively pessimistic view of developments in this era. The claim is refuted by the fact of women's enfranchisement alone. If we accept Keyssar's periodization, we must also acknowledge the adoption of the Thirteenth, Fourteenth, and Fifteenth Amendments in 1865–1870. This constituted real progress toward the eventual

empowerment of African Americans, notwithstanding developments after 1877.

14. "Concerning Men of Wealth," *The Outlook* 88, no. 16 (April 18, 1908): 907.

15. "Governor Johnson's Birmingham Speech," *The Outlook* 89, no. 6 (June 6, 1908): 322.

16. Alfred D. Chandler, *The Visible Hand: The Managerial Revolution in American Business* (Cambridge, MA: Belknap Press, 1977), 541.

17. Frank Norris, *The Octopus* (New York: Doubleday, Page, 1901), 289.

18. Chandler, *The Visible Hand*, 174.

19. An exhaustive list of attempted combinations, from acids to zinc, is provided by: Henry Demarest Lloyd, *Wealth against Commonwealth* (New York,: Harper, 1894), 537–544.

20. Horace L. Wilgus, *A Study of the United States Steel Corporation in Its Industrial and Legal Aspects* (Chicago: Callaghan, 1901), 4–5.

21. Commissioner of Corporations, *Report on the Petroleum Industry* (Washington, DC: Government Printing Office, 1907), 6–20.

22. Ida M. Tarbell, *The History of the Standard Oil Company*, 2 vols. (New York: McClure, Phillips, 1904), 2:229–230.

23. Pujo Committee, *Report on the Concentration of Control of Money and Credit* (Washington, DC: Government Printing Office, 1913), 129–133.

24. Louis D. Brandeis, *Other People's Money: And How the Bankers Use It* (New York: F. A. Stokes, 1914), 6.

25. "New Freedom on Way Here Says Senator Owen," *Rockford (IL) Morning Star*, November 18, 1914, 12.

26. George K. Holmes, "The Concentration of Wealth," *Political Science Quarterly* 8, no. 4 (1893): 589–600, 593.

27. Charles B. Spahr, *An Essay on the Present Distribution of Wealth in the United States*, 2d ed. (New York: T. Y. Crowell, 1896), 123–129.

28. Henry Laurens Call, *The Concentration of Wealth* (Boston: Chandler Publishing, 1907), 7.

29. "John D. Will Be First Billionaire," *Philadelphia (PA) Inquirer*, August 9, 1909, 9.

30. "The Story of America's Oldest Multimillionaire Family," *Colorado Springs Gazette*, October 22, 1905, 18.

31. J. Bruce Glasier, "Andrew Carnegie and His Millions," *New York Worker*, July 14, 1906, 3.

32. "The New Vanderbilt Villa," *Riverside (CA) Independent Enterprise*, June 22, 1895, 4.

33. "An Orgy of Vulgarity," *Boston (MA) Herald*, April 15, 1903, 3.

34. Walter Rauschenbusch, *Christianity and the Social Crisis* (New York: Macmillan, 1907), 253–254.

35. Roy G. Saltman, *The History and Politics of Voting Technology: In Quest of Integrity and Public Confidence* (New York: Palgrave Macmillan, 2006), 71–104; James L. Baumgardner, "The 1888 Presidential Election: How Corrupt?," *Presidential Studies Quarterly* 14, no. 3 (1984): 416–427, 418–419.

36. Lincoln Steffens, *The Shame of the Cities* (New York: McClure, Phillips, 1904). See also Joseph Lincoln Steffens, *The Struggle for Self-Government* (New York: McClure, Phillips, 1906).

37. Edward F. Dunne, "Why the Initiative and Referendum Should Be Incorporated in the Constitution," *Chicago Schools Journal* 2, no. 6 (1920): 9–12, 9.

38. "The Lobby," *National New Era* 20, no. 2 (1903): 14–15.

39. George Henry Haynes, *The Election of Senators* (New York: H. Holt, 1906), 51.

40. During the Stephenson investigation, Senator Atlee Pomerene asked Stephenson's campaign manager why any man would spend such a large amount of money to win a position that paid only $7,500 a year. The cryptic answer: "It is not supposed that a man goes to the Senate for $7,500 alone." "Stephenson Election Probe," *Lexington (KY) Leader*, October 10, 1911, 2.

41. See also "Lobbyists I Have Met," *Saturday Evening Post* 186, no. 5 (1913): 6–7.

42. David Graham Phillips, "The Treason of the Senate," *The Cosmopolitan*, September 1906, 525–535, 534.

43. Ernest Crosby, "Wall Street and the House of Dollars," *The Cosmopolitan*, 1906, 885–886, 886.

44. William Jennings Bryan, *The First Battle* (Chicago: W. B. Conkey, 1898), 482.

45. John Calvin Reed, *The New Plutocracy* (New York: Abbey Press, 1903), vii.

46. "New Freedom on Way Here Says Senator Owen," *Rockford (IL) Morning Star*.

47. Moisey Ostrogorsky, *Democracy and the Organization of Political Parties* (New York: Macmillan, 1902), 572–576 and 607–608.

48. Robert Michels, *Political Parties: A Sociological Study of the Oligarchical Tendencies of Modern Democracy* (New York: Hearst's International Library, 1915), 310 and 401.

49. Bill Winders, "The Roller Coaster of Class Conflict: Class Segments, Mass Mobilization, and Voter Turnout in the U.S., 1840-1996," *Social Forces* 77, no. 3 (1999): 833–862, 836.

50. Susan B. Carter et al., *Historical Statistics of the United States Millennial Edition Online*, ed. Joshua L. Rosenbloom (New York: Cambridge University Press, 2006).

51. Alasdair Roberts, *The End of Protest* (Ithaca, NY: Cornell University Press, 2013), ch. 2. Graham Adams called the years 1900–1915 "the age of industrial violence": Graham Adams, *Age of Industrial Violence, 1910–15* (New York: Columbia University Press, 1966), 228.

52. Commission on Industrial Relations, *Final Report* (Washington, DC: Government Printing Office, 1916), 29–30.

53. Bryce, *The American Commonwealth*, 2:355.

54. The work of the federal Bureau of Corporations after 1903 is also a good example.

55. Haynes, *Election of Senators*, 110.

56. "President Favors Direct Primaries," *Watertown (NY) Daily Times*, June 5, 1913, 2.

57. W. S. U'Ren, "Remarks on Mr. Herbert Croly's Paper on 'State Political Reorganization,'" *Proceedings of the American Political Science Association* 8 (1911): 136–139, 138.

58. Chester L. Jones, *Readings on Parties and Elections in the United States* (New York: Macmillan, 1912), 71. See also Allen H. Eaton, *The Oregon System* (Chicago: A. C. McClurg, 1912), 85.

59. Alan Ware, *The American Direct Primary* (New York: Cambridge University Press, 2002), 117–119. See also Charles E. Merriam and Louise Overacker, *Primary Elections* (Chicago: University of Chicago Press, 1928).

60. Eldon Cobb Evans, *A History of the Australian Ballot System in the United States* (Chicago: University of Chicago Press, 1917), 19–27. See also Lionel E. Fredman, *The Australian Ballot: The Story of an American Reform* (East Lansing: Michigan State University Press, 1968); Alan Ware, "Anti-Partism and Party Control of Political Reform in the United States: The Case of the Australian Ballot," *British Journal of Political Science* 30, no. 1 (2000): 1–29, 9.

61. "Oklahoma Outbursts," *Tulsa (OK) World*, April 9, 1920, 4.

62. Mark Sullivan, "Comment on Congress," *Collier's*, June 25, 1910, 9.

63. R. Earl McClendon, "Violations of Secrecy in Re Senate Executive Sessions, 1789-1929," *American Historical Review* 51, no. 1 (1945): 35–54, 35.

64. Dorman B. Eaton, *Secret Sessions of the Senate* (New York: H. Bessey, 1886), 8.

65. C. R. Atkinson and C. A. Beard, "The Syndication of the Speakership," *Political Science Quarterly* 26, no. 3 (1911): 381–414; "Press Opinion," *St. Albans (VT) Messenger*, March 31, 1910, 12.

66. Rauschenbusch, *Christianity and the Social Crisis*, 263.

67. On state precedents, see Frederick C. Clark, "State Railroad Commissions and How They May Be Made Effective," *Publications of the American Economic Association* 6, no. 6 (1891): 11–110.

68. "Roosevelt Stated His Political Creed in Speech at Osawatomie," *Grand Forks (ND) Daily Herald*, September 1, 1910.

69. W. W. Thornton, *A Treatise on the Sherman Anti-Trust Act* (Cincinnati, OH: W. H. Anderson, 1913), iii.

70. Arthur M. Johnson, "Theodore Roosevelt and the Bureau of Corporations," *Mississippi Valley Historical Review* 45, no. 4 (1959): 571–590.

71. Gilbert H. Montague, "Business and Politics at Home and Abroad," *Annals of the American Academy of Political and Social Science* 42 (1912): 156–171, 171.

72. "New Impetus to Business," *Springfield (MA) Daily News*, December 22, 1913, 1.

73. "Income Tax Defended," *Oregonian* (Portland, OR), March 25, 1910, 2. See also Holmes, "The Concentration of Wealth," 600.

74. E. J. Shriver, "The Income Tax," *Single Tax Review*, January 1914, 40–42, 41.

75. Bryce, *The American Commonwealth*, 3:289–301.

76. Keyssar, *Right to Vote*, tables A17 to A20.

77. Ida H. Harper, ed., *History of Woman Suffrage*, vol. 5, *1900–1920* (New York: Fowler & Wells, 1922), 2.

78. Sara H. Graham, *Woman Suffrage and the New Democracy* (New Haven, CT: Yale University Press, 1996); Harper, *History of Woman Suffrage*, 253, 287, and 315; Keyssar, *Right to Vote*, 197 and 203.

79. "Suffragists Have 'Strong Machine,'" *Boston (MA) Herald*, April 29, 1917, 23.

80. Keyssar, *Right to Vote*, 39–40, 218–219.

81. Harper, *History of Woman Suffrage*, 59.

82. "Suffrage a Good Thing," *Kalamazoo (MI) Gazette*, June 26, 1896, 9.

83. Harper, *History of Woman Suffrage*, 144.

84. "Equal Suffrage Notes," *Augusta (GA) Chronicle*, September 23, 1917, 14.

85. Janet Beer, Anne-Marie Ford, and Katherine Joslin, *American Feminism: Key Source Documents, 1848–1920*, 4 vols. (New York: Routledge,

2003), 345; Helen John, "Women Jeered and Jostled in Suffrage Parade," *Trenton (NJ) Evening Times*, March 4, 1913, 10.

86. Inez Haynes Gillmore, *The Story of the Woman's Party* (New York: Harcourt, Brace, 1921), 207–208.

87. "Anne Martin Backs Pickets," *Reno (NV) Evening Gazette*, June 29, 1917, 11.

88. "Text of President's Appeal for Federal Suffrage Amendment," *Boston (MA) Herald*, October 1, 1918, 13.

89. Just four states—Georgia, Mississippi, Alabama, and South Carolina—accounted for 40 percent of the African American population in 1900. The center of the African American population, a 1904 Census study concluded, was just east of Birmingham, Alabama: Walter F. Willcox and William E. B. Du Bois, *Negroes in the United States* (Washington, DC: Bureau of the Census, 1904), 19–25.

90. The amendment said that the representation of states in Congress and the electoral college would be reduced if the right to vote was denied to adult male citizens.

91. Eric Foner, *Reconstruction: America's Unfinished Revolution, 1863–1877*, 3rd ed. (New York: Harper Perennial Modern Classics, 2002), 353–355.

92. Jennifer Manning and Colleen Shogan, *African American Members of the United States Congress, 1870–2012* (Washington, DC: Congressional Research Service, November 26, 2012), 56.

93. For a description of the final phase of federal intervention, see Clarence C. Clendenen, "President Hayes' 'Withdrawal' of the Troops: An Enduring Myth," *South Carolina Historical Magazine* 70, no. 4 (1969): 240–250.

94. William E. B. Du Bois, *Black Reconstruction in America* (New York: Oxford University Press, 1935).

95. "What Is Bulldozing?," *Chicago (IL) Daily Inter Ocean*, November 15, 1876, 4.

96. Mark W. Summers, *The Ordeal of the Reunion* (Chapel Hill: University of North Carolina Press), 386–390.

97. Walter C. Hamm, "The Three Phases of Colored Suffrage," *North American Review* 168, no. 508 (1899): 285–296; Albert E. McKinley, "Two New Southern Constitutions," *Political Science Quarterly* 18, no. 3 (1903): 480–511; Keyssar, *Right to Vote*, 111–112. For an assessment of the effect of these measures, see Hanes Walton, Sherman C. Puckett, and Donald R. Deskins, *The African American Electorate: A Statistical History*, 2 vols. (Thousand Oaks, CA: CQ Press, 2012), ch. 17.

98. "Reduction of Southern Representation," *Kansas Semi-Weekly Capital*, July 3, 1900, 4.

99.   Cong. Rec., February 26, 1900, 2242–2245.

100. "When Law Protects Crime," *Sullivan (IN) Democrat*, June 14, 1906, 2.

101. George B. Tindall, "The Campaign for the Disfranchisement of Negroes in South Carolina," *Journal of Southern History* 15, no. 2 (1949): 212–234.

102. Du Bois, *Black Reconstruction in America*, 694.

103. John M. Mecklin, *Democracy and Race Friction* (New York: Macmillan, 1914), 11.

104. Henry Cabot Lodge and T. V. Powderly, "The Federal Election Bill," *North American Review* 151, no. 406 (1890): 257–273; Richard E. Welch Jr., "The Federal Elections Bill of 1890: Postscripts and Prelude," *Journal of American History* 52, no. 3 (1965): 511–526. Keyssar, *Right to Vote*, 108–111.

105. Charles F. Adams Jr. to James Bryce, December 31, 1913. Bryce Papers, MSS Bryce U.S.A. 20, fols. 148–150.

106. Robert J. Norrell, *Up from History: The Life of Booker T. Washington* (Cambridge, MA: Belknap Press, 2009), 123–128; Booker T. Washington, "Colored Men Advance," *New York Herald*, October 20, 1895, 5.

107. W. E. B. Du Bois, *The Souls of Black Folk* (Chicago: A. C. McClurg, 1903), 51.

108. "The Niagara Movement," *Chicago (IL) Broad Ax*, August 5, 1905, 1.

109. W. E. B. Du Bois, "The Crisis," *The Crisis*, November 1910, 10.

110. Norrell, *Up from History: The Life of Booker T. Washington*, 392, 407, 422.

111. "The Colored Voter and the Presidency," *Harrisburg (PA) Patriot*, August 15, 1912, 2.

112. John M. Cooper, *Woodrow Wilson: A Biography* (New York: Alfred A. Knopf, 2009), 205, 272–273, 407–409, 489, 510. See also Morton Sosna, "The South in the Saddle: Racial Politics during the Wilson Years," *Wisconsin Magazine of History* 54, no. 1 (1970): 30–49; Kathleen Long Wolgemuth, "Woodrow Wilson's Appointment Policy and the Negro," *Journal of Southern History* 24, no. 4 (1958): 457–471; "For Action on Race Riot Peril," *New York Times*, October 5, 1919; Department of Justice, *Investigation Activities of the Department of Justice* (Washington, DC: Department of Justice, 1919), 162.

113. Noriko Kawamura, "Wilsonian Idealism and Japanese Claims at the Paris Peace Conference," *Pacific Historical Review* 66, no. 4 (1997): 503–526, 520.

114. Yuichiro Onishi, "The New Negro of the Pacific: How African Americans Forged Cross-Racial Solidarity with Japan, 1917–1922," *Journal of African American History* 92, no. 2 (2007): 191–213, 199–200.

115. Ernest McKinney, "The Election Comes," *The Crisis*, October 1920, 274–276; W. E. B. Du Bois, "The Unreal Campaign," *The Crisis*, December 1920, 54–56, 56.

116. In 2015, there was a vigorous debate about demands to rename Princeton University's Woodrow Wilson School of Public and International Affairs, given his opinions and record on race relations.

117. J. Clay Smith, *Emancipation: The Making of the Black Lawyer, 1844–1944* (Philadelphia: University of Pennsylvania Press, 1993), 217.

118. *Guinn v. United States*, 238 U.S. 347 (1915).

119. Isabel Wilkerson, "When Will the North Face Its Racism?," *New York Times*, January 10, 2015. See also Nicholas Lemann, *The Promised Land: The Great Black Migration and How It Changed America* (New York: A. A. Knopf, 1991); Isabel Wilkerson, *The Warmth of Other Suns: The Epic Story of America's Great Migration* (New York: Random House, 2010).

120. Joseph Lee, "Immigration and Assimilation: Some Dangers from Unrestricted Inpour," *Springfield (MA) Republican*, July 6, 1908, 11.

121. Federal jurisdiction was confirmed by a Supreme Court decision, *Henderson v. City of New York*, 92 U.S. 259 (1875).

122. John Hawks Noble, "The Present State of the Immigration Question," *Political Science Quarterly* 7, no. 2 (1892): 232–243.

123. After 1855, immigrant wives of American citizens were simply deemed to be citizens as well. Of course, the 1805 law did not apply to imported slaves. The importation of slaves was prohibited in 1807.

124. Leon Aylsworth, "The Passing of Alien Suffrage," *American Political Science Review* 25, no. 1 (1931): 114–116; Keyssar, *Right to Vote*, 32–33 and table A.12.

125. Joint Special Committee to Investigate Chinese Immigration, *Report* (Washington, DC: Government Printing Office, 1877), v.

126. The 1882 law imposed a ten-year ban on immigration that was renewed once and then made permanent in 1902.

127. Campbell Gibson and Emily Lennon, *Historical Census Statistics on the Foreign-Born Population of the United States, 1850–1990*, Population Division Working Paper No. 29 (Washington, DC: Bureau of the Census, 1999), table 19.

128. Carter et al., *Historical Statistics of the United States Millennial Edition Online*.

129. "Opinions in Wakefield," *Boston (MA) Herald*, September 9, 1901, 8.

130. The Anarchist Exclusion Act of 1903.

131. Edward A. Ross, "Immigrants in Politics," *Century Illustrated Magazine*, January 1914, 392–398, 396.

132. Philip Davis and Bettha Schwartz, *Immigration and Americanization: Selected Readings* (Boston, MA: Ginn, 1920), 322–323. For a more sympathetic view of the relationship between urban political machines and immigrants, see Richard Hofstadter, *The Age of Reform* (New York: Vintage Books, 1955), 181–188.

133. Henry Cabot Lodge, "Efforts to Restrict Undesirable Immigration," *Century Magazine*, January 1904, 466–473, 469.

134. Immigration Commission, *Statements and Recommendations Submitted by Societies and Organizations Interested in the Subject of Immigration* (Washington, DC: Government Printing Office, 1911), 135.

135. Ibid., IX.129.

136. Ibid., I.14, I.491, I.541.

137. R. P. Bonham, "Protest against Alien Vote Made," *Oregonian* (Portland, OR), November 2, 1914, 15.

138. Keyssar, *Right to Vote*, 136–138; Aylsworth, "The Passing of Alien Suffrage," 114.

139. American Society of International Law, "An Act to Establish a Bureau of Immigration and Naturalization, and to Provide for a Uniform Rule for the Naturalization of Aliens throughout the United States. Approved June 29, 1906," *American Journal of International Law* 1, no. 1 (1907): 31–47.

140. This law was strengthened in 1918: Howard L. Bevis, "The Deportation of Aliens," *University of Pennsylvania Law Review and American Law Register* 68, no. 2 (1920): 97–119.

141. Kunal M. Parker, *Making Foreigners: Immigration and Citizenship Law in America, 1600–2000* (New York: Cambridge University Press), 170; Patrick Weil, *The Sovereign Citizen: Denaturalization and the Origins of the American Republic* (Philadelphia: University of Pennsylvania Press, 2013), 55–76.

142. Robert D. Ward, "The New Immigration Act," *North American Review* 185, no. 619 (1907): 587–593.

143. Immigration Commission, *Report* (Washington, DC: Government Printing Office, 1911), 45–47.

144. Davis and Schwartz, *Immigration and Americanization*, 380.
145. Henry Pratt Fairchild, "The Immigration Law of 1924," *Quarterly Journal of Economics* 38, no. 4 (1924): 653–665.
146. Carter et al., *Historical Statistics of the United States Millennial Edition Online*.
147. Jacob G. Schurman, *Philippine Affairs: A Retrospect and Outlook* (New York: Charles Scribner's Sons, 1902), 82–86.
148. John T. Morgan, "What Shall We Do with the Conquered Islands?," *North American Review* 166, no. 499 (1898): 641–649, 647.
149. Through the so-called "Insular cases" decided by the Supreme Court in 1901. For an early critique of these cases, see George F. Edmunds, "The Insular Cases," *North American Review* 173, no. 537 (1901): 145–153.
150. Cong. Rec., February 26, 1900, 2244.
151. Declaration of Philippine Independence, June 12, 1898.
152. Morgan, "What Shall We Do with the Conquered Islands?," 644.
153. James H. Blount, "Philippine Independence: When?," *North American Review* 184, no. 607 (1907): 135–149.
154. Stuart Creighton Miller, *"Benevolent Assimilation": The American Conquest of the Philippines, 1899–1903* (New Haven, CT: Yale University Press, 1982), 192; David Reynolds, *America, Empire of Liberty: A New History of the United States* (New York: Basic Books, 2009), 297–298.
155. John M. Gates, "War-Related Deaths in the Philippines, 1898–1902," *Pacific Historical Review* 53, no. 3 (1984): 367–378. For a much higher estimate, see Matthew Smallman-Raynor and Andrew D. Cliff, "The Philippines Insurrection and the 1902–4 Cholera Epidemic: Part I— Epidemiological Diffusion Processes in War," *Journal of Historical Geography* 24, no. 1 (1998): 69–89, 70.
156. United States Senate, *Session Laws of the Second Philippine Legislature* (Washington, DC: Government Printing Office, 1911), 87.
157. Philippine Organic Act of 1902, sec. 7. Parts of the Moro population of the Philippines, an indigenous Muslim group, continued to resist US authority until 1913: James R. Arnold, *The Moro War: How America Battled a Muslim Insurgency in the Philippine Jungle, 1902–1913* (New York: Bloomsbury Press, 2011).
158. Schurman, *Philippine Affairs: A Retrospect and Outlook*, 33.
159. J. A. Robertson, "The Effect in the Philippines of the Senate 'Organic Act,'" *Journal of Race Development* 6, no. 4 (1916): 370–387; Cooper, *Woodrow Wilson: A Biography*, 249.

160. The 1934 law provided for independence ten years after the drafting of a new constitution, which was done in 1935. Even if the war had not intervened, therefore, independence would not have been achieved until 1945.

161. Bryce, *The American Commonwealth*, 3:141.

162. Samuel P. Huntington, *Political Order in Changing Societies* (New Haven, CT: Yale University Press, 1968), 7.

163. The same was true of Chinese immigrants, who were denied the right to obtain citizenship and vote.

164. Bryce, *The American Commonwealth*, 1:2, 2:353.

165. "We live in a universe of changing environment, and political institutions, like other forms of life, must grow": Frederick Albert Cleveland, *The Growth of Democracy in the United States* (Chicago: Quadrangle Press, 1898), xii–xiii, 114, 242–244, 386–388.

166. See Frederick Jackson Turner, *The Frontier in American History* (New York: Henry Holt, 1920), 2, 205–206, 243–244, 321. Charles A. Beard had a similar but narrower view, describing the evolution of political institutions in response to "economic forces" alone: Charles A. Beard, *An Economic Interpretation of the Constitution of the United States* (New York: Macmillan, 1913); Charles A. Beard, *Contemporary American History, 1877–1913* (New York: Macmillan, 1914), 32. Thorstein Veblen also believed that "the scheme of institutions" was subject to "unremitting changes and adaptations": Thorstein Veblen, *The Instinct of Workmanship, and the State of the Industrial Arts* (New York: Macmillan, 1914), 17–18.

CHAPTER 3

1. Dave Johnson, "Longest Flight," *Idaho Sunday Statesman*, May 23, 1948, 9.

2. United Press, "Air Force Unveils B-36 Giant Bomber," *Richmond (VA) Times-Dispatch*, October 9, 1948, 7.

3. Douglas Holdstock and Frank Barnaby, *Hiroshima and Nagasaki: Retrospect and Prospect* (Portland, OR: Frank Cass, 1995), 2.

4. Don Whitehead, "A-Bomb Sinks 2 Ships, Damages 16," *Boston (MA) Herald*, July 1, 1946, 1.

5. Fred Norris Robinson, "Retrospect and Prospect," *PMLA* 60 (1945): 1292–1305, 1302.

6. Chester Wilmot, "If NATO Had to Fight," *Foreign Affairs* 31, no. 2 (1953): 200–214, 213.

7. James Bryce, *The American Commonwealth*, new ed. (New York: Macmillan, 1914), 1:295.

8. United Press, "Air Force Unveils B-36 Giant Bomber."

9. For more detailed histories of this period, see Barry Dean Karl, *The Uneasy State: The United States from 1915 to 1945* (Chicago: University of Chicago Press, 1983); Bruce A. Ackerman, *We the People*, vol. 2, *Transformations* (Cambridge, MA: Belknap Press, 1998); Ira Katznelson, *Fear Itself: The New Deal and the Origins of Our Time* (New York: Liveright, 2013); J. Adam Tooze, *The Deluge: The Great War and the Remaking of Global Order, 1916–1931* (New York: Viking, 2014); and also the three-volumes of *The Age of Roosevelt* by Arthur Schlesinger Jr.

10. "State capacity . . . is the institutional ability of the state to carry out various policies that deliver benefits and services to households and firms": Timothy Besley and Torsten Persson, *Pillars of Prosperity: The Political Economics of Development Clusters* (Princeton, NJ: Princeton University Press, 2011), 6. "State capacity refers to the ability of states to apply and implement policy choices within the territorial boundaries they claim to govern": Matthias vom Hau, *State Capacity and Inclusive Development: New Challenges and Directions*, Working Paper No. 02 (Manchester, UK: Effective States and Inclusive Development Research Centre, February 2013). "By state capacity we mean the degree of control state agents exercise over persons, activities, and resources within their government's jurisdiction": Doug McAdam, Sidney G. Tarrow, and Charles Tilly, *Dynamics of Contention* (New York: Cambridge University Press, 2001). Note that all of these definitions tend to emphasize the exercise of authority within national borders; that is, the execution of domestic policies. There is no reason to limit the definition in this way. The development of military forces or a diplomatic corps can also be viewed as exercises in capacity building.

11. Roy F. Nichols, "Book Review," *Mississippi Valley Historical Review* 28, no. 1 (1941): 127–128, 128.

12. Frederick Cleveland, "Creating Governmental Efficiency," *New Republic*, July 29, 1916, 326–328, 326.

13. John M. Gaus, "The Present Status of the Study of Public Administration in the United States," *American Political Science Review* 25, no. 1 (1931): 120–134.

14. Bryce, *The American Commonwealth*, 1:20.

15. Harold Laski, *Democracy in Crisis* (Chapel Hill: University of North Carolina Press, 1933), 47 and 52. In a similar vein, the British economist

John A. Hobson wrote: "There is in every people a half-conscious recognition of the fact that the will of the people is not really operative unless it is able to perform concrete acts of government": J. A. Hobson, *The Crisis of Liberalism: New Issues of Democracy* (London: P. S. King, 1909), 15.

16. Bryce, *The American Commonwealth*, 2:281.

17. *Historical Statistics of the United States*, tables Ad1, Aa46, Df931, Ba821, and Ba826. The industrial workforce includes manufacturing and railways.

18. George Gilboy and Eric Heginbotham, "China's Coming Transformation," *Foreign Affairs* 80, no. 4 (2001): 26–39; George Gilboy and Eric Heginbotham, "China's Dilemma," *Foreign Affairs*, October 14, 2010, http://www.foreignaffairs.com/articles/66773/george-j-gilboy-and-eric-heginbotham/chinas-dilemma; Susan L. Shirk, *China: Fragile Superpower* (New York: Oxford University Press, 2007).

19. Bryce, *The American Commonwealth*, 1:420.

20. Walter Edward Weyl, *The New Democracy* (New York: Macmillan, 1914), 1, 4, 313–318.

21. Walter Lippmann, *Drift and Mastery* (New York: M. Kennerley, 1914), 64, 170–171, 211, 267.

22. Edward Mandell House, *Philip Dru, Administrator: A Story of Tomorrow* (New York: B. W. Huebsch, 1912).

23. Graham Wallas, *The Great Society: A Psychological Analysis* (New York: Macmillan, 1914), 14, 289.

24. A. Hamon and H. Hamon, "The Political Situation in France," *American Journal of Sociology* 11, no. 1 (1905): 107–128, 107.

25. Georges Sorel, *Reflections on Violence* (New York: B. W. Huebsch, 1912).

26. Gladys M. Kammerer, "The Political Theory of Vichy," *Journal of Politics* 5, no. 4 (1943): 407–434, 411–413; Denis Gwynn, "A Prophet of Reaction: Charles Maurras," *Studies* 11, no. 44 (1922): 523–540, 530–532.

27. Arthur Moeller van den Bruck, *Der Preussische Stil* (1916).

28. David Stevenson, *1914–1918: The History of the First World War* (London: Penguin Books, 2012), 46–47.

29. Frederick Scott Oliver, *Ordeal by Battle* (London: Macmillan, 1915), 156.

30. Emile Faguet, *The Cult of Incompetence* (New York: E. P. Dutton, 1916), 15.

31. Albert Bushnell Hart, *The War in Europe, Its Causes and Results* (New York: D. Appleton, 1914), 215.

32. Henry Raymond Mussey, *National Conference on War Economy: A Series of Addresses and Papers Presented at the National Conference on War Economy Held under the Joint Auspices of the Bureau of Municipal Research and the Academy of Political Science in the City of New York, July 5–6, 1918* (Academy of Political Science, 1918), 29.

33. Edwin A. Alderman, "Can Democracy Be Organized?," in *Proceedings of the Sixteenth Annual Session of the State Literary and Historical Association of North Carolina*, ed. R. D. W. Connor (Raleigh, NC: Edwards & Broughton, 1915), 31–41, 38–40.

34. "Can Democracy Fight?," *Lawrence (KS) Journal-World*, June 10, 1940, 4.

35. G. T. Garratt, *Mussolini's Roman Empire* (Harmondsworth, UK: Penguin, 1938), 10. See also Karl R. Popper, *The Open Society and Its Enemies*, 2 vols. (London: G. Routledge, 1945), 2:59–67.

36. X (George F. Kennan), "The Sources of Soviet Conduct," *Foreign Affairs* 25, no. 4 (1947): 566–582.

37. Robert Strausz-Hupé, "The Great Powers in the New World Order," *Annals of the American Academy of Political and Social Science* 257 (1948): 47–56, 53.

38. "Taft Eulogizes the Regular Soldiers," *Denver (CO) Post*, May 31, 1909, 1.

39. James A. Drain, "Conscription Must Come," *Arms and the Man* 54, no. 12 (1915): 229.

40. In his farewell address of 1796, President George Washington asked: "Why quit our own to stand upon foreign ground? Why, by interweaving our destiny with that of any part of Europe, entangle our peace and prosperity in the toils of European ambition, rivalship, interest, humor or caprice?" Five years later, in his first inaugural address, Thomas Jefferson promised "honest friendship with all nations, entangling alliances with none."

41. Senator Joseph Underwood of Kentucky, in *Congressional Globe*, December 3, 1851, p. 26. "Possibly no nation in the world . . . is more desirous of being permitted to mind its own business than the United States": *The Dial*, November 5, 1900, p. 305.

42. Generally, see Russell Frank Weigley, *History of the United States Army* (New York: Macmillan, 1967), ch. 16.

43. "The 'iron ring' around Germany has passed into history.... Diplomatically and militarily, Germany has the initiative. It is her move in the great game of world war": Karl Von Wiegand, "Big Iron Ring Broken: Huns Have Initiative," *Seattle (WA) Daily Times* (1918): 9.

44. Andrew H. Bartels, "The Office of Price Administration and the Legacy of the New Deal, 1939–1946," *Public Historian* 5, no. 3 (1983): 5–29.

45. Irvin Stewart, *Organizing Scientific Research for War: The Administrative History of the Office of Scientific Research and Development* (Boston, MA: Little, Brown, 1948).

46. War Department, *War Report of the Office of Strategic Services*, 2 vols. (New York: Walker, 1976).

47. Martin Walker, *The Cold War: A History*, American ed. (New York: H. Holt, 1994), 29–58.

48. "War without End," *Canton (OH) Repository*, September 2, 1949, 6.

49. Michael J. Hogan, *A Cross of Iron: Harry S. Truman and the Origins of the National Security State, 1945–1954* (New York: Cambridge University Press, 1998), 23–68.

50. Amy B. Zegart, *Flawed by Design: The Evolution of the CIA, JCS, and NSC* (Stanford, CA: Stanford University Press, 1999), 163–184.

51. George B. Galloway, "The Operation of the Legislative Reorganization Act of 1946," *American Political Science Review* 45, no. 1 (1951): 41–68.

52. Rossiter Clinton, "The Impact of Mobilization on the Constitutional System," *Proceedings of the Academy of Political Science* 24, no. 3 (1951): 61–69; Harold D. Lasswell, "Does the Garrison State Threaten Civil Rights?," *Annals of the American Academy of Political and Social Science* 275 (1951): 111–116.

53. The address is reproduced and analyzed in: James Ledbetter, *Unwarranted Influence: Dwight D. Eisenhower and the Military-Industrial Complex* (New Haven, CT: Yale University Press, 2011).

54. *Everybody's Magazine* 10, no. 2 (February 1904): 278.

55. Clark was born in 1850. For a list of panics, see Clément Juglar, *A Brief History of Panics and Their Periodical Occurrence in the United States* (New York: G. P. Putnam, 1916), 20. For a description of the depressions, see Harold Glenn Moulton, *Principles of Money and Banking*, 2d impression ed. (Chicago: University of Chicago Press, 1917), 147–150. See also J. Steven Landefeld, "GDP: One of the Great Inventions of the 20th Century," *Survey of Current Business* 80 (January 2000): 6–14, 8.

56. "Pointed Straight out of the Woods," *Automobile Topics*, 1921, 527–529. See also James Grant, *The Forgotten Depression: 1921, the Crash That Cured Itself* (New York, Simon and Schuster, 2014).

57. Associated Press, "Rioting Marks Red Thursday in U.S. Cities," *Tampa (FL) Morning Tribune*, March 7, 1930, 1.

58. Walker S. Burl, "Bonus Army Is In Full Retreat; Camps Burned; Troops Use Gas," *Cleveland (OH) Plain Dealer*, July 29, 1932, 1.

59. Alasdair Roberts, *The End of Protest* (Ithaca, NY: Cornell University Press, 2013), ch. 2.

60. *New State Ice Co. v. Liebmann*, 285 U.S. 262 (1932), at 306.

61. Popper, *The Open Society and Its Enemies*, 2:120.

62. "Semi-Dictator?," *Barron's*, February 13, 1933, 12.

63. *Springfield (MA) Republican*, March 30, 1933, p. 4.

64. *Fortune*, May 1932.

65. Charles P. Stewart, "American Dictatorship Seriously Considered in Official Quarters," *Rockford (IL) Register-Republic*, May 14, 1932, 6.

66. Wolfgang Schivelbusch, *Three New Deals* (New York: Metropolitan Books, 2006), 31.

67. Inaugural address, March 4, 1933.

68. Edmund Wilson, *The American Earthquake* (Garden City, NY: Doubleday, 1958), 479.

69. "Congress . . . has made him the dictator of the economic life of the country": Lindsay Rogers, *Crisis Government* (New York: W. W. Norton, 1934), 60, 128, 130, 160.

70. Address at Oglethorpe University, May 22, 1932. Available at http://newdeal.feri.org/speeches/1932d.htm.

71. Timothy Mitchell, *Carbon Democracy* (New York: Verso, 2011), 124.

72. J. Adam Tooze, *Statistics and the German State, 1900–1945: The Making of Modern Economic Knowledge* (New York: Cambridge University Press, 2001), 1. See also Adam Tooze, "Imagining National Economies," in *Imagining Nations*, ed. Geoffrey Cubbitt (Manchester, UK: Manchester University Press, 1998), 212–228.

73. "Proposes Daily Business Reports," *Boston (MA) Herald*, October 6, 1921, 9.

74. Carol S. Carson, "The History of the United States National Income and Products Accounts," *Review of Income and Wealth* 21, no. 2 (1975): 153–181, 156.

75. Generally, see James W. Knowles, "Recent Developments in American Economic Statistics," *Incorporated Statistician* 9, no. 2 (1959): 35–46, 39–40; Carson, "The History of the United States National Income and Products Accounts"; Landefeld, "GDP: One of the Great Inventions of the 20th Century."

76. See Arthur D. Gayer, "Fiscal Policies," *American Economic Review* 28, no. 1 (1938): 90–112; Jay Franklin, "Seven Economists Persuade President to New Deal Spending Policy," *Washington (DC) Evening Star*, 1939, 11. The language of "pump-priming" was used as early as 1933.

77. Frederick A. Cleveland, "Evolution of the Budget Idea in the United States," *Annals of the American Academy of Political and Social Science* 62 (1915): 15–35, 21. For background on state initiatives and the effect of war finances on the budget reform movement, see Mussey, *National Conference on War Economy*.

78. "The [General Accounting Office, headed by McCarl] is a survival from pre-New Deal days, when economy was the watchword. . . . The GAO has been a nuisance to the Roosevelt folks. . . . McCarl has been 'anti' throughout": Charles P. Stewart, "Brown, Henderson Appointments Win General Acclaim," *Columbus (OH) Daily Enquirer*, April 7, 1939, 6.

79. "Last summer everyone was talking about pump-priming. The Public Works Administration was going to do it. . . . But the PWA money didn't flow out. . . . All sorts of things united to delay the actual expenditure of money, and the pump didn't get primed": United Press, "Hopkins Puts over CWA Program," *Charlotte (NC) Observer*, December 16, 1933, 2.

80. The Treasury calculated that the ratio of returns filed in 1933 to the total population was 3 percent: United States Treasury, *Statistics of Income for 1933* (Washington, DC: Government Printing Office, 1935), 5.

81. "Initials Do Heavy Duty under Roosevelt," *Oregonian* (Portland, OR), February 22, 1934, 4.

82. Milton Friedman and Anna Schwartz, *A Monetary History of the United States, 1867–1960* (Princeton, NJ: Princeton University Press, 1963), 321.

83. Chang-Tai Hsieh and Christina D. Romer, "Was the Federal Reserve Constrained by the Gold Standard during the Great Depression? Evidence from the 1932 Open Market Purchase Program," *Journal of Economic History* 66, no. 1 (2006): 140–176, 170–172; Gerald Epstein and Thomas Ferguson, "Monetary Policy, Loan Liquidation, and Industrial Conflict: The Federal Reserve and the Open Market Operations of 1932," *Journal of Economic History* 44, no. 4 (1984): 957–983, 968–972.

84. Because of the appointments, there was "some basis for the statement, frequently made, that the Federal Reserve Board had come largely under the domination of the Administration": Frederick A. Bradford, "The Banking Act of 1935," *American Economic Review* 25, no. 4 (1935): 661–672, 663. The appointments included a new board chairman, Marriner Eccles, who previously served as an appointee in the Roosevelt administration and who shared the view that the economy could survive only "under a modified capitalistic system controlled and regulated from the top by government": Arthur M. Schlesinger, *The Crisis of the Old Order, 1919-1933,* Mariner Books ed., *The Age of Roosevelt* (Boston: Houghton Mifflin, 2003), 189. Eccles served as chairman until 1948.

85. "The Federal Reserve was less independent of the administration from 1934 to 1941 than in any other peacetime period": Allan H. Meltzer, *A History of the Federal Reserve* (Chicago: University of Chicago Press, 2003), 1:490. Donald Kettl observes that by 1948, the Federal Reserve had "gone from an era when the president reverenced its independence . . . to a time when the agency had little if any independence": Donald F. Kettl, *Leadership at the Fed* (New Haven, CT: Yale University Press, 1986), 65.

86. Raymond Clapper, "Recovery Program Puts 2,000,000 to Work in 4 Months," *Seattle (WA) Daily Times,* October 16, 1933.

87. Luther H. Gulick, "Politics, Administration, and the 'New Deal,'" *Annals of the American Academy of Political and Social Science* 169 (1933): 55–66, 65.

88. An early illustration: James M. Beck, *Our Wonderland of Bureaucracy* (New York: Macmillan, 1932).

89. Pendleton Herring, "A Prescription for Modern Democracy," *Annals of the American Academy of Political and Social Science* 180 (1935): 138–148, 141.

90. President's Committee on Administrative Management, *Report* (Washington, DC: President's Committee on Administrative Management, 1937), 1.

91. On the Federal Reserve, see Bradford, "The Banking Act of 1935," 665.

92. Morton J. Horwitz, *The Transformation of American Law, 1870-1960* (New York: Oxford University Press, 1992), 230–232.

93. Galloway, "The Operation of the Legislative Reorganization Act of 1946."

94. G. Gould Lincoln, "House Votes to Debate Merger Bill after 'No Dictator' Pledge," *Washington (DC) Evening Star,* March 31, 1938, 1. On this controversy, see Richard Polenberg, *Reorganizing Roosevelt's Government* (Cambridge, MA: Harvard University Press, 1966).

95. Institute of Labor and Industrial Relations, *The Employment Act of 1946* (Urbana: University of Illinois, 1947), 6 and 10.

96. John M. Barry, *The Great Influenza* (New York: Viking, 2004); Donna Hoyert, "75 Years of Mortality in the United States, 1935–2010," *NCHS Data Brief*, no. 88 (2012): 1–8.

97. Barry Trevelyan, Matthew Smallman-Raynor, and Andrew D. Cliff, "The Spatial Dynamics of Poliomyelitis in the United States: From Epidemic Emergence to Vaccine-Induced Retreat, 1910–1971," *Annals of the Association of American Geographers. Association of American Geographers* 95, no. 2 (2005): 269–293; Tony Gould, *A Summer Plague: Polio and Its Survivors* (New Haven, CT: Yale University Press, 1995).

98. Drew Pearson and Robert Allen, "Permanent Drought," *Greensboro (NC) Daily News*, August 3, 1936; Donald Worster, *Dust Bowl: The Southern Plains in the 1930s* (New York: Oxford University Press, 1979), 12.

99. For similar assessments, see Ackerman, *We the People*, vol. 2, *Transformations*, ch. 1; Tooze, *The Deluge: The Great War and the Remaking of Global Order, 1916–1931*, 505.

100. Harold Joseph Laski, *The American Democracy: A Commentary and an Interpretation* (New York: Viking Press, 1948), 77. See also pp. 98–99.

101. "The administrative state [was] a counterweight to democratic corruption and populist excess . . . a check on the factionalism, populism, and other excessives of party politics. . . . [and] a bulwark against the irrationalities of the electorate and their representatives." Mark Bevir, *Governance: A Very Short Introduction* (Oxford: Oxford University Press), 14, 57 and 103.

102. Samuel P. Huntington, *Political Order in Changing Societies* (New Haven, CT: Yale University Press, 1968), 7.

CHAPTER 4

1. Jimmy Carter, *Address to the Nation* (Washington, DC: Executive Office of the President, July 15, 1979).

2. For a less critical appraisal of the speech, see Kevin Mattson, *"What the Heck Are You Up To, Mr. President?": Jimmy Carter, America's "Malaise," and the Speech That Should Have Changed the Country* (New York: Bloomsbury, 2009), ch. 5.

3. James Reston, "The Crisis of Democracy," *New York Times*, June 29, 1975. See also James Reston, "The Crisis of Democracy," *New York Times*, March 3, 1974; James Reston, "A Basis for Compromise," *New York Times*, January 14, 1975, 43; Reston, "'The American Commonwealth' Revisited," *New York Times*, October 12, 1975, 239.

4. Norman Crossland, "Talk of Brandt Resigning," *The Guardian*, February 19, 1974, 4; Michel Crozier, Samuel P. Huntington, and Joji Watanuki, *The Crisis of Democracy* (New York: New York University Press, 1975), 2.

5. Arnold Toynbee, "After the Age of Affluence," *The Observer* (London), April 14, 1974, 12.

6. Michael Flamm, *Law and Order: Street Crime, Civil Unrest, and the Crisis of Liberalism in the 1960s* (New York: Columbia University Press, 2005).

7. White, *America in Search of Itself: The Making of the President, 1956-1980* (New York: Harper and Row, 1982), 148.

8. Kay M. Knickrehm and Devin Bent, "Voting Rights, Voter Turnout, and Realignment: The Impact of the 1965 Voting Rights Act," *Journal of Black Studies* 18, no. 3 (1988): 283–296, 283–286; Wendell W. Cultice, *Youth's Battle for the Ballot: A History of Voting Age in America* (New York: Greenwood Press, 1992). By the early 1970s, Alexander Keyssar says, "virtually all formal restrictions on suffrage rights of adult citizens were swept away": Alexander Keyssar, *The Right to Vote* (New York: Basic Books, 2009), 256 and 281–282.

9. Anne N. Costain, "The Struggle for a National Women's Lobby: Organizing a Diffuse Interest," *Western Political Quarterly* 33, no. 4 (1980): 476–491.

10. Richard C. Leone, "Public Interest Advocacy and the Regulatory Process," *Annals of the American Academy of Political and Social Science* 400 (1972): 46–58.

11. For example, see John F. Kennedy's commencement address at Yale University in June 1962, and Lyndon Johnson's State of the Union address in January 1964.

12. From Johnson's 1964 State of the Union address. Deployment data: Department of Defense, Deployment of Military Personnel by Country, as of September 30, 1968.

13. Julian E. Zelizer, *The Fierce Urgency of Now: Lyndon Johnson, Congress, and the Battle for the Great Society* (New York: Penguin Press, 2015), 322.

14. Expenditure: Office of Management and Budget Historical Tables, Table 1.1. Employment: Historical Statistics of the United States, Series Ea917.

15. Theodore H. White, *The Making of the President, 1968* (New York: Atheneum Publishers, 1969), 155.

16. Scott J. Spitzer, "Nixon's New Deal: Welfare Reform for the Silent Majority," *Presidential Studies Quarterly* 42, no. 3 (2012): 455–481, 456.

17. Hugh Davis Graham, "Richard Nixon and Civil Rights: Explaining an Enigma," *Presidential Studies Quarterly* 26, no. 1 (1996): 93–106, 94 and 96.

18. Patrick G. Donnelly, "The Origins of the Occupational Safety and Health Act of 1970," *Social Problems* 30, no. 1 (1982): 13–25; Russell E. Train, "The Environmental Record of the Nixon Administration," *Presidential Studies Quarterly* 26, no. 1 (1996): 185–196. On the "regulatory binge" of the Nixon era, see Theodore J. Lowi, *The End of the Republican Era, The Julian J. Rothbaum Distinguished Lecture Series* (Norman: University of Oklahoma Press, 1995), ch. 2.

19. Paul W. McCracken, "Economic Policy in the Nixon Years," *Presidential Studies Quarterly* 26, no. 1 (1996): 165–177; Donald F. Kettl, *Leadership at the Fed* (New Haven, CT: Yale University Press, 1986), 120–131; Douglas A. Irwin, "The Nixon Shock after Forty Years: The Import Surcharge Revisited," *World Trade Review* 12, no. 1 (2013): 29–56, 30.

20. American National Election Studies, "How much of the time do you think you can trust the government in Washington to do what is right?," http://www.electionstudies.org/nesguide/toptable/tab5a_1.htm.

21. David H. Donald, *Lincoln Reconsidered: Essays on the Civil War Era*, 3d ed., Vintage Civil War Library (New York: Vintage Books, 2001), 57.

22. Samuel Huntington, *Political Order in Changing Societies* (New Haven, CT: Yale University Press, 1968), 430–431.

23. Crozier, Huntington, and Watanuki, *Crisis of Democracy*, 2, 7–9, 113–115, 173–174. These arguments were reprised in Samuel P. Huntington, "The Democratic Distemper," *The Public Interest*, no. 41 (1975): 9–38.

24. "Members of the Trilateral Commission . . . nearly demolished a study that the commission itself had requested be made": "Democratic Goals Upheld by Panel," *New York Times*, June 1, 1975, 17.

25. Samuel Brittan, "The Economic Contradictions of Democracy," *British Journal of Political Science* 5 (1975): 129–159, 130, 147–148, 156. Similarly, Charles Goodhart and Rajendra Bhansali asserted that "a pure democracy with all parties seeking to maximize political support is doomed to increasing inflation and political disintegration": C. A. E. Goodhart and R. J. Bhansali, "Political Economy," *Political Studies* 18, no. 1 (1970): 43–106, 82. For further discussion of the overload thesis, see Richard Rose, "Overloaded Government: The Problem

Defined," *European Studies Newsletter* 5, no. 3 (1975): 13–18; Richard Rose, *Challenge to Governance: Studies in Overloaded Polities* (Beverly Hills, CA: Sage Publications, 1980); Anthony Birch, "Overload, Ungovernability and Delegitimation," *British Journal of Political Science* 14, no. 2 (1984): 135–160.

26. James Douglas, "The Overloaded Crown," *British Journal of Political Science* 6, no. 4 (1976): 483–505, 485.

27. Government has "come to be regarded ... as a sort of unlimited liability insurance company, in the business of insuring all persons at all times against every conceivable risk": Anthony King, "Overload: Problems of Governing in the 1970s," *Political Studies* 23, no. 2/3 (1975): 284–296, 286 and 294–295.

28. James Q. Wilson, "The Rise of the Bureaucratic State," *The Public Interest*, no. 41 (1975): 77–104, 103.

29. Robert Y. Fluno, "The Floundering Leviathan: Pluralism in an Age of Ungovernability," *Western Political Quarterly* 24, no. 3 (1971): 560–566, 560. Also: "The ironic fact is that the post-1937 political economy had produced unprecedented prosperity, and as the national output increased arithmetically the rate of rising expectation must have gone up geometrically.... Public authority was left to grapple with this alienating gap between expectation and reality": Theodore Lowi, "The Public Philosophy: Interest-Group Liberalism," *American Political Science Review* 61, no. 1 (1967): 5–24, 12.

30. Aaron B. Wildavsky, "The Past and Future Presidency," *The Public Interest*, no. 41 (1975): 56–76, 57, 62.

31. Aaron B. Wildavsky, "Government and the People," *Commentary* (1973): 25–32.

32. Daniel Bell, *The Cultural Contradictions of Capitalism* (New York: Basic Books, 1976), 25, 145, 235, 239–240. For a similar assessment of the forces operating on fiscal and monetary policy, see Norman H. Keehn, "Liberal Democracy: Impediment to Anti-Inflation Policy," *Polity* 13, no. 2 (1980): 207–229, 220–221. Amitai Etzioni also subscribed to the overload thesis, although his prescriptions differed: Amitai Etzioni, "Societal Overload: Sources, Components, and Corrections," *Political Science Quarterly* 92, no. 4 (1977): 607–631.

33. *Historical Statistics of the United States*, Series Cc1.

34. An overview of American economic policy during this period is provided by: Jeffrey A. Frieden, *Global Capitalism: Its Fall and Rise in the Twentieth Century* (New York: Norton, 2006).

35. White, *America in Search of Itself*, 138.
36. Wilhelm Röpke, *Against the Tide* (Chicago: H. Regnery, 1969), 97; Wilhelm Röpke, *The Social Crisis of Our Time* (London: W. Hodge, 1950), 181.
37. Robin Bade and Michael Parkin, *Central Bank Laws and Monetary Policy* (London, Canada: University of Western Ontario, 1985).
38. Alberto Alesina and Lawrence H. Summers, "Central Bank Independence and Macroeconomic Performance: Some Comparative Evidence," *Journal of Money, Credit and Banking* 25, no. 2 (1993): 151–162, 154.
39. Bade and Parkin, *Central Bank Laws and Monetary Policy*, 4.
40. Sucheen Patel, "An Independent Bank of England: The Political Process in Historical Perspective," *Public Policy and Administration* 23, no. 1 (2008): 27–41, 29.
41. Paul Bowles and Gordon White, "Central Bank Independence," *Journal of Development Studies* 31, no. 2 (1994): 235–264, 243.
42. Dennis Mueller, *Public Choice III* (New York: Cambridge University Press, 2003), 1–2.
43. Richard E. Wagner, "The 'Calculus of Consent': A Wicksellian Retrospective," *Public Choice* 56, no. 2 (1988): 153–166, 153.
44. James M. Buchanan, "The Balanced Budget Amendment: Clarifying the Arguments," *Public Choice* 90, no. 1/4 (1997): 117–138, 119.
45. William C. Mitchell, "Virginia, Rochester and Bloomington: Twenty-Five Years of Public Choice and Political Science," *Public Choice* 56, no. 2 (1988): 101–119, 107.
46. James M. Buchanan, *Public Principles of Public Debt* (Indianapolis, IN: Liberty Fund, 1999), 120.
47. James M. Buchanan and Richard E. Wagner, *Democracy in Deficit: The Political Legacy of Lord Keynes* (Indianapolis, IN: Liberty Fund, 2000), 10; Buchanan, "The Balanced Budget Amendment," 119.
48. Buchanan and Wagner, *Democracy in Deficit*, 16.
49. Geoffrey Brennan and James M. Buchanan, *The Power to Tax: Analytical Foundations of a Fiscal Constitution* (Cambridge: Cambridge University Press, 1980), 177, emphasis added.
50. Many adopted constitutional limitations on borrowing after a string of state defaults on debt during the depression of the early 1840s: Alasdair Roberts, *America's First Great Depression: Economic Crisis and Political Disorder after the Panic of 1837* (Ithaca, NY: Cornell University Press, 2012), 49–83.
51. Buchanan, "The Balanced Budget Amendment," 118.

52. Joaquim Ayuso-i-Casals et al., *Beyond the SGP: Features and Effects of EU National-Level Fiscal Rules* (Brussels: European Commission, 2007), 651–652. For very similar explanations, see Gabriel Filc and Carlos Scartascini, *Budget Institutions and Fiscal Outcomes* (Washington, DC: Inter-American Development Bank, 2004), 4; Manmohan Kumar and Teresa Ter-Minassian, *Promoting Fiscal Discipline* (Washington, DC: International Monetary Fund, 2007), 3; Xavier Debrun, David Hauner, and Manmohan S. Kumar, "Independent Fiscal Agencies," *Journal of Economic Surveys* 23, no. 1 (2009): 44–81, 45.

53. International Monetary Fund, *Fiscal Rules: Anchoring Expectations for Sustainable Public Finances* (Washington, DC: Fiscal Affairs Department, December 16, 2009), 15; Jean-Louis Combes et al., *Inflation Targeting and Fiscal Rules: Do Interactions and Sequencing Matter?* (Washington, DC: International Monetary Fund, 2014), 3; European Commission, *Report on Public Finances in EMU 2013* (Brussels: European Commission, 2013), 45.

54. Ha-Joon Chang, *Bad Samaritans* (New York: Bloomsbury Press, 2008), ch. 2. On the pursuit of "import substitution" strategies by other countries, see Werner Baer, "Import Substitution and Industrialization in Latin America: Experiences and Interpretations," *Latin American Research Review* 7, no. 1 (1972): 95–122.

55. "Address to the Nation Outlining a New Economic Policy," August 15, 1971, http://www.presidency.ucsb.edu/ws/?pid=3115.

56. Stephen P. Magee, William A. Brock, and Leslie Young, *Black Hole Tariffs and Endogenous Policy Theory: Political Economy in General Equilibrium* (New York: Cambridge University Press, 1989), xv–xvi; Gene M. Grossman and Elhanan Helpman, "Protection for Sale," *American Economic Review* 84, no. 4 (1994): 833–850, 833–835. "Most recent models of trade policy have been based on interest group politics. Trade policy is viewed as the outcome of the relative political strengths of various factional, class, or sectoral interests": Jeffrey Sachs and Andrew Warner, "Economic Reform and the Process of Global Integration," *Brookings Papers on Economic Activity* 1 (1995): 1–118, 18.

57. "The purpose of a trade agreement is to tie the hands of its member governments in their interactions with private agents in the economy, and thereby to offer an external commitment device": Robert W. Staiger, *Non-Tariff Measures and the WTO*, ERSD-2012-01 (Geneva: World Trade Organization, 2012), 26.

58. Alfred E. Kahn, *The Economics of Regulation: Principles and Institutions* (New York: Wiley, 1970); Stephen G. Breyer, *Regulation and Its Reform* (Cambridge, MA: Harvard University Press, 1982).

59. Lowi, "The Public Philosophy"; Theodore J. Lowi, *The End of Liberalism: Ideology, Policy, and the Crisis of Public Authority* (New York: Norton, 1969); George J. Stigler, "The Theory of Economic Regulation," *Bell Journal of Economics and Management Science* 2, no. 1 (1971): 3–21; Richard A. Posner, "Theories of Economic Regulation," *Bell Journal of Economics and Management Science* 5, no. 2 (1974): 335–358.

60. Marver H. Bernstein, *Regulating Business by Independent Commission* (Princeton, NJ: Princeton University Press, 1955); Marver H. Bernstein, "Independent Regulatory Agencies: A Perspective on Their Reform," *Annals of the American Academy of Political and Social Science* 400 (1972): 14–26.

61. Anne O. Krueger, "The Political Economy of the Rent-Seeking Society," *American Economic Review* 64, no. 3 (1974): 291–303.

62. Rents are "rewards and prizes not earned or not consistent with competitive market returns": Roger D. Congleton, Arye L. Hillman, and Kai Andreas Konrad, *40 Years of Research on Rent Seeking*, 2 vols. (Berlin: Springer, 2008).

63. Robert B. Ekelund and Robert D. Tollison, *Mercantilism as a Rent-Seeking Society: Economic Regulation in Historical Perspective*, Texas A & M University Economics Series (College Station: Texas A & M University Press, 1981), 19.

64. George Will, "Rent-Seeking and Inertia," *Marietta (GA) Journal*, March 17, 1995, 53; Walter Williams, "Political Sugar Padders," *Washington Times*, August 22, 1989, 48.

65. Congleton, Hillman, and Konrad, *40 Years of Research on Rent Seeking*, 2.

66. Jagdish N. Bhagwati, "Directly Unproductive, Profit-Seeking (DUP) Activities," *Journal of Political Economy* 90, no. 5 (1982): 988–1002, 989.

67. Arye L. Hillman, "Rent Seeking," in *The Elgar Companion to Public Choice* (Northampton, MA: Edward Elgar, 2014), 307–330.

68. Krueger, "Political Economy of the Rent-Seeking Society." See also James M. Buchanan, Robert D. Tollison, and Gordon Tullock, *Toward a Theory of the Rent-Seeking Society*, Texas A & M University Economics Series No. 4 (College Station: Texas A & M University, 1980).

69. Mancur Olson, *The Rise and Decline of Nations* (New Haven, CT: Yale University Press, 1982), 44, 69, 73, 78, 87.

70. Jonathan Rauch, "Demosclerosis," *National Journal* (1992): 1998–2003. See also Jonathan Rauch, *Demosclerosis* (New York: Times Books, 1994).

71. Glenn R. Parker, *Congress and the Rent-Seeking Society* (Ann Arbor: University of Michigan Press, 1996), 2–3.

72. The mandate of the Federal Reserve was altered in 1977 and 1978, but the language was pitched broadly: Giuseppe Fontana, "The Federal Reserve and the European Central Bank: A Theoretical Comparison of Their Legislative Mandates," *Journal of Post Keynesian Economics* 28, no. 3 (2006): 433–450, 437.

73. Paul Volcker and Martin Feldstein, "An Interview with Paul Volcker," *Journal of Economic Perspectives* 27, no. 4 (2013): 105–120, 110–111.

74. For a discussion of the approach of the Carter and Reagan administrations, see Kettl, *Leadership at the Fed*, 173–191; Robert J. Samuelson, *The Great Inflation and Its Aftermath: The Transformation of America's Economy, Politics, and Society* (New York: Random House, 2008), ch. 4.

75. John Kenneth Galbraith, "The Public Sector Is Still Starved," *Challenge* 15, no. 3 (1967): 18–21, 21.

76. William Greider, *Secrets of the Temple: How the Federal Reserve Runs the Country* (New York: Simon and Schuster, 1989), 464 and 558.

77. Bob Woodward, *Maestro: Greenspan's Fed and the American Boom* (New York: Simon & Schuster, 2001), 227.

78. The Economist, "Monetary Myopia," *The Economist*, January 12, 2006.

79. James N. Danziger, "California's Proposition 13 and the Fiscal Limitations Movement in the United States," *Political Studies* 28, no. 4 (1980): 599–612, 609–611.

80. The pledge was widespread after the early 1970s, and promoted actively by Grover Norquist's Americans for Tax Reform after 1986: Josh Goodman, "Tax Pledge Permeates New Hampshire," *Governing .com*, November 1, 2012, http://www.governing.com/news/state/Tax-Pledge-Permeates-New-Hampshire-Politics.html; Howard Fineman, *The Thirteen American Arguments: Enduring Debates That Define and Inspire Our Country* (New York: Random House Trade Paperbacks, 2009), ch. 5.

81. James Saturno and Megan Lynch, *A Balanced Budget Constitutional Amendment: Background and Congressional Options* (Washington, DC: Congressional Research Service, December 20, 2011), 26. Strictly, the petitions asked Congress to organize a convention under Article V of the Constitution that would draft a balanced budget amendment and submit it to the states for ratification.

82. Iwan Morgan, "Unconventional Politics: The Campaign for a Balanced-Budget Amendment Constitutional Convention in the 1970s," *Journal of American Studies* 32, no. 3 (1998): 421–445, 423.

83. Saturno and Lynch, *Balanced Budget Constitutional Amendment*, 16.

84. Tom Morganthau, "Balance-the-Budget Boom," *Newsweek*, February 12, 1979, 28. Republican enthusiasm for an amendment was also tempered because of the effect of Reagan administration policies, which produced even larger deficits than in the 1970s. A balanced-budget requirement would have required a major retreat from Reagan's commitments on tax relief and increased defense spending.

85. Pub. L. No. 99-177.

86. Sung Deuk Hahm et al., "The Influence of the Gramm-Rudman-Hollings Act on Federal Budgetary Outcomes, 1986–1989," *Journal of Policy Analysis and Management* 11, no. 2 (1992): 207–234, 208.

87. President Reagan's chief budget official, James C. Miller III—a former student of James Buchanan—also described the law as "a kind of device ... that a Public Choice scholar would have advanced." Buchanan himself lauded the statute as the best alternative to a constitutional balanced-budget requirement. *Congressional Record*, July 30, 1987, p. 21733; Jane Seaberry, "GMU Teacher Wins Nobel in Economics," *Washington Post*, October 17, 1986, A1. Jane Seaberry, "Public Choice Finds Allies in Top Places," *Washington Post*, April 6, 1986; Jane Seaberry, "Nobel Winner Sees Economics as Common Sense," *Washington Post*, October 19, 1986, C1.

88. Pub. L. No. 101-508.

89. Bill Heniff Jr. et al., *Introduction to the Federal Budget Process* (Washington, DC: Congressional Research Service, 2010), 5 and 17–18.

90. Mindy R. Levit et al., *Reaching the Debt Limit: Background and Potential Effects on Government Operations*, R41633 (Washington, DC: Congressional Research Service, March 27, 2015).

91. D. Andrew Austin and Mindy R. Levit, *The Debt Limit: History and Recent Increases*, RL31967 (Washington, DC: Congressional Research Service, October 15, 2013), 19–33; D. Andrew Austin, *The Debt Limit since 2011*, R43389 (Washington, DC: Congressional Research Service, March 26, 2015).

92. Frederic Austin Ogg and P. Orman Ray, *Introduction to American Government* (New York: Century, 1922), 418.

93. "The purpose and effect of external liberalization, of trade as well as capital flows, is to limit the autonomy of national governments, albeit

in ways they have chosen to accept": David Henderson, *The Changing Fortunes of Economic Liberalism* (London: Institute of Economic Affairs, 1998), 148.

94. E. E. Schattschneider, *Politics, Pressures and the Tariff* (New York: Prentice-Hall, 1935), 282. See also Olson, *The Rise and Decline of Nations*, 142.

95. For a recent and favorable assessment of the fast-track method, see: William G. Howell and Terry M. Moe, *Relic: How Our Constitution Undermines Effective Government* (New York: Basic Books, 2016), Ch. 4.

96. Judith Goldstein, "International Law and Domestic Institutions: Reconciling North American 'Unfair' Trade Laws," *International Organization* 50, no. 4 (1996): 541–564.

97. Clyde Farnsworth, "Reagan and Mulroney Sign Pact to Cut U.S.-Canada Trade Curbs," *New York Times*, January 3, 1988; Richard Bilder et al., "The Canada-U.S. Free Trade Agreement: New Directions in Dispute Settlement," *Proceedings of the Annual Meeting (American Society of International Law)* 83 (1989): 251–271, 263–267; Allan Gotlieb, "Negotiating the Canada-U.S. Free Trade Agreement," *International Journal* 53, no. 3 (1998): 522–538, 528 and 532.

98. Samuel C. Straight, "GATT and NAFTA: Marrying Effective Dispute Settlement and the Sovereignty of the Fifty States," *Duke Law Journal* 45, no. 1 (1995): 216–254, 220–221.

99. David Sanger, "Senate Approves Pact to Ease Trade Curbs," *New York Times*, December 2, 1994.

100. Historical Statistics of the United States, Series Ee425–430.

101. "It is well-nigh universally recognized that the Interstate Commerce Commission is not only the oldest but the most powerful of the many federal agencies which exercise some measure of administrative control of economic conduct. . . . [It] has long been, and remains today, the outstanding agency of economic control in our government establishment": I. L. Sharfman, "The Interstate Commerce Commission: An Appraisal," *Yale Law Journal* 46, no. 6 (1937): 915–954, 915. The Commission was replaced by a smaller body, the Surface Transportation Board.

102. Ronald R. Braeutigam, "Consequences of Regulatory Reform in the American Railroad Industry," *Southern Economic Journal* 59, no. 3 (1993): 468–480.

103. Warren T. Brookes, "Best Way for Government to Help the Consumer? Promote Competition," *Boston Herald American*, September 18, 1976,

9; Steven A. Morrison and Clifford Winston, "Airline Deregulation and Public Policy," *Science* 245, no. 4919 (1989): 707–711.

104. Executive Order 12044, March 1978. This directive was tightened by Executive Order 12291, issued by the Reagan administration in February 1981. The two 1980 laws were the Paperwork Reduction Act and the Regulatory Flexibility Act. Title II of the Unfunded Mandates Reform Act extended these pre-adoption review requirements.

105. Alfred E. Kahn, *The Economics of Regulation: Principles and Institutions*, 2 vols. (Cambridge, MA: MIT Press, 1988), xv.

106. Alfred E. Kahn, "The Deregulatory Tar Baby: The Precarious Balance between Regulation and Deregulation, 1970–2000 and Henceforward," *Journal of Regulatory Economics* 21, no. 1 (2002): 35–56, 35–36.

107. Michael A. Crew and Paul R. Kleindorfer, "Regulatory Economics: Twenty Years of Progress?," *Journal of Regulatory Economics* 21, no. 1 (2002): 5–22, 16. Another observer, Marc Allen Eisner, argued in 1994 that "The regulatory reform and deregulation of the past two decades ... marked the emergence of a new [regulatory] regime": Marc A. Eisner, "Discovering Patterns in Regulatory History: Continuity, Change, and Regulatory Regimes," *Journal of Policy History* 6, no. 2 (1994): 157–187, 179. Eisner observed later that "where changes in regulation occurred [after Reagan], they were overwhelming deregulatory in nature": Marc Allen Eisner, *The American Political Economy: Institutional Evolution of Market and State* (New York: Routledge, 2011), 132.

108. A. Michael Froomkin, "Wrong Turn in Cyberspace: Using ICANN to Route around the APA and the Constitution," *Duke Law Journal* 50 (2000): 17–184.

109. William Niskanen, "The Peculiar Economics of Bureaucracy," *American Economic Review* 58, no. 2 (1968): 293–305, 293.

110. Alasdair Roberts, *The Collapse of Fortress Bush: The Crisis of Authority in American Government* (New York: New York University Press, 2008), 146–147; Donald P. Moynihan and Alasdair S. Roberts, "The Triumph of Loyalty over Competence: The Bush Administration and the Exhaustion of the Politicized Presidency," *Public Administration Review* 70, no. 4 (2010): 572–581, 573–574.

111. Government Performance and Results Act, Pub. L. No. 103-62.

112. A good example is the Prescription Drug User Fee Act of 1992, Pub. L. No. 102-571.

113. The case for public-private competition was laid out in: David Osborne and Ted Gaebler, *Reinventing Government* (New York: Plume, 1992), ch. 3.

114. Office of the Vice President, *Vice President Gore to Chair Global Forum on Reinventing Government* (Washington, DC: Office of the Vice President, December 21, 1998).

115. John Micklethwait and Adrian Wooldridge, *The Fourth Revolution* (New York: Penguin Press, 2014), 251.

116. "It would be desirable to modify [American] legislation in the direction of the Maastricht Treaty, which specifies that price stability is the overriding long-run objective of monetary policy": Ben Bernanke et al., *Inflation Targeting: Lessons from the International Experience* (Princeton, NJ: Princeton University Press, 2001), 325. See also Edwin M. Truman, *Inflation Targeting in the World Economy* (Washington, DC: Peterson Institute, 2004), 103–123.

117. Thomas F. Cargill and Gerald P. O'Driscoll Jr., "Federal Reserve Independence: Reality or Myth?," *Cato Journal* 33, no. 3 (2013): 417–435, 419.

118. Samuelson, *The Great Inflation and Its Aftermath*, 112–113.

119. Bureau of Labor Statistics Consumer Price Index, http://www.bls.gov/cpi/. There is a debate about the extent to which central bank independence contributed to inflation control, compared to other factors such as trade liberalization. Many economists agree with Kenneth Rogoff that independence "played a central role in the overall reduction of inflation": Kenneth Rogoff, *Globalization and Global Disinflation* (Washington, DC: International Monetary Fund, 2003).

120. Bryan D. Jones, *Reconceiving Decision-Making in Democratic Politics* (Chicago: University of Chicago Press, 1994), 117.

121. For example: Steven K. Beckner, *Back from the Brink: The Greenspan Years* (New York: Wiley, 1996), viii; Steven K. Beckner, "Squeezed," *New York Times*, June 11, 1979, A19.

122. The median age of the American population is 37 years—that is, a birthdate in 1978.

123. These rules apply to countries that agreed to use the euro as their currency after 1999. Strictly, the criteria are percentages of GDP: Alasdair Roberts, "No Simple Fix: Fiscal Rules and the Politics of Austerity," *Indiana Journal of Global Legal Studies* 22, no. 2 (2015): 1–33.

124. "Check Out the Check-Off," *Marietta Journal*, August 26, 1992, 4.

125. Roberts, "No Simple Fix," 415–416.

126. It must be noted that European leaders also struggled to obtain compliance with the 1992 Treaty requirements on deficits and debt: ibid., 416–417.

127. "Most people understand that the endless growth in federal spending is going to lead to disaster": Richard Rahn, "The Deniers of Economic Reality," *Washington Times*, December 16, 2013. "The expansionary dynamic is largely irreversible. ... Total government spending ... grows in good times and bad": Peter H. Schuck, *Why Government Fails So Often* (Princeton, NJ: Princeton University Press, 2014), 9 and 17. "Left to its own devices, [government] will expand inexorably": Micklethwait and Wooldridge, *The Fourth Revolution*, 21.

128. Admittedly, the trends change substantially after the financial crisis of 2008. Federal revenues collapsed, while bailouts and "pump-priming" expenditures were necessary. However it is difficult to present this as evidence of democratic overload. The emergency arose because of mistakes made by financial institutions, rather than the unreasonable demands of voters. Everyone recognized that the measures taken in response to this economic emergency were temporary.

129. Office of Management and Budget, Historical Budget Tables, table 8.2. https://www.whitehouse.gov/omb/budget/Historicals.

130. Office of Management and Budget, Historical Budget Tables, table 8.4. https://www.whitehouse.gov/omb/budget/Historicals.

131. Office of Personnel Management, Executive Branch Civilian Employment since 1940, excluding Post Office.

132. John J. DiIulio, *Bring Back the Bureaucrats* (West Conshohocken, PA: Templeton Press, 2014).

133. Jim Powell, "The Tempting Path of Protectionism," *Washington Times*, October 22, 2011. On softening public support: Arvind Subramanian, *Testimony before the Joint Economic Committee* (Washington, DC: Peterson Institute for International Economics, September 21, 2011). "The ghost of Smoot-Hawley is still around": Harish Mehta, "Many US Policymakers Tilt toward Trade Protectionism," *Business Times Singapore* (2015). Earlier, former Commerce Secretary Donald Evans also warned of a "new wave of protectionism": Donald Evans, "Protectionists on the Wrong Side of History," *The Banker*, June 1, 2006.

134. On the "protectionist impulse" throughout the G20 countries, see Simon J. Evenett, *The Global Trade Disorder* (London: Center for Economic Policy Research, 2014). Of course, the 2016 presidential race seemed to show a revival of protectionist sentiments. However,

we should be careful to distinguish rhetoric and policy outcomes. At the time of writing (June 2016) it was still too early to say whether, and how far, these sentiments would result in a shift in federal policies. On protectionist trends globally, see: "Protectionism may bark but it still has no bite," *Financial Times*, June 23, 2016.

135. Based on the trade-to-GDP ratio: total exports and imports as a percentage of GDP. See http://data.worldbank.org/indicator/TG.VAL .TOTL.GD.ZS.

136. Clyde Crews, *Ten Thousand Commandments: An Annual Snapshot of the Federal Regulatory State* (Washington, DC: Competitive Enterprise Institute, 2015), 21.

137. "Non-stop growth": Wayne Crews and Ryan Young, "Twenty Years of Non-Stop Regulation," *American Spectator*, June 5, 2013. Page count is used as evidence of persistent sclerosis by Charles Murray: Charles A. Murray, *By the People: Rebuilding Liberty without Permission* (New York: Crown Forum), 5–6, 83, 100–102. The definition of sclerosis comes from the *Oxford English Dictionary*. Other scholars and politicians have also used page count as evidence of regulatory expansion. For example: J. B. Ruhl and James Salzman, "Mozart and the Red Queen: The Problem of Regulatory Accretion in the Administrative State," *Georgetown Law Journal* 91 (2002): 757–850, 773–775; Niall Ferguson, "The Regulated States of America," *Wall Street Journal*, June 18, 2013; Schuck, *Why Government Fails So Often*, 9; Jason Miller, *Momentum Builds to Reform the Regulatory Process* (Washington, DC: Federal News Radio, March 12, 2014).

138. Maeve Carey, *Counting Regulations: An Overview of Rulemaking, Types of Regulations, and Pages in the Federal Register*, R43056 (Washington, DC: Congressional Research Service, July 14, 2015).

139. "The regulatory reform and deregulation of the past two decades ... marked the emergence of a new regime": Eisner, "Discovering Patterns in Regulatory History," 179. Eisner observes that "where changes in regulation occurred [after Reagan], they were overwhelming deregulatory in nature": Eisner, *American Political Economy*, 132.

140. To put it another way: the regulatory challenge today might not be one of controlling demands from special interests. It might be the distinct problem of deciding how best to control increasingly complex systems. This problem is discussed by: Donald N. Sull and Kathleen M. Eisenhardt, *Simple Rules: How to Thrive in a Complex World* (New York: Houghton Mifflin Harcourt, 2015).

141. Wolfgang Streeck, *Buying Time: The Delayed Crisis of Democratic Capitalism* (London: Verso, 2014), ch. 1.

142. Advisory Commission on Intergovernment Relations, *Changing Public Attitudes on Governments and Taxes* (Washington, DC: Advisory Commission on Intergovernment Relations, June 1974).

143. In 1979, for example, polls showed that three-quarters of the American public supported a constitutional balanced-budget amendment. Adam Clymer, "Carter Budget Gets Support in Survey," *New York Times*, January 31, 1979, A1. On taxpayer anger in 1978–1979, see also Mattson, *"What the Heck Are You Up To, Mr. President?"*, ch. 5. For an analysis of shifting attitudes toward taxes over the whole period of 1940–2000, see Andrea Campbell, "What Americans Think of Taxes," in *The New Fiscal Sociology*, ed. Isaac Martin, Ajay K. Mehrotra, and Monica Prasad (New York: Cambridge University Press, 2009), 48–67.

144. Sixteen elections between 1974 and 2006. Voter turnout data: United States Census Bureau, http://www.census.gov/compendia/statab/cats/elections.html.

145. James V. Higgins, "UAW Calls for Elected Fed Chairman," United Press International, October 12, 1981.

146. James Weyer, "Eyes on the Fed," *Cleveland (OH) Plain Dealer*, February 8, 1988.

147. "The Balanced Budget Amendment: An Inquiry into Appropriateness," *Harvard Law Review* 96, no. 7 (1983): 1600–1620, 1609.

148. Ralph Nader and Lori Wallach, "GATT, NAFTA, and the Subversion of the Democratic Process," in *The Case against the Global Economy*, ed. Jerry Mander and Edward Goldsmith (San Francisco, CA: Sierra Club Books, 1996), 92–107.

149. Robert B. Horwitz, "Understanding Deregulation," *Theory and Society* 15, no. 1/2 (1986): 139–174, 169.

150. Alasdair Roberts, *Blacked Out: Government Secrecy in the Information Age* (New York: Cambridge University Press, 2006), ch. 7.

151. Alan S. Blinder, *The Quiet Revolution: Central Banking Goes Modern* (New Haven, CT: Yale University Press, 2004), 34–62; Alan S. Blinder, *How Do Central Banks Talk?* (Geneva: International Center for Monetary and Banking Studies, 2001), 6 and 65–71.

152. Edmund Andrews, "Forget Aloof, Bernanke Goes Barnstorming," *New York Times*, July 27, 2009; Shirley Leung, "Janet Yellen Wants to Be the Fed Chair for All," *Boston (MA) Globe*, October 17, 2014.

153. Binyamin Appelbaum, "Central Bankers' New Gospel: Spur Jobs, Wages and Inflation," *New York Times*, August 24, 2014. Ernst Baltensperger, "Assessing the European Central Bank's Euro Crisis Policies," *CESifo DICE Report* 10, no. 1 (2012): 10–13.

154. Allen Schick, *Can the U.S. Government Live within Its Means?*, No. 141 (Washington, DC: Brookings Institution, 2005), 8.

155. Roberts, *Blacked Out*, 182–183.

156. Daniel W. Drezner, "The Traditional Political Economy of Trade Negotiations Has Ended," *Washington Post*, June 18, 2015.

157. Two examples: the Sarbanes-Oxley Act of 2002 and Dodd–Frank Wall Street Reform and Consumer Protection Act of 2010. For an illustration of the recent literature on re-regulation, see Eric Helleiner and Jason Thistlethwaite, "Subprime Catalyst: Financial Regulatory Reform and the Strengthening of US Carbon Market Governance," *Regulation & Governance* 7, no. 4 (2013): 496–511.

158. The federal government purchased shares in General Motors, Chrysler, and AIG. It also put two government-sponsored enterprises, Fannie Mae and Freddie Mac, into conservatorship: Financial Crisis Inquiry Commission, *The Financial Crisis Inquiry Report* (Washington, DC: Financial Crisis Inquiry Commission, 2011).

159. Straight, "GATT and NAFTA," 216.

CHAPTER 5

1. Although there was strong evidence that public dissatisfaction with the state of the country was deteriorating before that: Alasdair Roberts, "The Government We Deserve," ForeignPolicy.com, May 21, 2012. http://foreignpolicy.com/2012/05/21/the-government-we-deserve/.

2. Steve Fraser, *The Age of Acquiescence* (New York: Little, Brown, 2015); Darrell M. West, *Billionaires: Reflections on the Upper Crust* (Washington, DC: Brookings Institution Press, 2014). See also Chrystia Freeland, *Plutocrats* (New York: Penguin Press, 2012); Ronald P. Formisano, *Plutocracy in America* (Baltimore, MD: Johns Hopkins University Press, 2015).

3. Tova A. Wang, *The Politics of Voter Suppression: Defending and Expanding Americans' Right to Vote* (Ithaca, NY: Cornell University Press, 2012); Michelle Alexander, *The New Jim Crow* (New York: New Press, 2010); Ari Berman, *Give Us the Ballot: The Modern Struggle for Voting Rights in America* (New York: Farrar, Straus and Giroux, 2015).

4. Michelle Malkin, "Democrats' Cynical Push to Naturalize Thousands of New Voters," *National Review*, September 23, 2015. During the Republican presidential debate of March 10, 2016, Senator Ted Cruz also alleged that "The Democrats support illegal immigration because they view those illegal immigrants as potential voters." See transcript of debate, http://www.cnn.com/2016/03/10/politics/republican-debate-transcript-full-text/index.html.

5. Peter H. Schuck, *Why Government Fails So Often* (Princeton, NJ: Princeton University Press, 2014), 409–411.

6. *Morning Joe*, December 15, 2015.

7. Volcker Alliance, *Research Shows Growing Number of Federal Government Breakdowns* (Washington, DC: Volcker Alliance, December 11, 2015). See also Paul Light, *Vision + Action = Faithful Execution* (Washington, DC: Volcker Alliance, December 2015).

8. Elaine Kamarck, "Why Speaker Boehner Can't Govern," in *Brookings Institution FixGov Blog* (Washington, DC: Brookings Institution, 2015). http://www.brookings.edu/blogs/fixgov/posts/2015/09/25-john-boehner-speaker-cant-govern-resigns-kamarck.

9. Jonathan Rauch, *Political Realism* (Washington, DC: Brookings Institution, 2015).

10. Jason Grumet, *City of Rivals: Restoring the Glorious Mess of American Democracy* (Guilford, CT: Globe Pequot Press, 2014), xvii, 2, and 109.

11. Charles Murray, "Curing American Sclerosis," *The American Criterion*, June 2015, ch. 5. Donald Kettl concurs: few politicians, he says, are prepared to tell citizens that their appetite for government services is unreasonable: Donald F. Kettl, *The Next Government of the United States* (New York: W. W. Norton, 2009), ch. 4.

12. "A Few Words on the Crisis," *Dublin University Magazine* 17, no. 102 (1841): 777–780, 778–779.

13. For example, see W. Nordhaus, "The Political Business Cycle," *Review of Economic Studies* 42 (1975): 169–190, 178.

14. "People tend to be shaped throughout their lives by the events and ideals dominating the time when they arrived at political consciousness": Arthur M. Schlesinger, *The Cycles of American History* (Boston, MA: Houghton Mifflin, 1986), 30. An implication is that the mindset of an entire generation might be determined by events that are years in the past, and that the passing of a generation might be necessary to produce a significant shift in overall public opinion. See Karl Mannheim, "The Problem of Generations," in *Karl Mannheim: Essays*, ed. Paul

Kecskemeti (London: Routledge, 1952), 276–320; José Ortega y Gasset, *The Modern Theme* (New York: Harper, 1961); Alan B. Spitzer, *The French Generation of 1820* (Princeton, NJ: Princeton University Press, 1987), ch. 1. Tocqueville emphasized the importance of generational dynamics in his assessment of American politics: "Each fresh generation is like a new nation": Alexis de Tocqueville, *Democracy in America* (New York: Penguin Classics, 2003), 112. But the generational dynamic also operates in non-democratic regimes: Orlando Figes, *Revolutionary Russia, 1891–1991* (New York: Metropolitan Books, 2014).

15. For a survey of recent research, see Richard H. Thaler, *Misbehaving: The Making of Behavioral Economics* (New York: W. W. Norton, 2015). Three centuries ago, David Hume observed that "men are not able radically to cure . . . that narrowness of soul, which makes them prefer the present to the remote": David Hume, *A Treatise on Human Nature*, 2 vols. (London: Longmans, Green, 1898), 2:303. For a discussion of the effect of "psychological barriers" and their effect on the climate change debate, see Nicholas Stern, *Why Are We Waiting? The Logic, Urgency, and Promise of Tackling Climate Change* (Cambridge, MA: MIT Press, 2015), ch. 10.

16. Strictly, they tend to privilege self-interest or the needs of immediate family members. See Steven Pinker, *The Blank Slate: The Modern Denial of Human Nature* (New York: Viking, 2002), 241–268. Again, an older statement, this time from George Washington: "A small knowledge of human nature will convince us that, with far the greatest part of mankind, interest is the governing principle. . . . Few men are capable of making a continued sacrifice of all views of private interest or advantage, to the common good: it is vain to exclaim against the depravity of human nature on this account": United States Congress, *Journals of the American Congress from 1774 to 1788* (Washington, DC: Way and Gideon, 1823), 211.

17. The oldest known ocean quahog lived for five hundred years. It was inadvertently killed in 2013 during research to determine the lifespan of ocean quahogs.

18. Associated Press, "Weeks Says Lesson of Late War Is to Be Prepared for Another," *Denver Rocky Mountain News*, October 24, 1922, 4. Resistance to preparedness before the two world wars was motivated by ambivalence about entanglement in European affairs, and not just indifference about the future.

19. Catherine Dale, *The 2014 Quadrennial Defense Review (QDR) and Defense Strategy: Issues for Congress*, R43403 (Washington, DC: Congressional Research Service, February 24, 2014), 2.

20. George E. Sokolsky, "These Days," *Canton Repository* (1948): 15. Or as the 1962 Port Huron Statement of the Students for a Democratic Society said: "The enclosing fact of the Cold War . . . brought awareness that we . . . might die at any time."

21. Walter Sullivan, "Disaster Tolls Needlessly High," *New York Times*, February 20, 1979, C2.

22. Carbon dioxide is not the only "greenhouse gas," but for simplicity I will focus on it alone.

23. Barry Kramer, "Ancient Enemy: Droughts May Spread in Big Climatic Shift," *Wall Street Journal*, May 30, 1974, 1. See also: Donald Moffitt, *The Wall Street Journal Views America Tomorrow* (New York: Amacom, 1977), 65–70.

24. Intergovernmental Panel on Climate Change, *Climate Change: The IPCC Scientific Assessment* (New York: Cambridge University Press, 1990), xi and xvii. Craig Whitney, "Scientists Urge Rapid Action on Global Warming," *New York Times*, May 26, 1990. The ethicist Peter Singer has argued that this was the moment at which the world could no longer deny knowledge of the hazards associated with current patterns of human activity. Peter Singer, *One World: The Ethics of Globalization*, 2d ed. (New Haven, CT: Yale University Press, 2004), Location 406.

25. Intergovernmental Panel on Climate Change, *Climate Change 2014: Synthesis Report* (Geneva, Switzerland: Intergovernmental Panel on Climate Change, 2014), 2, 9–10, 16; Intergovernmental Panel on Climate Change, *Climate Change 2014: Impacts, Adaptation and Vulnerability* (Geneva, Switzerland: Intergovernmental Panel on Climate Change, 2014), 12–20 and 23 and 25; Intergovernmental Panel on Climate Change, *Climate Change 2014: Impacts, Adaptation and Vulnerability, Part B: Regional Aspects (North America)* (Geneva, Switzerland: Intergovernmental Panel on Climate Change, 2014). See also Andrew T. Guzman, *Overheated: The Human Cost of Climate Change* (New York: Oxford University Press, 2013).

26. Barry G. Rabe, "The Durability of Carbon Cap-and-Trade Policy," *Governance* 29, no. 1 (January 2016): 103–119.

27. United Nations Framework Convention on Climate Change, *Report of the Conference of the Parties on Its Fifteenth Session, Held in Copenhagen from 7 to 19 December 2009* (Bonn: Climate Change Secretariat, March 30, 2010).

28. Philip Shabecoff, "Bush Asks Cautious Response to Threat of Global Warming," *New York Times*, February 6, 1990, A1.

29. David Sanger, "Bush Will Continue to Oppose Kyoto Pact on Global Warming," *New York Times*, June 12, 2001.

30. Office of the Special Envoy for Climate Change, *Letter to the UNFCCC Secretariat on US Emissions Reduction Target* (Washington, DC: Office of the Special Envoy for Climate Change, January 28, 2010).

31. The Clinton administration proposed a BTU or energy tax in 1993, but it was not adopted by Congress.

32. Office of the Press Secretary, *Remarks by the President in State of the Union Address* (Washington, DC: Executive Office of the President, January 20, 2015).

33. See data for the Primary Energy Overview produced by the US Energy Information Administration: http://www.eia.gov/totalenergy/data/annual/.

34. United Nations, *Kyoto Protocol to the United Nations Framework Convention on Climate Change* (New York: United Nations, 1998), Annex B.

35. See data produced by the Environmental Protection Agency, http://www3.epa.gov/climatechange/science/indicators/ghg/us-ghg-emissions.html.

36. Jeff Goodell, "Obama Takes on Climate Change," *Rolling Stone*, October 6, 2015, 36–45, 42, 45.

37. See, e.g., Eric Pooley, *The Climate War* (New York: Hyperion, 2010); Naomi Klein, *This Changes Everything: Capitalism vs. The Climate*, hardcover ed. (New York: Simon & Schuster, 2015), 148–150. Recently disclosed documents show that scientists within Exxon Mobil were aware of the dangers in the early 1980s. One senior scientist wrote in 1981 that it was "distinctly possible" that warming would be "catastrophic" for much of the earth's population: Neela Banerjee et al., *Exxon: The Road Not Taken* (Brooklyn, NY: Inside Climate News, 2015).

38. For a similar assessment over a shorter time frame, see Yale Project on Climate Change Communications, *Global Warming's Six Americas in October 2104* (New Haven, CT: Yale University, 2014), 8. The propensity of Republicans to express skepticism about global warming increased sharply after President Obama's inauguration in January 2009. Gallup Poll, "Republican Skepticism toward Global Warming Eases," April 9, 2013, http://www.gallup.com/poll/161714/republican-skepticism-global-warming-eases.aspx.

39. Gallup Poll, "In U.S., Most Do Not See Global Warming as Serious Threat," March 13, 2014, http://www.gallup.com/poll/167879/not-global-warming-serious-threat.aspx.

40. See also Robert J. Brulle, Jason Carmichael, and J. Craig Jenkins, "Shifting Public Opinion on Climate Change: An Empirical Assessment of Factors Influencing Concern over Climate Change in the U.S., 2002– 2010," *Climatic Change* 114, no. 2 (2012): 169–188.

41. Goodell, "Obama Takes on Climate Change," 41, 45.

42. A slight majority of all countries that established targets under the Protocol met those targets, but several of these countries were new democracies in Eastern Europe, which met the targets mainly because of the collapse of their Soviet-era industries: Quirin Schiermeier, "The Kyoto Protocol: Hot Air," *Nature*, November 28, 2012.

43. James Massola, Peter Ker, and Lisa Cox, "Coal Is 'Good for Humanity,' Says Tony Abbott at Mine Opening," *Sydney Morning Herald*, October 13, 2014.

44. Stern, *Why Are We Waiting?*, 236.

45. Ibid., 23.

46. Intergovernmental Panel on Climate Change, *Climate Change 2014: Synthesis Report*.

47. Pope Francis, *Encyclical on Climate Change and Inequality* (Brooklyn, NY: Melville House, 2015), 26, 91, 97–98.

48. John Dunn, *Breaking Democracy's Spell* (New Haven, CT: Yale University Press, 2014), 5 and 138–139. Similarly, James Goodman and Tom Morton argue that the climate crisis poses an "existential challenge" and a "potentially fatal" threat to the democratic model: James Goodman and Tom Morton, "Climate Crisis and the Limits of Liberal Democracy?," in *Democracy and Crisis*, ed. Benjamin Isakhan and Steven Slaughter (London: Macmillan, 2014), 229.

49. David Runciman, *The Confidence Trap* (Princeton, NJ: Princeton University Press, 2013), xiii, 33, 290, 316–318.

50. David Runciman, "A Tide of Horseshit," *London Review of Books*, September 24, 2015, 34–36, 36.

51. Donella H. Meadows et al., *The Limits to Growth* (New York: Universe Books, 1972), 126.

52. Robert L. Heilbroner, *An Inquiry into the Human Prospect* (New York: Norton, 1974), 179.

53. William Ophuls, *Ecology and the Politics of Scarcity: Prologue to a Political Theory of the Steady State* (San Francisco: W. H. Freeman, 1977), 159–163.

54. Hans Jonas, *The Imperative of Responsibility: In Search of an Ethics for the Technological Age* (Chicago: University of Chicago Press, 1984),

146–147; Hans Jonas, *Mortality and Morality: A Search for the Good after Auschwitz* (Evanston, IL: Northwestern University Press, 1996), 111–112.

55. Karen L. O'Brien and Elin Selboe, *The Adaptive Challenge of Climate Change* (New York: Cambridge University Press, 2015), 32; Andrew Dobson, *Green Political Thought*, 4th ed. (New York: Routledge, 2007), 105–115.

56. Mark Beeson, "The Coming of Environmental Authoritarianism," *Environmental Politics* 19, no. 2 (2010): 276–294, 289.

57. Mark Triffitt and Travers McLeod, "Hidden Crisis of Liberal Democracy Creates Climate Change Paralysis," *The Conversation* (2015), https://theconversation.com/hidden-crisis-of-liberal-democracy-creates-climate-change-paralysis-39851.

58. Peter Wells, "The Green Junta," *International Journal of Environment and Sustainable Development* 6, no. 2 (2007): 208–220.

59. Bruce Gilley, "Authoritarian Environmentalism and China's Response to Climate Change," *Environmental Politics* 21, no. 2 (2012): 287–307; Beeson, "The Coming of Environmental Authoritarianism," 289.

60. David J. C. Shearman and Joseph Wayne Smith, *The Climate Change Challenge and the Failure of Democracy* (Westport, CT: Praeger, 2007), 130, 133–134, 141, 166.

61. Ibid., 125–126.

62. Gilley, "Authoritarian Environmentalism and China's Response to Climate Change," 292.

63. Thomas L. Friedman, "Our One-Party Democracy," *New York Times*, September 8, 2009.

64. For a similar but briefer argument, see Michael Mann, "The End May Be Nigh, but for Whom?," in *Does Capitalism Have a Future?*, ed. Immanuel Wallerstein et al. (New York: Oxford University Press, 2013), 71–98, 92–97.

65. Hendrik Spruyt, *The Sovereign State and Its Competitors* (Princeton, NJ: Princeton University Press, 1994), 3.

66. For example, see one of the first books written by Woodrow Wilson, while a professor of political science: Woodrow Wilson, *The State: Elements of Historical and Practical Politics* (Boston, MA: D. C. Heath, 1889).

67. There are debates about the extent to which state power has been undermined because of globalization and the increasing role of international organizations. For one illustration of the expansive literature

on this question, see Jessica Mathews, "Power Shift," *Foreign Affairs* 76, no. 1 (1997): 50–66. For a brief reply, see Alasdair Roberts, "The Nation-State: Not Dead Yet," *Wilson Quarterly*, (Summer 2015), http://wilsonquarterly.com/quarterly/summer-2015-an-age-of-connectivity/the-nation-state-not-dead-yet/.

68. We have constructed some organizations that attempt to provide such guarantees, such as the United Nations, but the United Nations is not an autonomous body with its own forces, capable of intervening when one state threatens the security of another state.

69. The general problem that I am referring to here is sometimes called the "security dilemma" of states. See Herbert Butterfield, *History and Human Relations* (London: Collins, 1951); John H. Herz, *Political Realism and Political Idealism* (Chicago: University of Chicago Press, 1951).

70. Joseph S. Nye, *Soft Power: The Means to Success in World Politics* (New York: Public Affairs, 2004).

71. William Gamble, "The Middle Kingdom Runs Dry: Tax Evasion in China," *Foreign Affairs* 79, no. 6 (2000): 16–20; Tucker Van Aken and Orion A. Lewis, "The Political Economy of Noncompliance in China: The Case of Industrial Energy Policy," *Journal of Contemporary China* 24, no. 95 (2015): 798–822; Andrew Wedeman, *Enemies of the State: Mass Incidents and Subversion in China*, APSA 2009 Toronto Meeting Paper (Atlanta: Georgia State University, 2009).

72. Bruce Gilley, *The Right to Rule: How States Win and Lose Legitimacy* (New York: Columbia University Press, 2009), 84.

73. Tom Bingham, *The Rule of Law* (London: Allen Lane, 2010), 3–4 and 66–67.

74. In rich countries, Nicholas Stern suggests, "there is an underlying feeling that . . . 'my sense of community responsibility for inequality does not extend strongly to the rest of the world' ": Stern, *Why Are We Waiting?*, 292–293.

75. Marc J. Hetherington and Thomas J. Rudolph, *Why Washington Won't Work: Polarization, Political Trust, and the Governing Crisis* (Chicago: University of Chicago Press, 2015), chs. 3 and 7.

76. A strong economy and strong tax revenues also improve the capacity of governments to invest in other domestic capabilities, such as policing, data-gathering, and economic regulation.

77. http://www.eia.gov/tools/faqs/faq.cfm?id=427&t=3.

78. For a recent history of attempts to control smog in the first industrial capital, London, see Christine L. Corton, *London Fog: The Biography* (Cambridge, MA: Harvard University Press, 2015).

79. "Climate change . . . must be regarded as market failure on the greatest scale the world has ever seen": Nicholas Stern, *Report on the Economics of Climate Change* (London: HM Treasury, 2006), 1.

80. Jeffrey A. Frieden, *Global Capitalism: Its Fall and Rise in the Twentieth Century* (New York: Norton, 2006), 392–412.

81. A recent report from the International Energy Agency observed that "the electricity demand of our increasingly digital economies is growing at an alarming rate": International Energy Agency, *More Data, Less Energy* (Paris: International Energy Agency, 2014).

82. Consider the set of advanced democracies that constitute the G7: Canada, France, Germany, Italy, Japan, the United Kingdom, and the United States. In none of these countries was the principle of popular rule, based on universal adult suffrage, established at the advent of industrialization. See also Raymond Aron, *The Opium of the Intellectuals* (Garden City, NY: Doubleday, 1957), 259–260.

83. W. Fordyce, *A History of Coal, Coke, Coal Fields, Iron, Its Ores, and Processes of Manufacture* (London: Sampson Low, 1860), 5–6.

84. "Exhausting Our Wealth," *Idaho Statesman*, July 12, 1943. "In Europe men are fighting and dying by the millions today for [oil]. . . . The defense of the U.S. is based upon the assurance of an unending supply of crude and its products": "Oil for Defense Pours out of Tri-State," *Evansville (IN) Courier and Press*, September 28, 1941, 64.

85. This turn was actively encouraged by bodies like the International Monetary Fund and the World Bank. In 1990 the economist John Williamson characterized the prevailing wisdom as being preoccupied with "free-market capitalism" and an "outward orientation." He called this the Washington Consensus: John Williamson, "What Washington Means by Policy Reform," in *Latin American Adjustment: How Much Has Happened?*, ed. John Williamson (Washington, DC: Institute for International Economics, 1990).

86. This transformation was encouraged by Deng Xiaoping, who became China's paramount leader in 1978. After a phase of internal contention, the shift to a market-friendly model was confirmed at the Fourteenth Party Congress in 1992. Deng promised that the policy of "reform and openness will not change for one hundred years": Orville Schell and

John Delury, *Wealth and Power: China's Long March to the Twenty-First Century* (New York: Random House, 2013), 321.

87.   Kerry Brown, *Hu Jintao: China's Silent Ruler* (Hackensack, NJ: World Scientific, 2012), 81.

88.   Francis Fukuyama, "The End of History?," *National Interest* 16, no. 3 (1989): 3–16.

89.   Michael Mandelbaum, *The Ideas That Conquered the World: Peace, Democracy, and Free Markets in the Twenty-First Century* (New York: Public Affairs, 2002), ch. 9; Frieden, *Global Capitalism*, ch. 17; Fukuyama, "The End of History?"; Jeffrey Sachs, "Twentieth-Century Political Economy: A Brief History of Global Capitalism," *Oxford Review of Economic Policy* 15, no. 4 (1999): 90–101.

90.   International Energy Agency, *Key World Energy Statistics* (Paris: International Energy Agency, 2015), 38–39.

91.   China Statistical Yearbook, 2014, table 18–25, http://www.stats.gov.cn/tjsj/ndsj/2014/indexeh.htm.

92.   International Energy Agency, *Key World Energy Statistics*, 45.

93.   Stern, *Why Are We Waiting?*, 86.

94.   Shearman and Smith, *Climate Change Challenge*, 92. See also Quan Li and Rafael Reuveny, "Democracy and Environmental Degradation," *International Studies Quarterly* 50, no. 4 (2006): 935–956; Hugh Ward, "Liberal Democracy and Sustainability," *Environmental Politics* 17, no. 3 (2008): 386–409; Stefan Wurster, "Comparing Ecological Sustainability in Autocracies and Democracies," *Contemporary Politics* 19, no. 1 (2013): 76–93; Per G. Fredriksson and Eric Neumayer, "Democracy and Climate Change Policies: Is History Important?," *Ecological Economics* 95 (2013): 11–19.

95.   Fredriksson and Neumayer, "Democracy and Climate Change Policies," 12.

96.   Christopher Mims, "Is China's Quasi-Dictatorship Better Prepared for the 21st Century Than Our Mess of a Democracy?," *Grist* (January 21, 2011), http://grist.org/article/2011-01-21-is-chinas-quasi-dictatorship-better-prepared-for-the-21st-centur/.

97.   National People's Congress, *Twelfth Five Year Plan (2011–2015)* (Beijing: National People's Conference, 2011), ch. 21.

98.   FS-UNEP Collaborating Centre, *Global Trends in Renewable Energy Investment 2015* (Frankfurt: FS-UNEP Collaborating Centre, 2015), 20–23.

99. Chris Buckley, "China Burns Much More Coal Than Reported," *New York Times*, November 3, 2015. Energy Information Administration, *Recent Statistical Revisions Suggest Higher Coal Consumption in China* (Washington, DC: US Energy Information Administration, September 16, 2015); Van Aken and Lewis, "The Political Economy of Noncompliance in China."

100. Office of the Press Secretary, *U.S.-China Joint Announcement on Climate Change* (Washington, DC: Executive Office of the President, November 12, 2014).

101. Liu Zhu, *China's Carbon Emissions Report 2015* (Cambridge, MA: Harvard Kennedy School, May 2015), 2–7; Stern, *Why Are We Waiting?*, 225.

102. Stern, *Why Are We Waiting?*, 225.

103. Richard Bitzinger, "China's Double-Digit Defense Growth," *Foreign Affairs*, March 19, 2015, https://www.foreignaffairs.com/articles/china/2015-03-19/chinas-double-digit-defense-growth.

104. "Many Chinese make a bargain with the party: as long as they are allowed to enjoy growing wealthier . . . they will not seek to challenge authoritarian rule": Schell and Delury, *Wealth and Power*, 334, 397.

105. On spending for internal security purposes, see William J. Dobson, *The Dictator's Learning Curve: Inside the Global Battle for Democracy* (New York: Doubleday, 2012), 281. On reasons for the expansion of social programs, see Mark W. Frazier, *Socialist Insecurity: Pensions and the Politics of Uneven Development in China* (Ithaca, NY: Cornell University Press, 2010), 1–6.

106. For a critical overview of civil and political rights in Singapore, see the assessment by Freedom House: https://freedomhouse.org/report/freedom-world/2015/singapore.

107. Martin Jacques, *When China Rules the World* (New York: Penguin Press, 2009), 268.

108. Data on GHG emissions is available from http://data.worldbank.org/topic/climate-change.

109. Benjamin Wong and Xunming Huang, "Political Legitimacy in Singapore," *Politics & Policy* 38, no. 3 (2010): 523–543, 528.

110. Tan Ern Ser and Wang Zhengxu, *Singapore Country Report: Second Wave of Asian Barometer Survey* (Taipei: Asian Barometer Project Office, 2007), 8.

111. "About Singapore," Office of Student Affairs, National University of Singapore, http://nus.edu.sg/osa/iss/about-singapore.

112. Erik Velasco and Matthias Roth, "Review of Singapore's Air Quality and Greenhouse Gas Emissions: Current Situation and Opportunities," *Journal of the Air & Waste Management Association* 62, no. 6 (2012): 625–641, 629–630.

113. Deutsche Welle, "What Issues Will Decide Singapore's General Election?," September 8, 2015, http://www.dw.com/en/what-issues-will-decide-singapores-general-election/a-18699620.

114. The term is introduced by: Shearman and Smith, *Climate Change Challenge*, 141.

115. Dennis F. Thompson, "Democracy in Time," *Constellations* 12, no. 2 (2005): 245–261, 256–257.

116. Rupert Read, *Guardians of the Future* (Weymouth, UK: Green House, 2012).

117. Joerg Tremmel, "Parliaments and Future Generations: The Four-Power-Model," in *The Politics of Sustainability*, ed. Dieter Birnbacher and May Thorseth (London: Routledge, 2015), 212–233, 224.

118. For a discussion of this idea, see Alasdair Roberts, *The Logic of Discipline: Global Capitalism and the New Architecture of Government* (New York: Oxford University Press, 2010), ch. 3.

119. Stephen E. Flynn, "The Neglected Home Front," *Foreign Affairs* 83, no. 5 (2004): 20–33, 29–33.

120. Dieter Helm imagines a more modest model. Congress might approve a carbon tax but give an independent body like the Federal Reserve the power to determine the level at which the tax should be set, based on its assessment of risks: Dieter Helm and C. March, "Credible Carbon Taxes," in *Climate-Change Policy*, ed. Dieter Helm (Oxford: Oxford University Press, 2005), 305–321.

121. The phrase is Nicholas Stern's: Stern, *Why Are We Waiting?*, ch. 2. The IPCC describes the needed change as "a fundamental departure from business as usual": Intergovernmental Panel on Climate Change, *Climate Change 2014: Synthesis Report*, v. Dieter Helm says: "The nearest analogy is the conversion of peacetime economies in the 1930s to wartime economies by 1940, but even this fails to do justice to the scale of the transformation required": Dieter Helm, *Carbon Crunch: How We Are Getting Climate Change Wrong and How to Fix It* (New Haven, CT: Yale University Press, 2012), 227. Mark Jacobson has also made the comparison to mobilization during World War II: Mark Z. Jacobson and Mark A. Delucchi, "A Path to Sustainable Energy by 2030," *Scientific American* 301, no. 5 (2009): 58–65, 59.

122. During the recent financial crisis, the Federal Reserve itself encountered a similar problem, but on a smaller scale. In normal times, the Federal Reserve worries mainly about controlling inflation. In the aftermath of the crisis, though, it also had to worry about the potential for a collapse in economic activity. That is, it had to weigh inflation control against the pace of economic growth. (In fact, its statutory mandate requires that consideration of both factors.) But the Federal Reserve's decision-making began to look more like "ordinary politics" as it moved away from simple inflation-fighting, toward balancing price stability and growth.

123. The Gallup Poll found that awareness of global warming was generally higher in the established democracies: Gallup Poll, "Top-Emitting Countries Differ on Climate Change Threat," Gallup Poll, December 7, 2009; Tien Ming Lee et al., "Predictors of Public Climate Change Awareness and Risk Perception around the World," *Nature Climate Change* 5, no. 11 (2015): 1014–1020.

124. A count of articles was made by James L. Powell: see http://www.james powell.org/PieChartI/piechart.html.

125. Hugh S. Gorman and Barry D. Solomon, "The Origins and Practice of Emissions Trading," *Journal of Policy History* 14, no. 3 (2002): 293–320.

126. Natasha Geiling, "How Paris Turned the Climate Movement into an Everyone Movement," ThinkProgress.org, December 14, 2015, available from http://thinkprogress.org/climate/2015/12/14/3731402/paris-climate-agreement-movement-is-power/. The climate change movement is described in: Riley E. Dunlap and Robert J. Brulle, *Climate Change and Society: Sociological Perspectives* (New York: Oxford University Press), ch. 8.

127. United Nations Framework Convention on Climate Change, Paris Agreement, December 11, 2015.

CHAPTER 6

1. Walter Lippmann, *The Public Philosophy* (Boston, MA: Little, Brown, 1955); Theodore Lowi, "The Public Philosophy: Interest-Group Liberalism," *American Political Science Review* 61, no. 1 (1967): 5–24.

2. This could be a rational calculation: if there really is a fundamental threat to the nation, excessive caution might be the prudent route. Europeans call this the "precautionary principle" in risk management.

3. Peter Miller, "The Dangers of Retrospective Myopia," *Journal of Portfolio Management* 6, no. 1 (1979): 67–73.

4. David Streitfeld, "Housing Fades as a Means to Build Wealth," *New York Times*, August 22, 2010.

5. This phrase was coined by Richard E. Neustadt and Ernest R. May in *Thinking in Time* (New York: Free Press, 1986), xiii.

6. Arthur M. Schlesinger, *The Cycles of American History* (Boston, MA: Houghton Mifflin, 1986), 30–31.

7. Andrew Healy and Neil Malhotra, "Retrospective Voting Reconsidered," *Annual Review of Political Science* 16, no. 1 (2013): 285–306; Larry M. Bartels, *Unequal Democracy: The Political Economy of the New Gilded Age* (Princeton, NJ: Princeton University Press, 2008), ch. 4.

8. Martin Jacques, *When China Rules the World* (New York: Penguin Press, 2009). Indeed, Chinese scholars tend to make the same analytic mistake. See, e.g., Wei-Wei Zhang, *The China Wave: Rise of a Civilizational State* (Hackensack, NJ: World Century, 2012).

9. Samuel P. Huntington, *Political Order in Changing Societies* (New Haven, CT: Yale University Press, 1968), 7.

10. Francis Fukuyama, "America in Decay," *Foreign Affairs* 93, no. 5 (2014): 3–26.

11. "The World's Most Powerful People," *Forbes*, November 4, 2015, http://www.forbes.com/powerful-people/.

12. For a short survey of pragmatism as a philosophy of governance, see Christopher K. Ansell, *Pragmatist Democracy: Evolutionary Learning as Public Philosophy* (New York: Oxford University Press, 2011), ch. 1. For a classic statement of this philosophy, see John Dewey, *The Public and Its Problems* (New York: H. Holt and Company, 1927).

13. "Interstate Commerce Commission Has Picture Taken for First Time," *Kalamazoo (MI) Gazette*, March 21, 1913, 1. The Commission was said to have "powers approaching absolutism": Victor Elliott, "Commission Government at Washington Is Increasing," *Fort Worth (TX) Star-Telegram*, February 17, 1915, 7.

14. For an illustration of the tendency to universalize the problem of corruption in public service, see Alasdair Roberts, *So-Called Experts: How American Consultants Remade the Canadian Civil Service, 1918–1921* (Toronto: Institute of Public Administration of Canada, 1996).

15. *New State Ice Co. v. Liebmann*, 285 U.S. 262 (1932), at 306.

16. Orville Schell and John Delury, *Wealth and Power: China's Long March to the Twenty-First Century* (New York: Random House, 2013), 268.

17. Zhang, *The China Wave*, 97 and 126.

18. Sebastian Heilmann and Elizabeth J. Perry, *Mao's Invisible Hand: The Political Foundations of Adaptive Governance in China* (Cambridge, MA: Harvard University Press, 2011).

19. Jeremy L. Wallace, "Juking the Stats? Authoritarian Information Problems in China," *British Journal of Political Science* 46, no. 1 (2016): 11–29.

20. Willy Wo-Lap Lam, *Chinese Politics in the Era of Xi Jinping* (New York: Routledge, 2015), ch. 3.

21. "An obvious requirement is freedom of social inquiry and of distribution of its conclusions. . . . Whatever obstructs and restricts publicity, limits and distorts public opinion and checks and distorts thinking on social affairs": Dewey, *The Public and Its Problems*, 166–167.

22. Article 19, *Asia Disclosed: A Review of the Right to Information across Asia* (London: Article 19, 2015), 27–29; Freedom House, *The Politburo's Predicament: Confronting the Limits of Chinese Communist Party Repression* (Washington, DC: Freedom House, 2015); ChinaFile, *Document 9: A Chinafile Translation* (New York: Asia Society, November 8, 2013), https://www.chinafile.com/document-9-chinafile-translation.

23. A. M. Simons, *Social Forces in American History* (New York: Macmillan, 1911), 141.

24. George Bancroft, *History of the Formation of the Constitution of the United States of America* (New York: D. Appleton, 1885), 2:324.

25. George Cary Eggleston, "Where We Got Our Government," *Proceedings of the New York State Historical Association* 3 (1903): 46–62, 48.

26. For a survey of the different types of institutionalism, see B. Guy Peters, *Institutional Theory in Political Science: The New Institutionalism*, 3d ed. (New York: Continuum, 2012).

27. Sven Steinmo, "The New Institutionalism," in *The Encyclopedia of Democratic Thought*, ed. Barry Clark and Joe Foweraker (London: Routledge, 2001), 462–465, 464.

28. John L. Campbell, "Institutional Reproduction and Change," in *The Oxford Handbook of Comparative Institutional Analysis*, ed. Gareth Morgan (Oxford: Oxford University Press, 2010), 87–116, 91.

29. For an introduction to historical institutionalism, see Paul Pierson, *Politics in Time: History, Institutions, and Social Analysis* (Princeton, NJ: Princeton University Press, 2004).

30. "The common sense conception of historical institutionalism—that institutions are often slow to change once created—is difficult to

contest": Peters, *Institutional Theory in Political Science*, 74. For an extended discussion of institutionalism's emphasis on "fixity over change," also see B. Guy Peters, Jon Pierre, and Desmond S. King, "The Politics of Path Dependency: Political Conflict in Historical Institutionalism," *Journal of Politics* 67, no. 4 (2005): 1275–1300; Walter Kickert and Frans-Bauke van der Meer, "Small, Slow, and Gradual Reform," *International Journal of Public Administration* 34, no. 8 (2011): 475–485, 475. There are some scholars within the institutionalist school who have questioned the prevailing view. For example, Kurt Weyland has asked why political scientists emphasize "inertia and persistence" when the world has recently experienced "waves of profound transformation and stunning changes of trajectory": Kurt Weyland, "Toward a New Theory of Institutional Change," *World Politics* 60, no. 2 (2008): 281–314, 281–282. Similarly Kathleen Steinmo and Wolfgang Streeck have wondered about "the prevailing emphasis on institutional stability even in the face of indisputable and important change": Wolfgang Streeck and Kathleen Ann Thelen, *Beyond Continuity: Institutional Change in Advanced Political Economies* (New York: Oxford University Press, 2005), 6. For further criticism of the prevailing attitude, see Stephen Bell and Hui Feng, "How Proximate and 'Meta-Institutional' Contexts Shape Institutional Change: Explaining the Rise of the People's Bank of China," *Political Studies* 62, no. 1 (2014): 197–215; Stephen Bell and Hui Feng, *The Rise of the People's Bank of China: The Politics of Institutional Change* (Cambridge, MA: Harvard University Press), ch. 2; Chris Howell and Rebecca Kolins Givan, "Rethinking Institutions and Institutional Change in European Industrial Relations," *British Journal of Industrial Relations* 49, no. 2 (2011): 231–255; Timo Fleckenstein, "Learning to Depart from a Policy Path: Institutional Change and the Reform of German Labour Market Policy," *Government and Opposition* 48, no. 01 (2013): 55–79; Bo Rothstein, *The Quality of Government: Corruption, Social Trust, and Inequality in International Perspective* (Chicago: University of Chicago Press, 2011), ch. 10.

31. The proposition that some institutions change slowly is different and more easily defended. See Gérard Roland, "Understanding Institutional Change: Fast-Moving and Slow-Moving Institutions," *Studies in Comparative International Development* 38, no. 4 (2004): 109–131, 116; Kenneth Shepsle, "Rational Choice Institutionalism," in *The Oxford Handbook of Political Institutions*, ed. R. A. W. Rhodes, Sarah A. Binder,

and Bert Rockman (New York: Oxford University Press, 2006), 23–38, 27 and 30.

32.   There are some scholars who define "institutions" only as that set of rules or routines that persist or endure. In this case, the proposition that "institutions change slowly" is meaningless; it is true by definition.

33.   Stephen D. Krasner, "Approaches to the State: Alternative Conceptions and Historical Dynamics," *Comparative Politics* 16, no. 2 (1984): 223–246, 234.

34.   James G. March and Johan P. Olsen, "The New Institutionalism: Organizational Factors in Political Life," *American Political Science Review* 78, no. 3 (1984): 734–749, 737.

35.   J. G. March and Johan P. Olsen, "Elaborating the 'New Institutionalism,'" in *The Oxford Handbook of Political Institutions*, ed. R. A. W. Rhodes, Sarah A. Binder, and Bert Rockman (New York: Oxford University Press, 2006), 3–22, 7.

36.   Michael Witt and Arie Lewin, *Dynamics of Institutional Change*, 2004/87/ABCM/EARC 9 (Fontainebleu, France: INSEAD, 2004).

37.   Francis Fukuyama, *The Origins of Political Order: From Prehuman Times to the French Revolution* (New York: Farrar, Straus and Giroux, 2011), 16.

38.   Nicholas Stern, *Why Are We Waiting? The Logic, Urgency, and Promise of Tackling Climate Change* (Cambridge, MA: MIT Press, 2015).

39.   A variation of this experiment: count the number of articles in political science or public administration in the JSTOR database that include the phrase, "within the last X years," while varying the value for X. Most articles use the phrase to refer to the last five or ten years. David Armitage and Jo Guldi have recently complained that a substantial amount of research by American historians is also shaped by "biological time-spans" such as a generation or human lifetime: Jo Guldi and David Armitage, *The History Manifesto* (New York: Cambridge University Press), 7, 45, and 86.

40.   Joseph Schneider, "Social Problems Theory: The Constructionist View," *Annual Review of Sociology* 11 (1985): 209–229.

41.   Joseph Nye has also questioned the practice of treating institutions as though they were human organisms: Joseph S. Nye, *Is the American Century Over?* (Cambridge: Polity Press, 2015), ch. 2.

42.   On the state of healthcare reform in the mid-1980s, see Theda Skocpol, *Boomerang: Clinton's Health Security Effort and the Turn against Government in U.S. Politics* (New York: W. W. Norton, 1996), 23–24.

43. James Bryce, *The American Commonwealth*, 3 vols. (London: Macmillan, 1888), 1:411.

44. Shirley Anne Warshaw, *Guide to the White House Staff* (Washington, DC: CQ Press, 2013), 28–34.

45. Harold D. Lasswell, "Does the Garrison State Threaten Civil Rights?," *Annals of the American Academy of Political and Social Science* 275 (1951): 111–116.

46. Jeffrey L. Pressman and Aaron B. Wildavsky, *Implementation: How Great Expectations in Washington Are Dashed in Oakland* (Berkeley: University of California Press, 1984).

47. There is dispute about the number of civilians killed as a result of the war. I have used the figures calculated by Iraq Body Count, https://www.iraqbodycount.org. Estimates of displacement, as of 2008, were made by the United Nations High Commissioner for Refugees, http://www.unhcr.org/pages/49e486426.html.

48. See a large number of polls on this question provided at http://www.pollingreport.com/iraq.htm.

49. Mark Landler, "Iraq, a War Obama Didn't Want, Shaped His Foreign Policy," *New York Times*, December 17, 2011.

50. For judgments about democracy that are based on the US decision to go to war in Iraq, see: John Dunn, *Breaking Democracy's Spell* (New Haven, CT: Yale University Press, 2014), 38; David Runciman, *The Confidence Trap* (Princeton, NJ: Princeton University Press, 2013), 273.

51. The literature on this subject is voluminous. See, in particular, Louis Fisher, "Deciding on War against Iraq: Institutional Failures," *Political Science Quarterly* 118, no. 3 (2003): 389–410; Thomas Ricks, *Fiasco: The American Military Adventure in Iraq* (New York: Penguin Press, 2006), ch. 6; Michael Massing, *Now They Tell Us: The American Press and Iraq* (New York: New York Review Books, 2004). There is some parallel to the explanation that the political scientist James C. Scott provided in 1998 for the "great human tragedies" of the twentieth century, such as Soviet agricultural collectivization in the 1920s and 1930s, the Holocaust, and China's Great Leap Forward in the 1950s, which together caused the deaths of perhaps fifty million people. Three key factors contributing to these catastrophes, Scott said, were hubris among rulers, a lack of adequate formal checks on state power, and a weakened or prostrate civil society. James C. Scott, *Seeing Like a State*

(New Haven, CT: Yale University Press, 1998), 3–6. In an earlier book, I have pointed out how earlier policy decisions laid down a pathway to invasion: Alasdair Roberts, *The Collapse of Fortress Bush: The Crisis of Authority in American Government* (New York: New York University Press, 2008), ch. 5.

52. Peter Grier et al., "The New Normal," *Christian Science Monitor* 93, no. 222 (2001): 1.

53. See data from the ABC News/Washington Post Poll and CNN/USA Today/Gallup Poll at http://www.pollingreport.com/bush_ad.htm.

54. "Buzzword," *New York Times*, May 11, 2003, 1.

55. Ian Davis, "The New Normal," *McKinsey Quarterly*, no. 3 (2009): 26–28.

56. Nellie Andreeva, "NBC Picks up 'New Normal,'" *Deadline Hollywood*, January 27, 2012.

57. Morning Edition, *New York Planners Prep for a 'New Normal' of Powerful Storms* (National Public Radio, 2012).

58. In a speech in Boston on May 14, 1920. Warren G. Harding and Frederick E. Schortemeier, *Rededicating America: Life and Recent Speeches of Warren G. Harding* (Indianapolis, IN: Bobbs-Merrill Company, 1920), 223–229.

59. "No Normalcy in Past in U.S.," *Jackson (MI) Citizen Patriot*, August 19, 1921, 1.

60. Gregory S. Berns et al., "Neurobiological Substrates of Dread," *Science* 312, no. 5774 (2006): 754–758.

61. Elaine Scarry, *Thinking in an Emergency* (New York: W. W. Norton, 2011), 3–18.

62. Mark Penn and Don Baer, "Americans Are No Longer Optimists," *The Atlantic*, July 1, 2014, http://www.theatlantic.com/politics/archive/2014/07/has-america-entered-an-age-of-impossibility/373744/.

63. In 2015, the leading Republican presidential candidate, Donald Trump, said that his administration would build a wall on the US–Mexico border, while Governor Scott Walker said that building a wall on the US–Canada border was a "legitimate issue for us to look at." Trump also said that he would establish a "deportation force" to manage the removal of eleven million illegal immigrants and impose a temporary ban on the entry of Muslims to the United States. Senator Ted Cruz said that he would "carpet bomb [ISIS] into oblivion." Trump advocated the torture of terrorists and said that the United States should kill the family members of ISIS terrorists as a deterrent.

64. An NBC/SurveyMonkey Poll released on January 5, 2016, asked respondents to identify the most important quality in a presidential candidate. "Strong leadership" was the top response, followed by the "willingness to stand up for principles, no matter what." Among likely participants in the Iowa Republican caucuses, Donald Trump was most highly rated for his ability to "get things done," according to a *Des Moines Register/* Bloomberg Poll released on December 14, 2015.

authoritarianism (*cont.*)
  "green authoritarianism" and,
    148–49, 157, 164
  institutional flexibility seen as
    virtue of, 14
  limits of government power
    within, 151, 157, 164, 166
Autonomy Act (1916), 64

B-36D long-range bomber,
  68–70, 72
Balanced Budget Act of 1985,
  117–18, 124
balanced budget amendment
  proposals
  Buchanan and, 109–10,
    117–18, 226n87
  Congress's consideration
    of, 117–18, 124, 225n81
  future decision-making limited
    by, 129
  popular support for, 128, 232n143
  ultimate failure of, 131
Bancroft, George, 178–79
Banking Act of 1933, 90
Banking Act of 1935, 90
Bank of England, 115
Beard, Charles A., 69
Bell, Daniel, 2, 104
Bikini Atoll nuclear tests (1940s), 70
The Birth of a Nation (film), 55
Borah, William, 45
Brandeis, Louis, 36, 84, 175–76
Brandt, Willy, 98
Brittan, Samuel, 103–4
Bryan, William Jennings, 40
Bryce, James
  on "absence of violent passions"
    in American politics, 65

  on African Americans, 33, 53
  on Americans' lack of desire for
    federal legislation, 184
  biographical background of, 32
  as British ambassador to the
    United States, 34
  on bureaucracy in the United
    States, 73
  democracy defined by, 193n1
  on division of powers in the
    United States, 74, 94
  on enfranchisement of women, 46
  on the failure of American
    cities, 74
  on immigrants to the United
    States, 33
  on moneyed interests in
    Congress, 33
  on presidential election of 1912, 34
  on rapid pace of change in the
    United States, 67
  Reston on, 97
  on U.S. foreign policy, 71
  on value of transparency in
    government, 41
  Wilson on, 32
Buchanan, James
  Constitutional balanced budget
    amendment proposed
    by, 109–10, 117–18, 226n87
  on "endless growth" in
    government spending, 124
  on individual self-interest, 107
  Keynesian economics criticized
    by, 108–9
  on "moral constraints" in
    policymaking, 109, 132
  Public Choice theory established
    by, 107